THE
BURDEN
OF EXILE

THE BURDEN OF EXILE

A Banned Journalist's Flight from Dictatorship

AARON BERHANE

Foreword by Brendan de Caires, Executive Director of PEN Canada

DUNDURN
PRESS

Publisher: Kwame Scott Fraser | Acquiring editor: Russell Smith
Cover designer: David Drummond | Cover image: shutterstock.com/JM Travel Photography

Library and Archives Canada Cataloguing in Publication

Title: The burden of exile : a banned journalist's flight from dictatorship / Aaron Berhane ; foreword by Brendan de Caires, Executive Director of PEN Canada.
Names: Berhane, Aaron, author.
Identifiers: Canadiana (print) 20220240566 | Canadiana (ebook) 20220240612 | ISBN 9781459748545 (softcover) | ISBN 9781459748552 (PDF) | ISBN 9781459748569 (EPUB)
Subjects: LCSH: Berhane, Aaron. | LCSH: Journalists—Canada—Biography. | LCSH: Exiles—Canada—Biography. | LCSH: Political persecution—Eritrea. | LCGFT: Autobiographies.
Classification: LCC PN4913.B33 A3 2022 | DDC 070.92—dc23

We acknowledge the support of the Canada Council for the Arts and the Ontario Arts Council for our publishing program. We also acknowledge the financial support of the Government of Ontario, through the Ontario Book Publishing Tax Credit and Ontario Creates, and the Government of Canada.

Printed and bound in Canada.

Dundurn Press
1382 Queen Street East
Toronto, Ontario, Canada M4L 1C9
dundurn.com, @dundurnpress 𝕏 f ⊚

CONTENTS

FOREWORD

BY BRENDAN DE CAIRES
Executive Director of PEN Canada

WHEN ELEPHANTS FIGHT, THE GRASS SUFFERS. THIS PROVERB COULD SERVE AS an epitaph for Aaron Berhane's life, and for his beloved Eritrea's swift descent into autocracy. It was the theme of an editorial he wrote in September 2001 for *Setit,* a newspaper he had co-founded four years earlier. In it he argued that President Afwerki's confrontation with the G-15 dissidents — who were calling for elections and the implementation of the constitution — would only harm those "already suffering from a shortage of medical supplies, justice, and administrative services." Afwerki responded with a crackdown, jailing eleven of the G-15 group and shuttering the independent press. Aaron escaped, barely; his colleagues at *Setit, Admas, Mekalih, Keste-Debena,* and *Zemen* did not. Two decades later, at least five of them have died in Eritrea's gulag, which holds anywhere between ten thousand and thirty thousand dissidents. The surviving journalists remain in a legal limbo, having never been formally charged or tried for a criminal offence.

This memoir recounts, occasionally in harrowing detail, what it is like to lose everything short of your will to live. Forced to abandon his wife and three young children, Aaron spends weeks agonizing over his escape from Asmara. Thereafter his life becomes an improvisation. When soldiers corner him near the border with Sudan, he bolts into the desert. Hours of running deliver him to the relative safety of Kassala, home to many ethnic Tigrayans. But there he must disguise himself in suitable clothes and trim his beard in the local fashion. Lesser men would give up at this point, but Aaron rises to the challenge. He mimics prayer in the mosque, dodges awkward questions about his family, and finesses a situation in which he is expected to speak Arabic. When he gets to Khartoum, he hides from Eritrean agents sent to abduct him and negotiates — often with only a minimal grasp of what is being said around him — further journeys toward his eventual deliverance in Regina, Saskatchewan. Why there, one might ask? Because "even though I had no relative or friend who lived there," Canada would expedite a refugee claim.

Among its other privations, exile overtaxes the imagination. It requires heroic amounts of self-belief and an inexhaustible capacity for reinvention. Aaron had evinced both by the time I first met him almost a decade later, relocated to Toronto and publishing *Meftih*. We worked on advocacy for Dawit Isaak and the other arrested journalists. I introduced him to Rui Umezawa, a PEN member who has sent Dawit a monthly letter for a decade, and we grew close. The three of us corresponded often and met periodically to plan events and campaigns, to ensure that Aaron's colleagues were not forgotten. He was always willing to speak up on their behalf and never surrendered his hope for their freedom, of their chance to return to something like normal life.

Eventually, he opened up about his family. I learned that beneath the disarming smile and slow, graceful manner there was deep anxiety. Their prolonged absence had taken a toll; his voice softened when he spoke of his children and he looked vulnerable. When, after a few years, he mentioned an escape plan, I was rattled. We were at the waterfront in Barrie, relaxing after a conversation with high school students about freedom of expression in Eritrea. Escape for the whole family sounded like a pipe dream, but Aaron was quietly confident — he spoke like a man who believed in the force of good intentions. Characteristically, I was more doubtful, fearing that something might go awry, forgetting that nearly everything had done so during his own escape. I was delighted when he proved me wrong, a few months later, by bringing his wife, Mielat, to PEN's annual general meeting in Toronto. Her presence felt like a miracle, living proof of Aaron's quiet determination to make a new life in Canada and to bring his family into it.

Aaron's life was a triumph of character. He shouldered the burden of exile with exemplary grace and built a second, happy life from the ruins of the first. I have so many warm memories of his easygoing manner, his polite, over-pronounced English, and his boundless patience in the face of difficulties that it is hard to accept he is no longer here. My late father was also the publisher of an embattled independent newspaper in a lesser-known country and his sudden demise twelve years ago has left an aching void to this day. When I miss either of them, I console myself with the thought that men like these are never truly absent; they may be gone, but they can never be forgotten.

CHAPTER 1

FAREWELL

IT WAS AROUND 1 A.M. WHEN I HEARD A CAR PULL UP OUTSIDE THE compound. Then its engine cut. I slipped out of the room I'd been pacing in and went to the gate to see who had arrived. Flat on the ground, I peered through a gap between the iron gatepost and the concrete wall that surrounded the compound. I couldn't see the car or the people inside it, but I could make out the voices of two people, a man and a woman.

Were they lovers, stealing away to this desolate part of Mai-Chihot, a district on the outskirts of Asmara, or something much worse?

I shifted and strained to see further and was able to make out a small car, a Fiat 600, parked in front of the gate, but I still couldn't see the people inside. I crept to the other side of the gate but could see no better. All I heard were unintelligible voices. Were there more than two people in the car? Had they finally come for me?

It was the night of January 6, 2002, and I had been in hiding in this remote part of Asmara for 103 days. This night was meant to be my last. Arrangements had been made for me to slip across the border to Sudan, away from the government agents who were hunting me.

The compound I was staying in belonged to a relative. It was only partially built, like many in Mai-Chihot. The main house, a type of villa, would eventually have three bedrooms, a large living room, two bathrooms, and a kitchen. There was also an outbuilding that contained two small rooms plus a bathroom and a modest kitchen — the only rooms in the compound that were fully completed. One of these was my makeshift bedroom, outfitted with a single bed and a small table. The other room was a storage room accessible through a door in my bedroom. It was piled with bags of cement, cans of paint, and stacks of broken tile. In the event that someone came into the compound, I'd made a hiding spot for myself among the bags of cement. A high concrete wall separated "my" compound from the neighbouring houses. An iron gate, much taller than a man and wide enough to admit a car, faced the street.

I was the only person living in the neighbourhood.

That night, I was waiting for my cousin Petros to arrive and take me to say my final farewell to my wife and children. Petros was one of the few people with whom I had contact while I was in hiding. He was over six feet tall but walked with a stoop, and that, along with his bald head, made him seem older than his thirty-two years. When circumstances dictated, he could disguise himself as an old man by draping a shroud about his shoulders and walking with a cane. He was my connection with the outside world and took me out to meet with my sources, the people who could smuggle me out of the country or forge false papers.

When Petros would come to see me, he always parked seven hundred metres from the compound, so as not to draw any attention to my location. Whoever it was in the Fiat, it wasn't Petros. To calm myself, I told myself that the people in the car were there by chance and weren't interested in me. But it did no good. I was restless. Had my escape plan been foiled?

In the unfinished living room of the villa was the backpack I had prepared for my escape. I slipped inside the villa and shouldered my pack, not sure what I should do next. I opened the back door of the villa so that I could easily cover the few metres to my hiding place in the dusty storage room. If the people outside did try to breach the compound, at least they would be slowed down by the shards of glass that protruded from the top of the wall. That was some small comfort. The delay would grant me a few precious seconds to reach my hiding place.

The engine of the car came to life and the headlights turned on. I had my face pressed up against the bars of a glassless window and I jumped at the sudden sound of the engine and the bright lights. I retreated several steps and gripped the straps of my bag tightly. Headlight beams shot through the gate and seemed to rake across the vacant yard. The car backed up in line with the gate. It struck me that perhaps they intended to drive straight through the gate. The engine kept running and the sharp smell of petrol wafted across the yard. My pulse raced, and my breath came rapidly. I wanted to run to the storage room, but also wanted to see precisely who had come for me. I remained by the window, feeling the coldness of the night and listening to the rattle of the Fiat's engine. Then, with a lurch, the car was thrown into gear and it pulled away.

Once the Fiat had gone, I took my backpack off and set it down on the floor. My heart was still racing and I sat on the steps at the rear of the villa to be soothed by the night's chill.

I jumped, startled, when a pebble landed in the front yard. I sprang to my feet and primed myself for whatever might come next. A second pebble landed. I stole along the wall and peeked through the gap between it and the iron gate. I saw Petros's familiar shape.

"Did you see the car?" I asked Petros.

"Yes, I was waiting for it to leave," he said.

I opened the gate to allow him in and shut it behind him.

"Did you see their faces?" I asked.

"No, but I don't think we have anything to worry about. If they tried to chase us with a Fiat 600 you could outrun them on foot," he laughed. "Everything is clear now. Let's go."

"What took you so long?" I asked, trying to read his expression.

"I had to wait until the maid left," said Petros, holding the door for me. "Your wife wanted her to finish washing clothes before the water was cut off."

"Oh, I see, today is Friday," I said. The authorities distributed water to different areas of the city on different days, but it didn't flow all day even on the designated days. That was one of the main complaints we used to hear from people whenever we went to cover stories. Despite that, improving the availability of water never seemed to be a high priority for the government.

The moon was full and lit our way. Apart from some dogs scavenging through a pile of garbage beside Petros's car, nothing else stirred. We climbed into the car and drove along the narrow, unpaved roads of Mai-Chihot. The streetlamps that lined the road were out. We crossed street after street before we reached a paved road that led to the centre of Asmara.

Asmara looked peaceful, especially now that the soldiers who had menaced the population for months had withdrawn. They had been deployed in September 2001 when the authorities cracked down on the press and arrested their political rivals. The office buildings glowed with the diffuse yellow light of the streetlamps. Behind the palm trees that lined the boulevards, they gave the impression of sharp dressers heading out for an evening. I felt obliged to commit to memory these last impressions of my city before I left it, my family, and everyone I loved.

Petros was driving fast, past Fiat Talegro, Gejeret, Bar-Jima, Godaif, and Kahawta, while checking the rearview mirror to see if we were being followed. I had the window open and was enjoying the feel of the wind blowing through the beard I had grown over my months in hiding.

"No one will recognize you with your long beard, including your wife," Petros said.

I looked at my face in the side mirror. I was thirty-two, but the beard made me look older.

Petros slowed to turn onto my street. My heart beat faster as we got closer to my house. The streetlights were on and the streets were starkly lit. You could recognize a person from half a kilometre away. Petros parked the car and surveyed the street before crossing the hundred metres to my house. We were the only people out.

Petros knocked on the gate twice, while I watched anxiously.

My wife appeared and unlocked the gate. "Mielat, my love," I whispered. I stepped inside and drew her to me. Petros took a last look up and down the street before locking the gate behind him.

We crossed the yard that fronted my house. Frieta's bicycle and Mussie's toys — a helicopter, a car, and soccer balls — were scattered in the yard. Petros remained in the yard as a sentry while I went inside the house, holding my wife's hand. I led us to the children's bedroom where I found all three of them sleeping peacefully. Frieta, my beautiful, energetic eight-year-old daughter, the boss of the house, lay diagonally across her bed, her blanket bunched up around her feet. Mussie, my chubby four-year-old, slept on his belly, and Evan, still only six months old, lay in his cradle. I watched them and listened to the sounds of their breathing. I wondered if I would ever see them again or if they too would have to be raised without a father, as I had been. What a miserable legacy that would be.

I kissed my children on their foreheads, careful not to wake them. My eyes filled with tears and I averted my face so my wife wouldn't see. She, however, did not conceal her tears from me. She stood by Evan's cradle, watching me kiss our children, her tears streaming down.

"Do you think we will see each other again?"

I put my left hand on her shoulder and wiped her tears with my right.

"Yes, Mielat. I will reunite us in a peaceful country."

"I don't know, Aaron," she said and looked up to meet my eyes. "If they catch you while you're trying to escape, the punishment will be worse. Isn't it better to stay in your hiding place for a while longer? Things may change."

We had discussed this topic whenever she came to visit me in my hiding place. My wife is very persistent; she returns to an issue until she gets the answer she wants. But this time the matter was settled.

"Mielat," I said, "my hiding place will not remain secret for long. The security agents are still sniffing around after me, but I have great people who will help me escape. Don't worry. I'm sure I will make it."

The truth was that I didn't know if I would make it or not. The dangers were many. But for my wife's sake, I projected confidence. I held her in my arms and gazed at her.

"You remember how I escaped from the Ethiopian soldiers in Kisad Molekseyto? You know how fast I can run."

"That's different, my love," she cried. "This is more dangerous. They have distributed your picture at every checkpoint. They will catch you before you even reach the border with Sudan."

Petros interrupted. "Come," he said.

I followed him outside and told Mielat to stay where she was. Through the fence we saw a green military vehicle, parked near Petros's Land Cruiser.

"They just came?" I asked.

"Yes, just now. No one has left the car yet," Petros said.

The full moon and the streetlights allowed us to see what was going on. Two soldiers came out of the car with a small ladder and rested it against the wall of my neighbour's house. They climbed over the wall and dropped down into the compound.

"Does that family have a son or daughter who might be evading national service?" Petros asked.

My neighbours' four children lived abroad and they didn't have anyone in the national service. I didn't know why the soldiers had targeted their house. Petros and I watched to see what would happen. After about five minutes, the gate opened and the soldiers came out leading a young man in handcuffs.

"Do you know him?" Petros asked.

"I don't think so. He could be a relative hiding from the hunters, like me." I put myself in the poor man's shoes and felt terrible. "Someone must have betrayed him," I said.

The soldiers drove off quickly and disappeared. I was gripped with apprehension. What were the chances that I too would be betrayed by the people who had promised to help me? None of them were being paid. They were doing it because they believed in me as the editor-in-chief of our country's first independent newspaper, who had tried to bring freedom and change to our country. They were ready to sacrifice themselves to save my life. I had no choice but to trust them.

"We should go," Petros said.

I went back inside my house. Mielat was still standing in the children's room, gazing upon them as if she were seeing them for the first time. Tears still streamed from her eyes. They landed on her pink pyjamas and left dark splotches. I stood next to her, embraced her, and cast a final look at my children. Mielat buried her head in my chest and sobbed. After a time, she calmed down, and I kissed her lips softly.

"I have to go now, Mielat," I said. "Please, be strong, and believe we will meet again."

We held each other tightly.

"Please, tell our kids how much I love them," I said.

She nodded silently.

Petros returned. "We should go, Aaron. It's almost three."

Mielat grabbed me again and kissed me fiercely. "I love you very much. Don't forget us, please. You have to survive for us, for your children," she said, and released me.

I fought back my own tears and followed Petros toward the gate, Mielat trailing after us. In the yard, I picked up Frieta's bicycle and leaned it gently against the wall. Then Petros and I went through the gate and hurried into his car.

CHAPTER 2

PICKING UP GEBRAY

PETROS DROVE IN SILENCE, ALLOWING ME TIME TO COMPOSE MYSELF AS I looked back toward my house receding into the distance. Away from my wife, I allowed my own tears to fall. In my culture, a man did not cry or show vulnerability, especially in front of the people he was meant to protect. A man was expected to swallow his pain, to look tough, to always show strength and never betray any weakness. But now, in the darkness of the Land Cruiser, beside Petros, my tears ran like a stream down a hill.

After a time, I wiped my face and rested my chin on my arm in the open window. The road was badly rutted and my head bounced up and down. It wasn't wise to ride this way and I sat up properly and straightened my back against the seat.

"Do you think she will be okay?" I asked Petros, my eyes fixed on the road.

Petros glanced at me and nodded. He reached forward and pressed play on the tape deck on the car's console. Both of us fell silent again and listened to prominent Eritrean singer Abeba Haile's sentimental music.

More time passed and then Petros asked, "By the way, where are we meeting Gebray?"

I understood that his question was intended to distract me, to reorient my mind onto the trip ahead, for he was the one who had arranged the pickup location and knew better than I where we were going.

Gebray was my colleague who'd co-founded the newspaper with me. He and I were the same age. He came from the outskirts of Asmara and we had met in Arareb high school. However, I started to know him better when we both attended the University of Asmara, and he joined my study group. He was smart and very conscious about the political climate of the country. We both opposed the action the Eritrean government took to quash the demonstrations of ex-fighters and war-disabled veterans when they demanded salaries and adequate welfare in the early nineties.

Our ambition was to have a role in society. To launch an independent newspaper was our dream.

He took care of sales as I took care of editing. However, he had trouble making decisions, either personal (such as marrying the girl he loved) or professional (such as buying computers for the office). He tended to find faults in any idea proposed, while I would try to build ideas up. He saw the weakness that I didn't see, and I saw the victory that he didn't see. We were a perfect match on that. He liked to debate, but if the conversation didn't go his way or he felt uncomfortable, he would use humour or laughter to divert the issue.

Like me, he'd been forced into hiding since the crackdown on the independent press. But our circumstances were not quite the same, and so fifteen days after the security agents had raided my house seeking to arrest me, he approached my wife near the school where she taught and asked her to arrange a meeting between us. She rebuffed him and insisted that she didn't know my whereabouts. So he had left his telephone number and disappeared.

My wife and Petros visited me that night, bringing my three-month-old son.

"Gebray cornered me outside of my workplace today and wanted to meet you," she said, in a disturbed voice.

"What did you tell him?"

"You said trust no one, so I told him I didn't know where you were and not to bother me again," she said, and adjusted the head of my son who was sleeping on my lap.

"That's good," I said, but couldn't help wondering about what information Gebray might have had for us. After a pause I said, "Maybe it is okay to meet him and find out what he knows or wants."

"That's not a good idea," my wife declared. "You shouldn't trust him and you shouldn't meet him at all."

"But what if he has some information that could help us or knows someone who will smuggle him out of the country?"

"I think I agree with Mielat," Petros said. "How do you know you can trust him?"

"I've known him for many years. I doubt he has any ill intent for wanting to meet me. He's the godfather of our son after all," I said.

"That means nothing," my wife said angrily. "We've seen brothers betraying one another."

I understood my wife's and Petros's concerns but I felt I had to trust my instincts about Gebray. We had been in business together to bring change to Eritrea and I knew how dedicated he was. So, despite their apprehensions, I decided to meet with him. It took us about a month to arrange it, partly because I was sorting out my own escape plans and partly because Petros wanted time to monitor Gebray's movements to determine if he was indeed trustworthy.

When we finally met in Tiravolo District, a few blocks away from Expo Bar, in a car, on the night of October 27, 2001, I was disappointed to find that he had no new information and was in fact looking to me to help him find a way to get out of the country. Meeting him served only to complicate my own plans, because my own departure was imminent and now I had to decide whether to include him. The smuggler who had agreed to guide me could likely take an additional person, but only if that person had the necessary documents, which Gebray did not. Nobody could travel even from one city to another without the proper permits. Soldiers would demand to see these documents at each of the numerous checkpoints we would have to cross to reach the border with Sudan.

Gebray pleaded with me to delay my plans for one week to allow him time to secure the permits. I was torn. To delay would risk losing the smuggler's cooperation and also give the authorities one more week to discover my hiding place. However, I couldn't help putting myself in his position and sympathizing with his plight. I understood how desperate and frightened he was. I also felt I owed him a debt of friendship. He had always been generous to me, and never withheld help when I'd needed it. When I had moved with my wife from my parents' house to the one I'd built in Kahawta District, Gebray had volunteered to help with the move. I knew Petros would be furious with me for assenting to Gebray's request, but I decided to help him, even if against my own better judgment.

"You're insane," Petros had spat. "What's wrong with you? Don't you know your life is at stake? No one is pursuing Gebray right now. He's not your concern. He's safe on shore while you're flailing in the sea."

Since Gebray's main task in the newspaper had been in the administration, he hardly wrote.

"Petros, I'm sorry" I said. "If they're not after him today, they'll be after him tomorrow. Please ask the smuggler to give us a week."

Petros was the one who'd found the smuggler. He'd made the payment arrangements, chosen the meet-up location, devised the communication code, and organized the fallback plans if things went wrong. So he was the only one who could revise the arrangements. It would also raise our costs. But Petros succeeded in convincing the smuggler to wait the extra week. Unfortunately, it was to no avail. Gebray still failed to secure his permits in time.

Petros delivered this news to me in my hiding spot on the day we were supposed to make our escape. Gebray was pleading for a couple more days. At first, I thought Petros was joking, but then I saw the fury and indignation on his face. I was just as furious, although I didn't know where to direct my rage. At Gebray? At myself? I had been holding a book in my hands and I hurled it across the room.

Petros sat in the only chair in the room and stared at me. He waited for me to speak first.

"How confident is he that he can get the permit if we extend him another two days?"

"You're not serious about giving him more time?"

"What do you propose instead?"

"Let him fend for himself. You owe him nothing. Look after yourself. This isn't a game. No more extensions," Petros said.

"Did he really think he could get a permit in two days?" I asked again.

"He insisted that he was one hundred percent sure, but I don't believe him. There's absolutely no guarantee that he can do it. Just pack your stuff now. We only have three hours."

Acquiring a permit paper was not easy, especially if you didn't have the right connections. Generals, colonels, or their representatives could issue permit papers to individuals who served in the administration as national service conscripts. They might risk providing you with a permit as if you belonged to their unit when you did not, particularly if you were a friend or relative. Otherwise, you had to find the right person who could forge one for you, and such people were very difficult to find.

The burden Petros bore was huge. He risked his life every day to protect me, to find and deliver information, and to liaise with my sources. And now I was saddling him with responsibility for Gebray. Petros hardly thought about himself. He was willing to sacrifice anything to help others, especially if they were family. He wanted to get me to safety before it was too late. He seemed to care about my well-being as much as his own.

"Petros, I am very grateful to have you as my family, you are always here for me. But Gebray may not have family. He is not from Asmara, you know that. I know it is in your DNA to help others. I don't want you to knock on any doors to get him a permit paper, but only to wait and give him one last chance," I said. "If he fails, we'll leave him."

Grudgingly, out of respect for me, Petros went to the smuggler and asked for one final extension. But the smuggler refused. I wasn't the only fugitive he was helping. Someone else was supposed to go with us and the smuggler wasn't prepared to ask this person to wait any longer.

The news devastated all of us, Petros most of all. He informed me on November 6, 2001, at 10 p.m. He came to the house with a long face, holding his daughter's backpack in his hand. I opened the gate for him, and he entered the room without saying a word. I followed him without speaking either, but wondered why he'd brought his daughter's bag. He sat on the chair and started to unzip the bag. I stood near the door, my hand in my pocket.

"You don't seem to have good news," I said.

"You screwed up, Aaron," Petros said.

"He refused?"

"The smuggler said no." He pulled a bottle of whisky from the bag and put it on the table. "Get us the cups now, let's drink. Gebray will always be a burden."

What was worse was that this trusted and experienced smuggler disappeared after that. He crossed the border himself and never came back. We had to basically start again from scratch because of my decision to help Gebray. A new, reliable smuggler had to be found. I had to secure another permit, because the one I had was due to expire. I still see the disappointed and accusatory looks from my wife and Petros. I had behaved foolishly. I hadn't listened to them.

But now I was finally going to leave and take Gebray with me.

"Pull over, Petros," I said, as we reached the Alitena-Mereb Road, the main road that ran north-south from Kahawta District. "Let me drive now."

One of the things that Petros had discovered during the several trips he made to Gash-Barka near the border of Sudan was that the checkpoint officers didn't ask him anything about his passengers. Once they saw him driving a Land Cruiser, they assumed he worked for the government. The government owned 99 percent of the Land Cruisers in the country, but not the one I drove. My brother had borrowed it from a friend, as we didn't want to rent through the official line from the legitimate car rental companies. So it was safer for me to be in the driver's seat. It would help to avoid any potential suspicion.

We jumped out of the car and switched places. I adjusted the seat, fixed the rear-view mirror, and inserted a cassette of the music of Abraham Afewerki, my favourite singer, into the cassette deck. I love his songs. They blend a traditional instrument, the kirar, with modern jazz and R&B. I put the car into gear and drove into the night, comforted by his music. My wife's favourite song, "Mistir Fekri" (Secret of Love), was playing. The words describe a perfect union in which each partner shares the other's misery and love.

Mielat used to say that she learned those lyrics from me. I don't have a good voice, but she enjoyed listening when I sang with the singer. Sometimes she even used to joke, "I like your version better than Abraham Afewerki's."

That was, until she found out I had had an affair with Nadia, the head of guest services at the InterContinental Hotel.

Mielat's screaming in my ears: "Did you sing it for her, too?"

My train of thought was interrupted. Guilty memory flooded in. Silently, I cursed myself for leaving a scar on our love. I stopped humming along with the song and drove quietly.

"Where are we meeting Gebray?" I asked.

"Sembel."

"Why Sembel?" I asked in shock. Sembel was out of our way, twenty-five minutes southwest of Asmara. "Why didn't he just stay in Paradiso?"

"I think he was afraid," Petros said. "He moved last week to his uncle's house."

"Where exactly?"

"Near the bus station in Sembel," he said.

"Jesus, Petros!" I said, and stopped the car in the middle of the road. "Why didn't you tell me?"

"I thought I did."

"You didn't."

Petros turned his face away and scratched his head.

"Maybe you're right. I'm sorry. But it changes nothing. When he felt unsafe where he was, he hid at his uncle's, which is in Sembel. I visited the neighbourhood several times. I don't think there's any need to worry."

"Did you visit it in the middle of the night?" I demanded.

"Aaron, let's go," Petros replied.

"What about the air force barracks? The airport? The prison camp, or the police station? We have to pass under their noses to

16

get to Sembel. God knows how many soldiers patrol that area at night."

Petros let me bark about all the threats we stood to face.

"I have already figured it out," Petros said.

"To take a longer route instead of a short one?"

"It's the only way. Drive."

There was nothing else for it now but to drive on toward Blokko Godaif along Alitena-Mereb Road. We turned north at route P-3, the main road to downtown, and turned left when we reached St. Anthony's Catholic Church in Godaif. From there we took several unpaved streets to avoid driving right past the air force base. Though I knew the Godaif district very well, I felt anxious driving on the narrow, rundown streets, which were often strewn with broken glass, nails, and any number of other sharp objects that could slash into our tires. I gripped the wheel and listened to the grinding of the tires over the derelict back streets. As soon as we were clear, I stopped the car to inspect the tires. They were fine. I was relieved.

I drove straight toward Mogoraybe Street. We had to be past the air force base now.

"What are you doing?" Petros asked. "We don't need to drive up Mogoraybe. Go north along the side streets."

"Petros, it is better to risk the patrols than our tires," I said. "If we get a flat we'll lose time and bring attention to ourselves."

"I disagree," Petros said, but there was little he could do as I had stepped on the gas and was speeding toward Mogoraybe. He said nothing more, and gazed out at the vegetable plots that stretched alongside the road.

"Did you know one of those belongs to Uncle Thomas?" I asked.

Petros ignored my question and kept his gaze fixed out the open window.

I saw a car coming from the direction of the air force base along Mogoraybe toward the P-3 highway. I was a few metres short of the turnoff onto Mogoraybe and I slowed down to buy time. There was no place for us to veer off. We were the only other vehicle on the road. The car sped up to cut us off before we reached the intersection of Mogoraybe Street.

"What are you going to do now?" Petros asked gravely.

"We'll just take it easy and not show any fear," I said and rolled down my window. I drove slowly toward the intersection and the other car did too. It came to a stop and two soldiers piled out and stood beside their grey Land Rover. I stopped at the intersection and waited to see what the soldiers would do. They came toward us.

"Petros, just relax and let me do the talking," I said. "Our permits are in order. There's no reason to suspect us."

The soldiers, who wore green uniforms, came along my side of the car and peered inside. They were in their twenties or early thirties. One stood beside my window while the other, standing behind him, looked into the back of our vehicle. It was not hard to guess that they were doing their national service. Ever since the government had made it compulsory in July 1994, both women and men between the ages of eighteen and forty years old were required to serve in the army or government agencies, schools, courts, or hospitals. Ninety percent of the youth population were in national service. Seeing us in a Toyota Land Cruiser, they would believe whatever I would say.

"Hello, fellows," I said. "You also have the bad luck to have to serve on Christmas Day?"

"Yeah, it sucks!" said the younger soldier, who sported a John Travolta haircut.

"Well, that's the beauty of being a soldier," I said. "You patrol at night while everyone is sleeping; you guard the road while everyone is celebrating." We all laughed. To my surprise, it felt natural. I was relaxed.

The soldier bent his head to look inside the car at Petros. "So where are you heading?" he asked.

"We're heading to Keren," I said. "He's a doctor on an urgent call."

I reached into my wallet for my permit but the soldier seemed only mildly interested in it. He glanced at it quickly by the light of his flashlight without taking it from my hand.

"That's okay, have a great trip," he said and took a step back from the car.

"Thank you, sir!" I said. "Merry Christmas, if you can believe it's Christmas!" I called.

I drove off as they waved goodbye, laughing.

I turned right onto Mogoraybe Street and headed north for a few hundred metres, then turned left toward Sembel Complex, also known as Enda-Korea, because it was built by a Korean company.

"Better than risking a flat tire, Dr. Petros?" I said, needling him.

"Just because you got lucky doesn't make it less of a stupid idea," Petros said.

We reached Enda-Korea and took Hiday Street, lined with tall palm trees, toward Asmara International Airport. We drove on Hiday for about five minutes, past the Soplar meat processing plant, and proceeded straight to Sembel. Along the way we were forced to pass between the prison camp and the police barracks. I drove at speed so as not to appear suspicious. Some soldiers congregated outside the barracks but they seemed preoccupied with whatever they were doing and hardly looked up in our direction. We kept on until the bus station. I consulted my side mirrors to see if anyone was following us but there was no one. At the end of the road we turned left by a convenience store and onto an unpaved road. At the end of this road was the house where Gebray was hiding. Petros instructed me to stop near the convenience store.

"It's about two hundred metres from here. Wait while I go get him," Petros said, and made his way down the dark road.

I turned off the engine and decided to get out of the car. I took my backpack and sought shelter behind a damaged house some fifty metres away. Its roof was collapsed, likely from an Ethiopian bombardment. The place reeked of urine, as though its main purpose now was to be a latrine. The stench was very bad and I covered my face with my hand. Through a gap in the wall, I could see the Kidane-Mihret Orthodox Church nearby. That was the southwest end of Asmara. Beyond were farms, open fields, and small villages. I thought to myself that if anything went wrong I could run into the fields and try to escape from pursuers.

My thoughts were interrupted by the sound of footsteps. I couldn't quite determine where they were coming from. They were slow and shuffling — *shefah, shefah, shefah* — as if the people were sweeping the ground with their feet. I was quite certain that they weren't coming from the direction of Gebray's hiding place. Rather, they emanated from the street behind me. I crept out and pressed myself against the wall of the house. I saw two old men walking side by side, wearing *gabi* (white cotton cloaks) over their heads and shoulders to protect themselves from the chilly wind. A third man followed a few metres behind them. The first two headed to the Kidane-Mihret Orthodox Church, while the third made a beeline for the damaged house. Once inside, he passed gas and defecated loudly and at great length. The odour wafted over the wall to where I stood and I nearly gagged. I thought I might meet my end here, before I even made it to the border. The man finished his business and proceeded toward the church. I watched him go, then saw another figure approach. This time a woman, walking swiftly, covered head to foot in a white cloak. I looked at my watch and saw it was 4 a.m. Soon many elders would be making their way past toward the church.

I thought about my mother. It had become her custom to rise early and go to church to pray for me ever since the regime had called for my arrest. "It is early in the morning that I get God's attention."

I heard footsteps once more. This time I saw a tall man and a short man coming toward me. I tried to convince myself they were Petros and Gebray, but since I couldn't be sure I had no choice but to conceal myself back inside the putrid house. The smell of feces was almost unbearable but I had to endure it until I could determine if it was indeed Gebray and Petros. As they drew nearer I could see the shorter Gebray trying to keep pace with Petros's long strides. Every few feet Gebray glanced back over his shoulder. There was obviously nobody behind them: I couldn't understand what he kept looking for. It looked almost as if he was wanting to be rescued by someone so as to avoid having to go through with the escape.

I remained where I was until they reached the car. Gebray asked where I was and Petros silently scanned the surroundings. When I came out into the open, Gebray jumped.

"Is everything all right?" I asked him, and offered my hand. I noticed his shirt collar was folded over and his shirt was only partially tucked into his khaki pants. He looked like a child who had been hurriedly dragged out of bed.

"Yeah, everything is fine," he said in a shaky voice.

I unlocked the car and ushered him into the front passenger seat. As I went around behind the car I had a quick word with Petros before he took his place in the back. "Is there anything I should know?"

"He seems a little unsteady. I don't know if it's from fear or anxiety," Petros said and climbed inside.

I sat behind the wheel and paused before starting the engine. "Let's go now," Petros said.

I turned to Gebray. "Do you really want to go? Now is the time to make your final decision."

"What do you mean? Yes, I want to go," Gebray said.

"You look terrified."

"I'm not."

"Your voice is shaking and your hand is sweating, and your clothes —"

"I am fine," Gebray cut me off. "I decided," he said, thrusting his bag at me. "All my things are packed. Let's go."

"All right, that's what I wanted to hear," I said, "but you have to know, things are going to be tougher from now on."

"I know, we spoke about this before, Aaron. You like to repeat things."

"Only if it is very important."

"I said I'm ready."

"All right," I said. "But for the last time, you understand we will be confronted by checkpoint officers, and we may be shot or captured crossing the border. Whatever happens to us, you can't betray anyone who was involved in helping us. Do you understand?"

"Yes, sir," he smiled.

"I'm not joking," I said sternly. "Do you understand?"

He looked at me and saw how deathly serious the matter sat. His face blanched and his eyes narrowed with anger. I could see how he resented my question, but I didn't care. I had much more at stake than he did. I'd involved my brother, my cousin, my friends, and certain intelligence officers in the escape. I'd gotten him a permit using my network of contacts after he'd failed to manage on his own. Everyone who had played a part had put their life on the line — for me, not for him. I'd convinced them that Gebray was worthy of their trust so I wanted to be absolutely sure he understood the full extent and gravity of the situation.

"Do you understand?" I asked one last time.

Gebray exhaled heavily and peered back at Petros. Petros met his gaze with a cold, lizard-like stare. He'd find no sympathy there.

Gebray turned to me again and said, "Yes, I do understand."

"Good," I said and handed him his permit. "Act as if there is nothing to fear. Petros *has* made three trips to the border. We have all the information we need — the number of checkpoints, how many soldiers at each, and which checkpoints are more dangerous than others. I'll do the driving. Show your permit only when you're asked."

"Where are we going to meet the smuggler?" Gebray asked.

"At the border," I said. "We will drive to Girmayka. Petros will take the car and we'll meet the smuggler there. Then we'll cross the border on foot."

I started the engine and we started back north through the city toward the border. We would have to drive about three hundred kilometres to get there. Seven bumpy hours. Lost in our thoughts, we drove without uttering a word or even humming along with Abraham Afewerki's song. Gebray peered at the intersections we passed; Petros relaxed, leaning his head back on the seat. I concentrated on the drive. We had to cruise north through four of the thirteen districts of the city — Tiravolo, Tsetserat, Paradiso, and Mai-Temenai.

When we arrived at Mai-Temenai District, near another Kidane-Mihret Orthodox Church and the Ghirmay Hotel, Petros directed me to stop the engine. I knew what he wanted. Whenever he left Asmara, he had to pray for five minutes in front of a church near the place of the departure. That was his ritual.

"Please do it from here. We have little time left," I replied.

"If you say so," he said. He crossed the air in front of him with his hand, facing the church to send his worship that way, in silence. I was not a typical churchgoer like Petros. That was one of the unresolved arguments we had long kept going between us. I believe you can pray to God from anywhere, but Petros would reply that that is not sufficient. But on this occasion we didn't argue.

"Bless our journey, God," said Petros loudly. "Now you can ride as fast as you can. The first checkpoint is in Serejeka, twenty kilometres from here."

"What about the Adi-Abieto Blokko?"

"That's only for people coming into Asmara."

"Good God! Goodbye Asmara!"

We reached Adi-Abieto in five minutes. Despite the presence of five soldiers, there was no barrier to regulate the movements of automobiles at the checkpoint. We passed through without stopping.

"I hope we get through all the checkpoints this way," Gebray said.

"That's a wonderful hope, but get ready. From now on we'll be stopped at every checkpoint we run into," Petros said.

I travelled fast, to make distance before the highway became busy, not particularly with vehicles but with goats and sheep. Sometimes peasants taking their herds to market drove them on the pavement, or occasionally might graze their sheep on the shoulders. The landscape was rocky mountains with small plants scattered here and there. The roads zigzagged and twisted down the cliffs and ridges like snakes.

After a while I saw a vehicle ahead of us, travelling fairly slowly. Sixty kilometres per hour. As we drew closer I saw it was another Toyota Land Cruiser.

"I will pass this car, so pay attention to how many individuals are in it and jot down its plate number," I said. I got closer and closer to the car. The driver moved to the right so I could pass. I slowed beside him for a few moments, then sped up to pass. Gebray waved his hand to say hi.

"He is alone," Petros said. "It belongs to the state, according to its plate number." I was not happy with Gebray's wave.

"That was dumb," I said. "Please act as normal as you can. We don't need to attract attention."

"What is not normal about saying hi?" Gebray demanded.

"You would never have done that if we were not going away," I said.

"I think you are paranoid," he said.

"You should be, too. We are not heading out for a vacation. We don't have the luxury of making even a single little mistake."

"It is not a big deal."

"Yes, Gebray," Petros said. "It is not a big deal because nothing happened. But you shouldn't do it again."

Gebray sighed heavily and nodded. He turned to look at an intersection.

Dawn broke over the eastern escarpment as we pulled closer to the market town of Serejeka. It's a hub for roads that lead on to Keren or divert to Filfil and the evergreen forest, a tourist destination, and Massawa, Eritrea's largest port. We came over a hill, and I saw the security checkpoint gate was only two hundred metres ahead. I slowed down.

"Here comes the first checkpoint," Petros said.

Danger messages started to kick into my system and vibrate on my skin. I was breathing fast.

"Remember, Gebray, just show your permit paper only if they ask you," I said.

He nodded. We noticed that we were that day's first clients. No car was before us. I drove briskly, straight ahead, and halted the automobile in front of the wooden gate. There were three officers standing in the road, beside a small house. A short, well-built fellow in his twenties came toward us. He had an Afro and a military uniform but carried no gun. He greeted us warmly.

"*Selamat bitsot*," he said. In Tigrigna, it means, "Hi, comrades."

"*Selamat*," I said.

He stared at Petros and Gebray.

"Can I look at your permit papers?" he asked.

Petros pulled his ID and handed it over promptly. Petros didn't need to have a permit paper, as the ID he carried showed his government department, allowing him to visit anywhere in the region.

"So, you work for the Ministry of Health?" the guard said. He didn't wait to hear an answer and returned the ID.

"And you," he said, pointing to Gebray.

Gebray glanced at me before he pulled out his permit paper. I just looked the other way. He stretched out his hand slowly to present the paper. The officer squeezed the paper hard with his hand to test its validity: not too flimsy, not too stiff. Gebray stared at the officer and looked uncomfortable.

"Great," the soldier said. He yielded the paper back to Gebray and signalled to his companions to raise the wooden gate.

"Thank you," I said.

As we drove away, I kept checking the rearview mirror.

"One down, fourteen checkpoints to go," Petros said. He popped the back of my head with his hand. "Do you believe now?"

"I always believed you," I said.

"Speak the truth."

"Okay, when you mentioned that they don't ask for the driver's papers, I assumed they would ask for which department or division of the ministry I work at. But he didn't even try to ask me anything," I said.

"That's what I said."

"That's fascinating," Gebray added.

"They realize it's a meaningless task. He guessed you are on service," Petros said. "They created the checkpoints only to detect national service conscripts who are trying to avoid doing their duty, not terrorists. They're not particularly dangerous unless their supervisors are around."

We turned slowly into an avenue. It was too early for stores to be open. Three mothers carrying empty jerricans on their shoulders walked with their donkeys on the roadway, on their way to get water from a well.

I honked to get past them. One of them slowly herded the donkeys off the pavement.

"This pathway leads to Filfil," Petros said. He pointed to the gravel roadway that veered to the right from the asphalt road.

This was the place where my great-grandpa had been assassinated.

I remember when my grandfather would tell us the story. Petros and I were six years old then. Once a month, the whole clan got together in my grandparents' house to celebrate Kidanemihret, one of the sacred feasts of Orthodox Christianity. My grandpa always took this opportunity to tell stories of the past to his grandchildren, born from his ten offspring. I still remember how thrilled he was to have us all crowded into the home. There were between forty and fifty of us there every time, and the place sounded like a classroom. Sometimes, our fathers joined us to tune in to the history, even though they had heard it many times before.

"Is it true, Italian soldiers killed your father?" my older brother would ask, after my grandpa told us how the Italians invaded Eritrea and ransacked our treasures.

"Yes, Yosief," my grandpa said.

"Why?" I asked.

"Because he didn't want to give them his land," my older brother explained. Then Grandpa would tell tales of heroic resistance against the Italian colonizers, and the terrible retributions that followed.

As we drove past this spot, the sky that stretched over the peaks of the eastern escarpment glowed a bit more.

"Anyone hungry?" Petros asked. He reached for the backpack on the left side of his seat.

"Yes, I am," I said. "What have you got?"

"Everything that you can eat on the road." He hauled the bag up.

"That is huge."

"Yeah, you'll love it. We've got nuts, biscuits, grapes, oranges."

"Let me have nuts," I said.

"Me too," Gebray added. "You are a great host."

"He should be. I raised him well," I said. We all giggled.

We reached Adi-Tekelezan and navigated the security checkpoint gate without an obstacle. Then we drove as fast as we could to Elabered, still finding no major menace. We passed vans, small cars, buses, and horsecarts.

So we loosened up a bit. We bantered, sang, and laughed.

As we passed through Halib-Mentel, Petros alerted us. We were getting close to one of the strictest security checkpoints — Blokko Keren, set up between two small cliffs. I slowed down as the buses and small cars ahead of me slowed down. About fifty soldiers were perched on top of the hills in groups of four or five. There were crowds of civilians lined up beside the highway. I stopped the car behind a truck loaded with rock.

"What is this?" I asked.

"I'm not sure. I've never seen them asking passengers to leave the minibus or bus," Petros said. About ten armed soldiers stood on either side of the roadway. Two of them were reviewing permit papers. There were two minibuses, one truck, and two Toyota Land Cruisers ahead of us. More trucks had piled up behind us.

One of the two Land Cruisers drifted out of the line and headed straight to the security checkpoint gate.

"Great idea," I said. "That's what we should do. We don't need to line up with the civilians."

One of the checkpoint officers addressed the Land Cruiser. After a brief exchange, he authorized it to cross. As I contemplated doing the same, the other Land Cruiser pulled out and approached the checkpoint.

"I will follow that car," I said. There was no comment. I eased over to the left, passed the truck in front of me, and stopped behind the Land Cruiser. The checkpoint officer let him pass immediately and closed the gate behind.

"That was fast," Petros said.

"He didn't have any passengers," I said.

It was my turn to get closer. I drove forward. The checkpoint officer closed the rusty steel gate and went back to the ramshackle army checkpoint booth.

"*Testa di gallina*, where are you running to?" Petros muttered. I grinned because the shape of the soldier's hair did make his head look like a rooster.

"Be careful, *testa di gallina* might understand Italian," I said.

"Don't worry, he doesn't," he said.

"Everybody knows *testa di gallina*, unless he is one," I said. Petros giggled, but Gebray was silent as he stared at the soldiers.

The checkpoint officer might have been gone three minutes, but it felt like three hours. We were all getting uneasy. We tried to stare straight ahead. An officer yelled and poked a youth with his rifle butt. The young fellow appealed to be let go, but the trooper was determined. The soldier kicked him, snapped, "*Hilef!*" (go this way), and took him away.

"Unlucky fellow," I said.

"They are cruel," Petros said. "They like to take you down."

Gebray's eyes were wide with fear. He was breathing like a toad out of water.

The soldier emerged from the checkpoint building with a smoke in his left hand. He inhaled and puffed the fog out of his lips as he came toward us.

"Here he is now. Gebray, just sit back, you have a valid permit paper," I said.

The soldier stood beside me. He looked in his late thirties and seemed to have never smiled in his life. He had wrinkles on his forehead and around his eyes, and talked through clenched teeth. He leaned in to study Gebray first. "Permit paper?"

Gebray stuck his hand into the inside compartment of his jacket. Then he froze.

"Hey," the soldier yelled, finally freeing his locked teeth. Gebray was not there. Fear had overcome his nervous system, and disabled his body. I burned inside and wanted to grab the paper from his pocket and hand it over to the officer. But, instead, I pretended to have nothing to do with him. The soldier arched his back and sucked the smoke and puffed it through the window. He decided to use more force.

"Show me your permit paper," he snarled. His angry voice attracted the attention of his compatriots. Two of the soldiers dashed toward us to reinforce him.

Yes, Gebray had a valid permit paper, but now he had given them a reason to be suspicious. They would probably demand that he produce supplementary documents to back it up, which he didn't have. I did not know how or whether it would incriminate me. I just felt the weight of all the time and the work my family, my friends, and I had devoted to aiding Gebray, who was now cracking in front of my eyes like a squeezed egg. The soldiers besieged us.

How had I got here?

CHAPTER 3

STARTING A NEWSPAPER BUSINESS

I NEVER THOUGHT OR EVEN DREAMT I WOULD LEAVE MY HOME CITY —
Asmara. That was the city of my ancestors, the origin of my being.
I have a strong attachment to this place, as if it belongs only to me.
I built my family there, and I meant to raise my kids there. So I
assumed it was my duty to fight the corrupt system with my pen
to assure fairness in the justice system, transparency in its govern-
ance, accountability in the administration that hadn't existed for
ages. It was love for my country that fired my heart — and drove
me out of it. What irony!

One afternoon in the summer of 1994, I sat under the shade of
a grape arbour in the compound of my parent's house in Gejeret
District, reading a newspaper. I was in my early twenties and lived
there with my wife and four-year-old daughter, Frieta. My younger
brothers, Amanuel and Medhanie, and my two younger sisters,
Senait and Natsenet, also lived in the large, eight-room house.
I turned page after page in the newspaper, but found only the
same stories that were broadcast on radio and television. All media
uniformly trumpeted that the government was doing a wonderful
job in the economy by creating jobs, in education by opening new

schools, and in health care by building new clinics. Still more annoying, even the opinions published in the "Letters to the Editor" section parroted the party line. Which was exactly the opposite of what I heard on the streets and when I travelled outside the city. The rural communities were coping with a shortage of clean water and with poor health services.

I had recently written a letter complaining about government officials who arrived at their offices at ten in the morning instead of eight, and then kept people waiting for hours to access services.

"Let me guess," my wife said, coming out from the kitchen with two cups of tea and a plate of snacks. She placed them on the small table in front of me. "They didn't publish your letter."

"This newspaper will never publish any dissenting opinions."

"What do you expect from a government-owned newspaper," Mielat said. "The government likes to be praised, not criticized. But you never give up."

Like most young people, I was very ambitious. Eritrea had recently won its independence after a bloody thirty-year war with Ethiopia and I wanted to play my part in restoring our culture, preserving our language, and keeping my country from repeating the mistakes made by other African countries after they gained their independence.

One of the contentious issues was the way the government handled the protests of ex-fighters. Without trying to understand the dire situation of the veterans, the government issued a statement in April 1993 to inform the soldiers that they would have to serve for two additional years without pay. This incited anger. Thousands of soldiers organized themselves and occupied the streets of Asmara, the international airport, banks, and the president's office. They took Isaias Afwerki, the head of the country, from his office to Cicero Stadium — now called Asmara Central Stadium — where thousands of soldiers flocked to confront him personally.

I was in the university library studying with my friends when someone came to tell us about the demonstration. We grabbed our bags, thundered down three flights of stairs, and poured like beans from a can onto the campus. Just beyond it, hundreds of soldiers were moving along the road. There was no chanting or yelling, they just marched along Mai Bela Avenue with Isaias in their midst, and turned right on the small street that led toward Cicero Stadium. They carried AK-47s, RPGs, and machine guns, as if headed to war.

My friends and I didn't understand what it was all about, but we followed behind to watch like everyone else. They didn't arrest Isaias or harass him, but let him walk to Cicero Stadium, only five minutes from the University of Asmara. Despite their burning anger, the soldiers retained their discipline and walked toward the wide open gates of the stadium.

We entered after them, eager to see and hear what would happen. Soldiers and many curious civilians packed the northern part of the stadium. Two soldiers brought Isaias in front of the microphone and told him to discuss the issue and answer whatever questions the soldiers had. The meeting went well. The soldiers even seemed persuaded by his story. He explained the reality of the country's position and told them he would do his best to resolve their issue. He also said that if they thought he was the problem, he would be happy to resign. Finally, three soldiers accompanied him out. A few soldiers persisted in their complaints, but most seemed satisfied and filtered out.

A few days later, the government arrested hundreds of soldiers for organizing the demonstration. Some of them were sentenced to four and some to ten years. Some died from torture. I expected to hear a balanced story from the media about the strike, how civilized and fair the soldiers' demands had been but, on the contrary, the government-owned media attacked the demonstrators.

I thought of my brothers, Kesete, Yosief, and Mussie, who had died in their teens and early twenties fighting to build a free and democratic Eritrea, and I resolved to write letters to the government-owned newspaper, *Hadas Ertra*, about the issues that mattered to me and a majority of the people. They never published a single one.

"I have to own the media to write whatever I believe is right," I said to Mielat, as I sipped tea and stared at the blue, cloudless sky.

"That would be nice," Mielat said. "But who will let you do that?"

She was right. Three years had passed since we'd attained our independence, but the government didn't intend to introduce laws that would allow citizens to exercise their basic rights — freedom of speech, freedom of assembly, or freedom of peaceful demonstration. So we had no choice but to wait. In 1994, the government issued a proclamation to provide for the establishment of an Eritrean Information System Agency, a revised land reform proclamation, and a customs and related taxes proclamation. In 1995, it issued a proclamation to legally standardize and articulate religious institutions and activities, and a proclamation on national service.

Those proclamations could be important. They might show the government intended to put the country on track. However, I wasn't sure if that was what the people needed to happen first. Allowing the people to express themselves freely about the priorities in their lives would have been preferable. But how could the people do that if there was no platform where they could express their opinions without fear of repercussions? For instance, in 1994, when the government forced many university students to suspend their studies and used them to fill the shortage of high school teachers, we had no platform for debating the government's decision. I was assigned to teach in St. George High School at

Mendefera, fifty-four kilometres south of Asmara. I wrote a letter to *Hadas Ertra*, stating how wrong I believed it was to coerce us to quit our studies and teach. Of course it wasn't published.

But on June 10, 1996, the day I had been waiting for arrived. The government issued a press law that allowed private ownership of print media. I couldn't let the opportunity pass and started to think about how I might carve out my place. The law represented a significant moment in the history of Eritrea.

Missionaries had introduced the modern printing press to Eritrea in 1866. However, newspapers began to proliferate only after Italy colonized the country in 1891. Aside from the propaganda newspapers that supported the agenda of the colonizer, there were several independent newspapers that served the Italians living in Eritrea. Their target readers were always the Italians, not Eritreans. As a result, Eritreans didn't have a forum of their own to practise freedom of the press or their basic rights and remained marginalized until the British replaced the Italian colonizers.

During the British colonial period, from 1941 to 1952, Eritreans could form political parties and exercise their basic rights. A small radical press of the indigenous political parties appeared for the first time and, when the British relaxed censorship in 1947, Eritreans were able to address issues that affected them. They discussed what was good for the Eritrean people and Eritrea's future. They debated the forced federation of Eritrea and Ethiopia that the UN imposed in 1952. There were heated arguments between the parties that advocated for Eritrean independence and the unionists who backed Ethiopia. However, this freedom didn't last long. It ended when Emperor Haile Selassie voided the federation and annexed Eritrea in 1962. Later, he banned independent newspapers. From then until Eritrea's independence in 1991, the government owned all electronic and print media and used them as a mouthpiece of Ethiopian rule.

This was why June of 1996 felt like a turning point for Eritrea and, personally, for me and my ambitions. I remember the day well. I was due to go back to my workplace in Mendefera. I spent the weekdays in Mendefera, but returned to Asmara on the weekends, heading back early Monday morning. This was my routine from the time I'd been forced to suspend my university studies. But that Monday, June 10, 1996, I didn't go, because my wife and I had to take Frieta to the hospital for a tonsil infection.

When we came back from the hospital around noon and assured everyone Frieta would be okay, my mother called everyone to lunch. Eating together was one of the most common customs in Eritrea, which our family always observed. Lunch or dinner, we would sit around a big plate to dine together. We used this time to reconnect, laugh, share news, tell amusing stories, and sometimes discuss serious issues.

Mielat and I told them about our visit to the doctor, in an overcrowded clinic where patients had to wait inordinate amounts of time. Amanuel, a land surveyor two years my junior, told us about the new contract he had received from the government. My father told us about the new proclamation of the press law, issued in *Eritrea's Gazette*, allowing citizens to publish a magazine or a newspaper. At that, Mielat and I exchanged a look. She knew this was exciting news for me. I wanted to go right away to read what the *Gazette* had to say, but lunch was not over and our tradition didn't allow anyone to leave before my father recited the final prayer. Since a meal usually lasted from forty-five minutes to an hour, I became restless. I did sometimes break our house rules when I had a pressing appointment, but it was not fun to deal with my father afterwards. He would sit me down for an hour and lecture me about how I should behave so as to be a good role model for my siblings. By default I'd become the eldest brother, after the deaths in battle of my three brothers who were older. So I waited, and pretended to listen to the conversation going on around the table.

When lunch was finally over, I ran to the living room. I picked up *Eritrea's Gazette* from the table and disappeared into the bedroom. I remember reading every section of the law, to absorb the terms and conditions of the proclamation. Crucial aspects of the law were ambiguous, leaving plenty of room for interpretation. For instance, section five of the proclamation stated that a journalist was not to disseminate "any document or secret information of supreme interest to the nation and people, and national security and defence secrets" but it didn't define the terms. So interpreting that law would be in the purview of the courts, which were not independent from the executive body. Consequently, if someone criticized a minister of defence or of internal affairs for ill conduct, it could be interpreted as a matter of national security. If you disclosed secret information about the abusive or corrupt activities of generals, that could also be construed as acting against the law. Government officials or the courts would always have the ability to interpret the proclamation to suit themselves.

Mielat entered the room.

"Here you are," she said. She lay down in the bed beside me and threw her arm across my chest. "Your father is looking for you."

"This is exciting, Mielat," I said, kissing her warmly. "Read it and we will chat later. I have to go now."

My father and I went to the Land and Property Registration Office to collect the final documents for our properties that the Ethiopian regime had confiscated in 1975. I helped him to put the paperwork in order. It had taken us several months to get those papers because some of the officials seemed to know nothing about the departments they ran. They had been assigned because they were members of EPLF, the Eritrean People's Liberation Front. The regime was preferring loyal ex-fighters for key government jobs, over non-soldiers who were better qualified. It was frustrating to deal with such managers.

When my dad and I returned home it was nearly six, and we found Frieta in the yard riding her bicycle. As soon as she saw us she dropped her bicycle and ran toward us. She kissed me and hugged my father.

"You're feeling better?" I said, while checking her temperature by placing the back of my hand against her forehead.

"Yeah. Let's play hide and seek," she demanded.

"Okay, but can I eat my snack first?" I asked.

"No, let's play first." She sprang up and down to show me her impatience. I covered my eyes and told her to hide. She ran to the living room. I went to the study and found Mielat with the *Gazette*, taking notes.

"Hey, you are still reading it," I said, getting closer to see what she'd written. She had noted several points that could imperil our young family if we weren't careful.

"It is very vague," Mielat said. Her eyes stayed on the *Gazette* while I called out to Frieta that I would definitely find her.

"So, what do you think, Mielat?" I asked her.

"I am not sure, Aaron, it is risky," she said. "If you publish articles like the ones you used to send to *Hadas Ertra*, they could throw you in jail. This press law will not protect us."

"Ba … ba …" Frieta yelled from the other room. "Come find me. I am in the kitchen."

"Mielat, I understand. Let's talk later after Frieta goes to bed."

"Ba … ba … I am in the kitchen," came her voice from the living room.

"I will find you now, Frieta," I yelled so she'd know I was on my way to find her. "Are you in the cupboard?"

The next day, I didn't go to Mendefera, but met two old friends, Gebray and Habtom, who both worked as teachers. Knowing that they'd have an interest in such a noble undertaking, I invited them to meet at City Park — a café at the centre of Asmara.

The open-air café and bar was a popular destination with locals and with tourists. There was a hut in the middle of the space surrounded by a three-foot wall, flowers, and palm trees. There were about twenty tables, most of them occupied, when I arrived at about five in the afternoon. As the waiter took my order, Gebray arrived. I knew Habtom would be late, not because he had two young children at home, which he did, but out of habit. He was always late. He hadn't changed much in this respect since our time together in Arareb High School.

Habtom was three years older than Gebray and me. He was a talented cartoonist and had already made a name for himself by publishing several cartoons in *Hadas Ertra*. He was six feet tall and always wore a golf hat to cover his bald pate. While waiting for him, Gebray and I dissected the agenda for our meeting. Half an hour later, Habtom appeared.

"My apologies," he said as he grabbed a chair from the table beside us. "The day to start our publication has arrived."

"Today, you're forgiven," I said. "But next time, be punctual. This is serious business."

"Okay, tell us what you have," he said, taking off his hat and wiping his bald head with his hand.

I briefed them on the potential opportunities and the potential risks. They were intrigued and excited, in spite of the ambiguities and the attendant dangers. From past discussions, I knew how fed up they were about the dysfunctional administration of the government and how badly they, like me, wanted to do something about it.

"How much money will we need?" Gebray asked.

"Right now, I know about the proclamation but not very much about the business. That part we'll need to research," I said, and

I drew several sheets of paper from my bag. "I have assigned a task for each of us. Habtom, can you find out how many printing houses are there? And get us a quote for what it will cost to print an eight-page newspaper from each printing house. Gebray, I thought you could find out about the distribution network of *Hadas Ertra*: where, how, and what commission they pay to their distributors across the country."

I set a sheet of paper in front of each of them. Gebray picked his up and started to read.

"I will research *Hadas Ertra*," I said. "Its circulation, how many copies actually get sold, its printing costs, and the human resources needed to produce a weekly newspaper, as well as the equipment we'd need to get started. I'll also conduct a random survey to learn what columns are popular and try to gauge how people truly feel about the paper."

It was a very productive meeting. We agreed to go about our tasks quietly, so as not to tip off too many people about our aspiration to launch the country's first independent newspaper. We parted full of excitement, and eager to start on our respective tasks.

Two weeks later, schools closed for the summer break. Now I didn't have to go to Mendefera, but could remain with my family in Asmara. I used the time to focus on my research and learn as much as I could about running a newspaper. Every morning I went to the British Library to read books about the newspaper business and about starting a new business in general. Mr. Kiflom, the sixty-year-old librarian, was a great help. Every day, he would give me a new book, often indicating the chapters I should read. I felt I was gaining a solid grasp of what I needed to know.

I also created a questionnaire and surveyed people wherever I went — at the bars, in schools, on buses, and at work. It took us about six months to compile our findings. Unfortunately, our findings proved even more discouraging than the vague Eritrean press law. The next time we met it was at Genet Lateria, near the University of Asmara.

It turned out that there was only one printing house in Eritrea with the capacity to print a newspaper, and it was owned by the government. It was also very expensive — 1.25 Eritrean nakfas (Nfk1.25) per newspaper for a print run of three thousand copies or less. There was only one distributor in the entire country, and its area of distribution was limited to Asmara. The circulation of *Hadas Ertra* was ten thousand copies, in a country whose population at the time was 3.5 million. And even though the paper sold for only Nfk0.50 per copy, half of the copies went unsold.

We were worried about being reliant on a government-owned printing house. We were concerned about the poor reading habits of our people. We didn't understand why the printing costs were so high and feared we couldn't afford them. The weak distribution network also troubled us. According to our projections, we wouldn't make any profits until, at best, our third year of publication.

"This is ridiculous," Habtom said. He pulled a cigarette from his pack and lit it. "The future of our business is very bleak. I don't think we'll make a penny by publishing this newspaper." Habtom had expected to see a quick profit.

"Come on, Habtom," Gebray said. "We said from the start that we want to get into this business not for money but to become the voice of the people." Gebray elaborated on the importance of starting the first independent newspaper in the country and the changes we could bring about. Habtom countered with how badly we could fail and become laughingstocks to our friends.

I let them snipe at each other before I interrupted.

"Listen, guys," I said. "We conducted this research to discover what obstacles we'd have to face. So now we know. But there's no way for us to know whether we will succeed or fail if we quit now. If we decide to do it we should agree not to take a penny out until the third or fourth year. Our goal should be to build the biggest newspaper in the country. Not just a newspaper but the biggest one."

"Are you crazy?" Habtom exclaimed. "How are we supposed to work for free? We'll burn what little savings we have?"

"I don't see another choice," I said. "As our high-school teacher Mesfin used to say, 'We are the future.' So, we have to have the courage to take the wheel."

Mesfin had been our biology teacher, but he loved to talk politics, cultivate critical thinking in his students, and challenge conventional wisdom. We often hung around and spoke with him after class.

Habtom was unconvinced. He wanted to be in and he wanted to be out. He couldn't make up his mind. He kept puffing clouds of smoke.

On the other hand, Gebray, despite his usually indecisive character, saw the project as an opportunity to gain status and influence and so was determined to be involved.

Gebray and I painted a bright future for the newspaper we were envisioning and reminded Habtom about the opportunities he'd lose and the regret he'd suffer for the rest of his life if he pulled out.

In the end, Habtom came around and we dispersed with a mutual imperative to raise funds to meet our challenges.

There were so many obstacles ahead of us. I had to convince the Ministry of Education to lay me off from the unpaid teaching I was being forced to do. Otherwise, I wouldn't have the flexibility I needed to start the paper. Three times I submitted applications to the ministry and the president's office, highlighting all the services I'd already provided. Gebray did the same thing: he too had been forced to quit his university studies. To my great relief, I was finally granted permission to resign from teaching in October 1996. Gebray was given leave in early 1997.

Since I had no money to start a newspaper business, I planned to ask my father to help me get started. I tried several times to bring the subject up, only to be interrupted by my daughter, who loved to seize our attention. I wanted to find a time when I could talk to him alone, when Frieta wasn't around. She was his world. He loved to play with her, speak with her, and laugh with her. He would cease any serious conversation if she came to talk to him or to hug him in her little arms. At which point he would take her in his arms and say to me, "Let's talk about this tomorrow."

Mielat and I made a plan. On a Sunday morning, when my father finished drinking coffee, Mielat would take Frieta for ice cream and stay away for two hours. Then I would deliver the presentation I had rehearsed so many times.

So on Sunday, January 19, 1997, with a sheaf of pages in my hand, I found him and my sister, Senait, in the living room. She was knitting and he was sitting down with his Bible. I motioned for Senait to give us some privacy. She picked up her knitting and left the room. My father looked at me over his reading glasses.

"Do you have a minute?" I asked and sat down. He removed his reading glasses and looked at me silently but with a smile.

"I would like to start a newspaper business, and I need your help," I said directly.

"Well, are you a good writer?" he asked.

"I will be."

"So, you are not."

"That doesn't matter. I have ideas and ambition, and I will make it work," I said. I was caught off guard — he had posed a question I hadn't anticipated and I started to lose my composure.

"Okay, I am listening," he said, and placed the Bible on the sofa beside him.

I launched into my presentation and described, with excitement and passion, the results of our research and the amount of money I needed to fulfill my dream. I laid the research results and various graphs on the table in front of him. I picked up the graph for *Hadas Ertra*, and spoke about its weaknesses, and explained how we would produce a newspaper superior to theirs. I spoke of the power I could have to influence official policies and hold government officials accountable. I went on and on in an effort to impress him and to convince him to support my vision. He allowed me finish and then folded his hands on his lap.

"This is a great idea, but the time is not right," he said.

"Why not?"

He looked at me before he went further. He didn't want to hurt my feelings, but he wanted me to hear what he had to say.

"First," he said with a very gentle tone, "this is not a profitable business. You have already found that out in your research. Second, it is a risky business. This government is not ready to be challenged. You are young, and there are a great many things you don't know. You always say what is on your mind. That's fine in front of two or three people. But you will reach thousands with this weapon in your hand. That's dangerous."

He continued and identified many obstacles my partners and I hadn't contemplated or encountered in our research. This was the first time I'd debated with my father so intensely. And I grew frustrated because I found myself running out of convincing arguments. I felt I was failing. But I also got the feeling that, though my father didn't want to encourage me, he also didn't want to disappoint me. So in the end he promised to give me a one-room office and a small amount of money — Nfk30,000.

I thanked him, but left the room disappointed nevertheless. I had hoped and even expected that he would provide more than he did. I went to the bedroom and lay face down on our bed, not even bothering to remove my shoes. Ten minutes later, I heard Frieta's voice. Mielat came into the room and I sat up to meet her gaze.

She read the expression on my face. She'd waited all morning for this.

"You don't look happy," she said.

I told her what my father promised. But, unlike me, she was excited.

"This is excellent, Aaron. I thought he would reject your idea. You should be happy."

Mielat grasped, as I had not, that with my father's offer we could see a profit much sooner than we had anticipated, since we wouldn't need to spend money for an office. "Imagine," she said, "that's one third of your business expenses."

Since neither Gebray or Habtom had any better luck raising money, we started small by opening our first office in Asmara's Gejeret District. We furnished it with two tables and four chairs from my parents' house. Instead of buying a computer that would command a large chunk of our budget, we hired the Adulis printing press to typeset and lay out the newspaper. Instead of printing weekly as we'd first envisioned, we decided to print every two weeks. As for getting the right to establish the paper, I simply applied for a permit under my name from the Ministry of Information.

We named our paper *Setit*, after the only river in Eritrea, since we wanted our newspaper to flow unimpeded, like a river.

We wrote about four months' worth of articles in advance. We wrote at night and tried to sell advertisements during the day. We worked this way for months before most of our friends knew what we were doing.

In May, Mielat came to the office and handed me a letter. "When are you planning to print the first issue?"

"When would you suggest?"

"What about in three weeks? May 24, 1997, Independence Day," she said.

I didn't want the birth of the newspaper to be overshadowed by Independence Day. There also remained some work to be done. Editing took us more time than we expected, partly because we were relying on Adulis to correct by computer the errors we made on paper.

"What about October, when you deliver this baby?" I said, as I gently touched her pregnant belly. Mielat was carrying our second child.

"I don't want to have twins," she laughed. "This newspaper has to be born first. I will need your full attention in October. So, make it May or June."

"Only if you want me to deliver a premature 'baby,' right?" She pinched my ear.

"It is not possible. Let's aim for July or August, then," I said, quickly reading the letter. Then I laughed out loud. "This is hilarious. How would you like to upset the president in our first issue?"

One day a bus driver was driving his passengers to their destinations. He bumped a car parked on his left, saying, "This is for Sudan!"

The passengers were surprised and started asking each other what the driver was doing. Before they finished, he bumped again another car parked on his right, saying, "This is for Yemen!"

"What is this driver doing?" A young man who was knocked from his seat yelled loudly.

An older gentleman with grey hair said loudly, "I think he is imitating the president."

After Eritrea got its independence, there had been tension between Eritrea and Sudan. Eritrea broke diplomatic relations with Sudan in December 1994. Just a year later, Eritrea got into a dispute with Yemen over the Hanish Islands, and they fought for three days in December 1995. Seeing these unprecedented developments, some people used to mock the president's behaviour, in bars or at the university.

"I heard that joke from my uncle," Mielat said. "I hope it is not too political."

Our strategy for the start of publication was to not be aggressive or very critical of the authorities until we established ourselves and familiarized ourselves with our readers. The main columns were interviews, art, entertainment, news analysis, opinion, and sports.

We agreed to print five thousand copies per issue to reduce the unit price. At five thousand copies, each paper would cost Nfk1.00 instead of Nfk1.50. It was a calculated risk, but if we could sell every copy we printed, it could work to our advantage.

On August 21, 1997, the first issue of our newspaper was printed. Gebray and I drove around noon to Adulis, the printing house, south of the Ministry of Information in Forto. The receptionist, an elderly woman with grey hair, greeted us warmly.

"We're here to pick up our newspaper, printed this morning," I said genially. "It's our first time here, so please tell us where we should pay and where we should pick up the newspaper."

"You pay in that office," she said, and pointed to a room across the way. "And you will present a copy of your receipt at the warehouse through that door."

I paid Nfk5,000 in cash, took the receipt, and proceeded to the warehouse with Gebray. An older gentleman wearing a blue uniform escorted us through to the stacks of newspapers. Drawing close, I saw a copy of *Setit* atop a bundle of two hundred papers. I beamed and plucked the top copy. I smelled the heady aroma of fresh newsprint and thrilled at the notion that I was finally holding my newspaper in my hands. I turned the eight pages of the issue and saw that it was perfect, just as we'd dreamt.

This was the starting point of the first independent newspaper in Eritrea. That's history and it will never be rescinded. It opened a vital forum for public discussion. Gebray and I grinned from ear to ear. We carried the papers to a Toyota pickup truck and drove back to our office.

We recruited shopkeepers and children to work on commission to distribute the paper. Though we believed that the content of our paper was rich, entertaining, and informative, we still worried about selling all the copies. Our distribution network was modest — limited to Asmara — and the price per copy was more than double that of *Hadas Ertra*.

It's hard to be a pioneer. You have no one to look to. You're entirely on your own. So, we had to test the waters ourselves, learn from our mistakes, and be ready for surprises — good or bad. It was an emotional rollercoaster.

I felt the burden of my responsibilities upon my shoulders. I experienced everything my father warned me about. I had placed myself in a very influential position, set agendas of discussion, and shaped the culture and politics of the country.

To our surprise, the five thousand copies that we hoped to sell in two weeks, sold out in just one day. People consumed *Setit* like a delectable treat in cafés, restaurants, bars, parks, and their homes. Wherever we went, we heard people's excitement at having an independent newspaper, a platform where they could genuinely express their opinions.

Gradually, we expanded our distribution system to all the major cities of Eritrea and abroad. The frequency of publication increased from twice a month to twice a week. Our circulation grew from five thousand to forty thousand copies per issue, and our staff grew from three to twelve people. *Setit* became the largest and most powerful newspaper in the country.

The fledgling independent press didn't take long to take wing. It seemed we opened the way for newspapers all over the country. Two months after we launched our first issue, another independent newspaper called *Liela* appeared (October 10, 1997), followed by *Tsigienay* (November 19), and *Mestiat* (November 30); in 1998 *Wintana* (in March), *Kestedebena* (November 24), and *Mekalih* (December 29); in 1999 *Keih-Bahri* (January 30), *Zemen* (February 21), *Asmara Lomi* (March 21), *Admas* (May 1), *Maebel* (July 1), *Adal* (July 14), *Selam* (September 3), *Timnit* (also September 3), and *Millennium* (October 6). At one point, there were eighteen private newspapers, though most of them didn't survive the stiff competition.

The four-year period during which *Setit* operated (1997 to 2001) was difficult, particularly after the two-year border conflict with Ethiopia ended in 2000. We attempted to exert pressure on the government to implement the constitution, fight corrupt generals, focus on education, improve health care, and review the land and investment policy.

Of course, government officials were not happy with content critical of the regime. Intimidation and threatening phone calls by government spokespeople and other senior People's Front for Democracy and Justice (PFDJ) officials became part of our daily routine.

Nevertheless, the government could not halt the newspaper's momentum. We persistently called on the government to respect the rights of citizens and to implement our constitution. We published stories about the arrest of two thousand university students, including the student union president, for refusing to sign up for a compulsory work program set up by the government. We became the voice of the people by echoing their pain and concerns.

The tipping point came on June 5, 2001, when I published an open letter by fifteen senior government officials known as "the G-15." The G-15 criticized the president and called for democratic reforms. The intimidation and harassment intended to block the free press escalated. Enforced and unjustifiable conscription, interrogation, and arrest of my fellow journalists became standard practice. It was a routine matter for me to be summoned once or twice a week to answer serious or trivial questions about the G-15's letter or the editorial I wrote about it. "Who gave you that letter? What are you trying to say in this line? What do you mean? Where did you get this information? Why do you write this story while the country is at war?" (The country was not at war at the time.) The tactics were symptomatic of a paranoid government, but the government did not fully cross the line until September 11, 2001.

CHAPTER 4

THE INVISIBLE PRESSURE

ON TUESDAY, SEPTEMBER 18, 2001, ONE WEEK AFTER THE TERRORIST attacks on the World Trade Centre in New York and the Pentagon in Washington, D.C., at 7 a.m., the news came over the radio that, effective immediately, the Eritrean government had ordered all private presses to cease publication. I was in bed with Mielat when we heard the words of the presenter on Radio Dimtsi Hafash, the government station.

"They are shutting down our newspaper. I can't believe this," Mielat cried.

The pretext the government gave for their decision was that we had broken the laws by failing to pay taxes.

"This is a total lie," she said.

"I know."

"What does it mean? Why are they doing that? Does it mean they will come after you?" I had no answers.

"I have to go now, Mielat," I said. "I need to find out what is going on before we can discuss our next moves."

I dressed hurriedly, got the keys to my Toyota Land Cruiser from the drawer, and drove downtown. *Setit* was distributed on Tuesdays and Fridays. I suspected the government would have already confiscated the copies before they left the printing house, but as it turned out my paper had already hit the market. I saw the last edition of my newspaper being sold on the street as I drove through Asmara. *Setit* was the first independent newspaper to appear and, as fate would have it, the last to disappear.

The business that took us years to build was abolished by the stroke of a pen by a paranoid president. I thought about the impact of such an unjust decision on the democratic functioning of the country and its impact on the more than fifteen hundred people whose livelihood depended on these papers — the children who supported their parents and themselves by peddling papers, and the many employees at the newsrooms and printing houses. I felt unspeakable grief at the loss of *Setit*, which was so dear to me. And I feared where the government might strike next.

I parked the car on Maryam Gumbet Street and walked toward Bar Folia to place a call to one of my most trusted sources from a public phone. The man's name was Goitom, and he occupied a senior position in the Ministry of Interior Affairs. He provided me with news that hadn't been reported by Radio Dimtsi Hafash. Of the fifteen senior government officials who had written an open letter criticizing the president for refusing to implement the constitution and hold open elections, "the G-15," eleven had been arrested.

Goitom advised me to watch my back because the situation was volatile. It was then that I truly grasped that the regime had taken an irreversible step. I went back to my car and sat for a long time, mulling over everything I'd heard and considering my next move. Then I went to my office.

I found the staff of my newspaper sitting in the front yard, debating that morning's developments. The oldest member of our staff, a talented writer named Fesseha Yohannes (Joshua), evinced optimism. The feeling seemed to be shared by most of the journalists.

"They just shut us down because they don't want us to write about the jailed senior officials," he said. "They will let us continue our work once they settle that issue."

I didn't truly believe this, but allowed myself to at least hope that he was right.

Around noon, I met Matewos Habteab, the editor of *Mekalih*, and Amanuel Asrat, the editor of *Zemen*, at Rendez-Vous, a café near Cinema Roma, a relic of Italian colonial, art deco architecture. We had been friends since our time at the University of Asmara. Matewos and Amanuel had also been valued contributors to *Setit* before they launched their own papers. Now we were confronted with the most critical moment of our young journalistic careers. We needed each other's advice more than ever.

As Matewos and I drank tea and Amanuel sipped an espresso macchiato, we resolved to write a letter to the Ministry of Information to demand clarifications about the government's decision and to condemn the false accusations levied against us.

Medhanie Haile, deputy editor of *Kestedebena*, Yusuf Mohamed Ali, editor of *Tsigienay*, and Said Abdelkader, the editor of *Admas*, joined us and signed the letter, too. I didn't realize this would be the last time I would see all these talented and dedicated editors together. Amanuel and I delivered the letter to the Ministry of Information on September 21, 2001.

Sometimes, I wonder how we survived for four years. The government's intention was clear right from the beginning: they didn't want us to succeed. They tried to weaken us systematically by censoring our work, denying access to information, ignoring our requests for interviews, and refusing to give us permission to establish a journalists' union. Once we began to influence public opinion, the regime turned to intimidation and threats to try to silence us.

Censorship was one of the first weapons the regime used to slow us down. When the border conflict with Ethiopia erupted in May 1998, the Ministry of Information ordered all independent newspapers to submit all final proof copies to them before they went to the presses. The ministry ordered the printing house not to print any newspaper if there was no signature from the ministry on the proofs. It was a painful process. The proofs had to be submitted to the censorship committee one day before publication. If the committee deigned the articles too critical of the regime or that they broached a sensitive topic, they rejected them. Sometimes we would be forced to revise 50 percent of the copy, so we had to have additional content on standby to submit for approval to substitute in, to avoid missing publication. Even though it was futile, I often appealed the committee's decision to the minister, particularly when the censored material touched upon the war.

For example, I had gone to the battlefield of Zalambesa in July 1998 soon after the border war escalated. I interviewed a young soldier who had been wounded in the battle and wrote a piece depicting his willingness to defend our country and the lessons he'd learned at the front. However, the censorship committee and the minister of information, Beraki Ghebresilassie (now imprisoned as one of the G-15), wouldn't allow it to be published.

To my protestations, Beraki had said: "You will terrify the people if you write about conscripts who fulfill their national service and get wounded."

This was ridiculous. Everyone understood what could happen to their sons and daughters at the front, but the government was initially unwilling to talk about the war. The state media barely mentioned that battle and did their best to obfuscate and cover up. So — when we could sneak past the censors — my newspaper offered the only account of the battles before August 1998. The government was not only sensitive about news from the battlefield, but wary of any piece of information of value to the public interest.

Censorship continued until 1999, but that didn't discourage us. We were pursuing the dream. The government finally stopped censoring the press because the committee itself complained that it was ineffective. Sometimes they rejected articles that contained only mild criticism of the regime, while other times they approved articles with far harsher criticisms. The end of censorship felt like a victory for us, but the government merely resorted to other tactics. For instance, officials declined to cooperate with independent journalists, not because they were ordered to do so, but because they lacked confidence in their own standing. They always referred journalists to their superiors, rather than providing the information requested about their departments. The superiors would then pass the buck and refer you to their superiors, and so on up to the ministerial or even the presidential level. Rarely if ever would a minister or the president comply with a journalist's request, so the journalist usually just abandoned the idea of writing the article or, if they were enterprising, engaged foreign journalists to ask the questions: spokespeople for the government were more inclined to speak to foreign correspondents than to Eritrean journalists. So we often found ourselves quoting the BBC or Voice of America about our own country's internal affairs — a ludicrous and maddening process.

Unjustified arrest was another tactic the government used to hamper us. In October 2000, a group of thirteen Eritrean academics and professionals called in a letter to President Isaias Afwerki for a critical review of post-independence development and the nature of Eritrea's leadership. Their letter was written in English and published online. The government worried that the private press would translate this powerful letter and share it with their readers. So, before we could so, security agents raided all the independent newspaper offices and arrested eight journalists. Two journalists for *Setit*, Gebray and Yacoub, were arrested because they had the misfortune of being in the office that day. To justify their arrest, the government blamed the journalists for evading their national service. An utter lie. Some of them had valid student exemptions, while others had in fact done their service.

I evaded arrest and informed the BBC correspondent about what happened. Coverage in the international media and criticism from the international organizations that advocate for journalists played significant roles in pressuring the government to release the detained journalists. After a week, they were freed. But, because of the detentions, the affected papers couldn't go to press during that time, including *Setit*.

In mid-2000, the price of sugar increased rapidly. I investigated and found that the main cause was a secret regulation on the exchange rate of the dollar that involved levying a fee on currency exchange. Merchants had difficulties getting hard currency to import sugar.

As I pursued the investigation, I got a telephone call from the ruling party's office, the PFDJ.

"I've learned that you are writing about sugar," the voice said.

"Hello. May I ask who I am speaking with?"

"From PFDJ office. It is a very sensitive issue. Don't write anything about it," he said.

I asked him to elaborate and tried to persuade him, but he was adamant. "I said, don't write about it if you want to stay in business." I had no choice but to change the angle.

Telephone threats were the common technique the ruling party used to intimidate independent journalists. Calls from intolerant officials were part of my daily experience. For instance, officials at the Ministry of Defence would call to complain or threaten about our letters to the editor. Many national service conscripts were submitting letters about how some army generals forced them to work on private farms and construction projects. We would try to get a response from a spokesperson of the Ministry of Defence about the conscripts' complaints, but if they refused or ignored our requests, we would go ahead and publish the letters. That infuriated the Ministry of Defence.

"Stop insulting our generals who defend this country." "Don't mock our president." "Don't publish incorrect information." "I will roast you in your office." I received several calls, purportedly from the army, by people who claimed to be lieutenant colonels, colonels, and generals.

The threatening phone calls that I took seriously were the ones that came from the president's office. Yemane Ghebremeskel, adviser and spokesperson for the president, would call whenever he was upset about an editorial I'd written — which was much of the time.

In December 2000, I criticized some elements of the Comprehensive Peace Agreement signed by Eritrea and Ethiopia in Algiers. Both countries had signed an agreement to end their border conflict by accepting the decision of a boundary commission. A UN cartographic unit was assigned to do the demarcation. I was afraid this agreement would benefit Ethiopia at the expense of Eritrea. Ethiopia tried to insert a boundary map it had prepared in 1997. This violated the legal borders established by treaties signed with Italy in 1900, 1902, and 1908. The Ethiopian government wanted to change these borders, arguing they had not been demarcated.

When the comprehensive Peace Agreement was suddenly signed in December 2000 to end the border conflict according to the decision of the boundary commission, I assumed the issue would get out of Eritrea's control. The technical issues involved with border demarcation would open the door to political influences adverse to the interests of the people of Eritrea. It would undermine the existing treaties between Italy (the former colonizer of Eritrea) and Ethiopia. I criticized the Eritrean government and highlighted how the agreement would benefit Ethiopia because of its greater diplomatic influence in the world arena. Yemane was angry and had already called twice in the morning before I got to my office. He had used harsh words with my secretary, who was trembling when I arrived. She ran toward me.

"Oh, Yemane is furious about today's editorial," she said. "He wanted you to call him immediately." Even after I comforted her, she continued to shake.

"Don't confuse people," said Yemane before he even greeted me. "There is nothing new in our stance. Watch what you write."

I asked him if he would give me an interview that would corroborate his argument. He refused and hung up.

When the telephone threats and all kinds of intimidation failed to garner results for the regime, the legal committee stepped in. The committee was created by PFDJ in early 2000 and busied itself digging up transgressions by the independent newspapers so the regime could file suit against us. They resented our growing influence over the people and our insistence on asking contentious questions. "Why did we go to war in the first place with Ethiopia?" "Why is the constitution not implemented yet despite its ratification by the parliament?" "Why doesn't the government take action against the corrupt generals who abuse the national service conscripts?" etc.

It was a real headache for the regime, and they knew they had to do something about it. So, in July 2001, the government hired Dr. Teferi, a well-known lawyer, to prosecute us. A secret meeting was held, and the legal committee presented three or four charges against each newspaper. *Setit* faced three potential charges, all of them connected to an editorial I published in 2001 about the demonstration by students of the University of Asmara, and how the government should handle the G-15 and the land issues. But when Dr. Teferi compared the original documents with the documents drafted by the committee, he told them he saw no evidence of any crime. He criticized the work of the committee and refused to take the matter to trial. It was a big blow to the regime — they abandoned their plans for legal action, and the legal committee dissolved for good.

In the absence of a legal process, the government resorted to social pressure.

It was particularly stressful when pressure also came from your loved ones. My mother, brother, wife, uncle, and many relatives often advised me to temper the tone of my paper's criticism — particularly if they had been approached by people who had better access to the executive branch of the government than I did. They also feared that my activities would harm their lives. The subject was often raised when we sat down for meals together. To avoid these uncomfortable conversations, I joined my family for meals less and less. It was a frustrating time.

In June 2001, my son Evan was born. Rather than congratulate me on the new baby, relatives spoke to me instead of their apprehensions about my work and the dangers it posed to everyone connected to me. They told Mielat that my life and the lives of everyone I loved were in danger.

"Sahale was here this morning," Mielat informed me one afternoon as I entered the dining room for lunch. I looked at her without saying a word. She was distressed and looked like she had been crying.

"Colonel Sahale?"

She nodded. Colonel Sahale was Mielat's relative. This was his third visit to us in two months. Instead of sharing her happiness about the new baby, he came to warn and to frighten her. I was furious. He told her about my various editorial misdeeds, and the anger they were arousing in the generals.

Our maid appeared in the doorway and asked if she should prepare our lunch. I knew I wouldn't have any appetite. My anger boiled over, and I tersely declined lunch. I waited until she left before resuming my conversation with Mielat.

"What did Sahale say today that he hasn't said before?"

"I'm scared, Aaron," Mielat replied. Her eyes filled with tears. "They'll kill you if you don't stop. That's what he said."

I drew my chair close to her and sat beside her. I laid my hand on her shoulder to comfort her, but she brushed my hand away and rose from her seat.

"Do you want me to stop?" I asked.

"Yes."

"What's changed?"

"Because I am a mother of three now. I don't want to lose you. I don't want to worry every evening that you might not return to us."

Though I understood her concerns, I remained unwilling to surrender to the regime. I stood up to go.

"Where are you going?"

"To the office so I don't have to hear this anymore."

"Do you know how selfish you are? You only care about what you can accomplish, not about us, the people you say you love. What's wrong with you?"

Her words wounded me. I rushed from the room before she could hurl another one.

Relations between me and Mielat deteriorated and I started coming home later and later, absenting myself more and more from the life of my family. And it was then I strayed into even more perilous territory — an affair with Nadia.

I had known Nadia since the end of 1999. She worked at the InterContinental Hotel as head of guest services, and she was one of my primary sources at the hotel, which was the main destination for the United Nations Mission in Eritrea and Ethiopia (UNMEE). The UN Security Council established UNMEE on July 31, 2000, to monitor the ceasefire at the border of Eritrea and Ethiopia. With Nadia's help, I gained insights into the commanders of UNMEE, the challenges the peacekeeping forces faced in the field, and the cohesiveness of the UNMEE command structure. Sometimes Nadia also shared information she'd overheard from senior officials of the government. She played a significant role in elevating the contents of my paper.

Nadia had been raised in Kenya and was fluent in English, French, Swahili, and Amharic. She was tall, beautiful, and poised. But what impressed me most was her charismatic personality. She could chat with kids and make them laugh like crazy. She could speak with equal ease with intellectuals or the most common people. She was also very savvy and knew how to steer a conversation to get what she wanted. She was two years older than me. When she was in her early twenties, her first boyfriend died and she never married. Though we met once or twice a week and knew a great deal about each other, our relationship remained strictly professional until July 2001.

But one Friday evening, as I sat alone in my office, reading the columns written by some of my journalists and avoiding going home, the phone rang. It was Nadia.

"Hey, I have something," she said. "Can you meet me now?" As a rule, she didn't identify herself over the phone. Our receptionist used to call her the nameless woman.

"Where are you?"

"Near your office, I'm calling from the public phone, near Nakfa House. I saw your car."

I locked up the office and went to meet her.

"You look like you're going out on a date," I said.

"I am. With you," she laughed. I kissed her on the cheeks, as is the custom between men and women in our country.

"You look great as always," I said.

"Thank you!"

She twirled around to display her dress and fell backward toward me. I caught her, and she laughed loudly. She'd never flirted that way before. I didn't mind, flattered and glad for the distraction.

"So where do you want to go?"

"Whatever fancy place you choose," she grinned as she put her hand in mine.

"Caravel."

"Good choice."

We walked to Caravel Bar and Restaurant, which was also a nightclub, located just two blocks from where we were. That evening, our business relationship turned personal. We drank, danced, and ended up in bed together. After that, it became a routine. I enjoyed spending time with her. I used her place as a shelter from the tensions at home. Our affair continued until the end of August — when I learned some secrets about Nadia.

On a Monday afternoon, one of my colleagues came to tell me that a middle-aged man was waiting for me outside the compound of the office. I went to meet him. Furtively, looking to make sure no one was observing us, he took an envelope from his pocket and handed it to me.

"He instructed me to bring him your answer."

I inspected the envelope. It bore no identifying information. When I tore it open, I found a typed message that read, "Hi Aaron, Can we meet today or tomorrow after 6 pm in my office. It's important. T.B."

I immediately knew who it was — Tekie Beyene, the Governor of the National Bank of Eritrea. He was my relative, my father's cousin. This wasn't the first time he had contacted me this way. I returned to my office, wrote "Tuesday 6:30 pm" on a slip of paper, and put it in the envelope.

The following evening I went to see him. Since he was my relative, I went with an open mind to hear what he had to say. I parked near the Central Post Office and walked toward the National Bank. A security guard escorted me inside. There was no one in the building but him. He greeted me warmly and offered me tea.

"Your father would have been so proud of you," he said, looking at the day's copy of *Setit*, which was laid out on his table. From a drawer in the desk he extracted a folder and put it before me.

"People talk about what's reported in *Setit* instead of *Hadas Ertra*."

I didn't know where this conversation was headed, so I kept quiet and just listened.

"Do you know what this means?" he paused, presumably waiting for my answer, but I remained silent and sipped my tea.

"The government sees you as a threat now. This is precisely what your father feared before he died. He knew one day you would aggravate the authorities and become a target." He stared at me, his eyes tight and worried.

Tekie had been very close with my father. Since my father's death at the end of 1997, he'd tried to serve as a surrogate father to me, offering his advice when he felt it would do me good. Despite his busy schedule, he always made time to meet me. This time, I sensed that he had something critical to tell me.

"I will tell you something important as my nephew," he paused. "But whatever happens, you can never implicate me."

"Of course, I would never do that."

"A friend of mine who works in intelligence told me he saw your name on the list of people under scrutiny." He looked at the folder on his table.

"What does it mean?"

"They have been spying on you for a while. They have assigned people to watch your activities, the people you meet, the places you visit, conversations you've had."

Though I knew from other sources that I was being watched, I didn't know all the details. I felt my chest constrict.

"What did they find?"

He pulled a page from the folder and glanced at it as he spoke. It had many bullet points.

"It says you refused to become a member of the PFDJ in 1994. You started the first newspaper. You became a strong critic of the government. Now your paper has become the mouthpiece of the G-15. You are perceived as being one of the people who would like to overthrow the government, an agenda you have been pursuing since you were in Mendefera," he said.

"Overthrow the government! Wow!"

"I know it's ridiculous," he said. "The point is, don't take this lightly. You are being watched. You should be aware of every activity you engage in and all the people you interact with." He paused and stared at me. "Including Nadia."

I froze. I didn't know what to say. I merely gazed at him.

"Do you know she works for National Security?"

I didn't.

"My friend said that they usually assign her to spy on foreigners. She is one of their best assets. She is smart and sophisticated. But in your case, my friend believes that they are using her because she is your friend. Maybe more than that? So watch out for your marriage." Tekie shot me a stern look. "Your father would have been very upset."

When I left his office, I felt light-headed. A great deal of information to digest and a load of embarrassment to deal with. Of course what troubled me most was Nadia's role. I couldn't wait a day or an hour. I drove to her house in the affluent, bougainvillea-lined district of Tiravolo. It was around 8 p.m. and I found her getting ready to go to an event at the Embasoyra Hotel. She was surprised to see me, since I'd said I wouldn't come that day.

"What's happening? I'm just on my way out."

She appeared utterly relaxed while I roiled with anger.

"I have to ask you. This can't wait," I said and sat down on her sofa.

"I'm all yours," she said, trying to sit in my lap. I slipped free.

"What's going on?" she asked.

"Is it true you work for National Security?"

She gasped and averted her eyes.

"Yes," she said.

"So, I am your assignment?"

"Not at all."

"Tell me the truth, please. What did you report about me?"

She rose and settled herself down beside the phone. She checked the time. It was clear she would be late to the event.

"Can I call first to let my boss know I'm going to miss tonight's event?" she said and reached for the phone. I nodded in assent.

After she informed her boss, she leaned back against the sofa and recounted what she'd reported about me. Most of the reports had no value at all — interviews I'd conducted with UNMEE officers and whatever meetings I'd had with foreigners at the InterContinental Hotel. She reported to her bosses either in advance or during these interactions. She insisted that the focus of her assignments was to follow the activities of the foreigners, not me. She swore that she had no intention to destroy my marriage or to sell me out. She maintained that she loved and respected me. As she spoke, tears streamed down her face.

"Why didn't you tell me?"

"I was afraid you wouldn't see me the same way," she said, and wiped her tears with her scarf. "You'd imagine that I support this government. The truth is, I don't. I hope you know that already. I share your belief that elected leaders should be accountable to the people. To have a democratic society, not a dictatorship. You have no idea how much I hate the job I do with National Security, but I have no way out. They refuse to let me go, so I can't try to have a normal life like you and your beautiful wife have."

I went to sit beside her and wiped away her tears. I stroked her shoulder to soothe her, and she buried her head in my chest and sobbed. I felt her pain. After all, she was also a victim of the regime. They trapped thousands of young people like her in the national service against their will.

"I believe you," I said. "But we will not see each other again. I have to go to my wife and beg her forgiveness."

As I drove toward home to confess my sins to Mielat, I thought about the early days of our acquaintance and the family we built together.

My wife is the light of my life. She is bright, beautiful, caring, loving, and a wonderful mother. We met at Arareb school. I'd had a crush on her since I was fourteen and my feelings for her didn't abate until I won her heart. She was my high-school sweetheart and I courted her until we got married at the end of 1992. We'd come a long way, and I considered it one of my life's greatest accomplishments.

She had a strong and magnetic personality — neither very showy nor shy — her beauty and charm seemed to attract the attention of many of my schoolmates. There were two in particular who intimidated me. They were older and bigger than me. And they showered her with precious gifts like chewing gum — a scarce luxury in Eritrea at the time. Mielat neither encouraged nor discouraged them but chatted with them in the presence of her friend Hanna, who was always by her side. I would wait for both of my rivals to leave before I approached her. Sometimes I had time to chat with her and her friend for a few minutes but sometimes there wasn't even the opportunity for that. The other boys never regarded me as a threat since I was younger than them and didn't ply Mielat with flashy gifts. It mystified me how exactly I'd bested the other boys and won her heart, just as it mystified me now how I'd been so stupid and reckless to jeopardize everything we had built together.

I went home that day unsure how I would even broach this painful subject with Mielat. It was late, around eleven, and my kids were in bed. I regretted not being able to see them, since I felt that seeing them would have fortified me.

"Hey," I said with a dead voice.

"Hey," Mielat replied. She'd been lying on the sofa and watching television. She sat up and I kissed her and sat down beside her. My guilt gnawed at me like never before. Reluctant to broach the subject, I stared at the TV, which was showing a Crocodile Dundee movie.

"How was your day?" Mielat asked.

"Fine," I replied, still too scared and sickened to say what I'd come to say.

"Are you okay?"

"Yeah, I just had a long day."

"As always?" she said wearily.

It seemed at that moment as if she could see through me and detect what was on my mind. I felt I should confess my sin immediately before she discovered it by some other means — which would be far worse for the both of us — and yet I couldn't bring myself to speak the words. We went to bed with this dense uneasiness between us.

The next day we left our kids with my parents and drove a couple of kilometres east of Asmara to Biet Giorgis, Eritrea's only zoo. Mielat always liked it there, not only for the animals but because she enjoyed walking in the eucalyptus forest that ringed the zoo. There was also quite a good bar and restaurant for visitors. We paid the entrance fee and drove straight through the eucalyptus forest toward the restaurant. The restaurant and the zoo were busy that day. Mielat got out of the car and went toward the monkey enclosure.

"Can we go for a walk in the forest? I'd like to speak to you."

She read my face carefully and followed me toward the forest, which offered more privacy and quiet. We walked in silence for about a hundred metres along a narrow path.

"Mielat, I am here to ask your forgiveness," I said and stopped to look her in the eye. "I have lost my way."

She glanced at me and, seeing the pain and guilt in my eyes, averted her face and looked down at the ground.

"Our home isn't how it used to be," I said. "And I'm to blame."

I started walking again to gather my thoughts and find the courage to say what I needed to say. But before I could, Mielat spoke.

"I understand," she said. "I know you have been under tremendous stress and that you have many people at work who depend on you, but it's my responsibility as a mother and a wife to remind you to give us priority. I'm glad to hear that you're ready to talk about it now. It hasn't been easy for me, too."

Of course, her words only made what I had to say next even harder. I tried to find a suitable way to confess my infidelity, but I could think of none. There's no easy way to describe cheating, no matter how hard you think about it. So I had to say it and be prepared to receive my wife's hurt and fury.

"Not only that, Mielat," I said and then pried the most difficult words out of myself. "I have also strayed."

"What do you mean?"

"I have had an affair."

"What?" She stared at me with horror. I kept quiet.

"You cheated on me? You betrayed our marriage?" Her beautiful eyes filled with tears and she looked away from me as her tears rolled down. She brushed the tears away with her hands.

"You hurt me, Aaron, so badly! You disrespected me. How ... how could ... ?" she burst into tears again.

"I know what you feel," I said.

"You can't imagine what I feel inside," she barked. "You humiliated me."

I said nothing, but absorbed every word she spoke. I put my hand on her shoulder to comfort her. She shrugged it away and sat down on a log at the edge of the path. She wore white pants but was indifferent to the dirt that would surely stain them. She hung her head and refused to look at me. She was in a different state of mind. I sat beside her and tried to explain further and confess my sins in detail, but she didn't want to hear it. I was full of remorse.

"Please shut up!" she shouted at the top of her voice. It was the first time I had ever seen her lose her temper so. She was always composed, in control of herself. She shouted and cursed, her tears flowing bitterly. I let a few moments tick by and then offered her a handkerchief I had in my pocket. She grabbed it from my hand and fixed me with a wounded and furious look.

"Why did you do it?"

I knew there was no answer that could justify my misdeed.

"I'm so sorry, Mielat. I made a stupid mistake. It's over now."

She wiped her eyes with the handkerchief and straightened her spine.

"Is it your secretary?"

"No."

"Who is she then?"

"You don't know her. What's important is, it's over."

"You can't tell me what is important for me." She leaped up and stood in front of me. She was boiling with anger again. "I don't think you understand what I feel right now. The peaceful life I have been leading is in turmoil. I don't know if I will be the same again. I want to know her name. Where does she work? How long have you been seeing her? Everything!"

"Of course!" I said. I rose and met her eye. I confessed everything.

Mielat looked at me with steely focus.

"Do you love her?"

"No," I said but I could see she didn't believe me.

"Why did you decide to tell me? Is it because you were seen by someone?"

"Yes, but that's not the reason. It has been eating me up and now I feel relieved." I closed the short distance between us and placed my hands on her shoulders. "I love you very much. I don't expect you to forget this, but I hope you will forgive me." I hugged her, and she buried her head in my chest, slackened, and then pressed herself to me.

Two days after I confessed my affair, Mielat visited Nadia at the InterContinental Hotel. She told me about her interaction with Nadia months later.

Mielat asked one of the receptionists to call for her and sat in the café ordering tea. Nadia showed up shortly and froze when she saw her. Mielat didn't bother to introduce herself, but Nadia knew who she was, having seen her from a distance.

"Nadia?" Mielat asked when she saw a woman staring at her from a distance of five metres.

"Yes, how are you?" Nadia approached Mielat feeling awkward and shook her hand.

"Do you have five minutes? I would like to speak to you."

"Yes," Nadia checked her watch and sat in front of her.

"Do you know who I am?"

"Yes, you are Aaron's wife," she sighed.

"And do you know why I am here?" Mielat asked.

"I guess so. I am very sorry."

"How would you feel in my place?"

"I'm sorry. It was never my intention to hurt you," Nadia said with regret.

"Did you know he was married?"

"Yes."

"Children?"

"Yes." Nadia answered reluctantly. She wanted to answer frankly and get over it as quickly as possible.

"Why would you want to get involved with a married man with three young children? I don't understand. You are young and beautiful. What were you after?" Mielat thundered.

Nadia shook her head with regret and kept silent.

"Do you love him?" Mielat asked.

Nadia looked around and looked at Mielat for a while. She took a moment to answer.

"Yes."

"Does he love you?"

"I don't know. You have to ask him. Look, I said I was sorry. I'm ashamed of what I did. Isn't it enough? Or are you here to humiliate me?"

"No, I'm not here to humiliate or intimidate you, but to make you understand that you're mistaken if you think he will ever choose you over his family. Aaron was my first and he will be my last. We will see our children grown and be together until the end of our days."

Mielat faced Nadia with firm resolve.

"Please stay away from my husband." She picked her purse from the table and left.

In early September 2001, two security officers visited my home around 10 p.m. They waited outside for me. I had driven home mentally replaying the conversation I had had with a gentleman about that day's editorial, which invoked an Eritrean proverb: *When elephants fight; it is the grass that suffers.* In my editorial I argued that the quarrel between the president and the G-15 would most hurt the people already suffering from a shortage of medical supplies, justice, and administrative services. The gentleman had appreciated the editorial and suggested that it might bring both parties to their senses. If only the president thought that way.

I pulled up at my house and got out to open the gate. The two security guys rushed from the shadows and barred my way, standing mere inches away from me. Their faces were half covered by their baseball hats, so I could not make out their features.

"We're here to give you one final piece of advice," said a short guy as he pushed a gun concealed in his jacket into my ribs. "If your paper publishes any more criticism of the government, it will be your final byline."

I could feel the point of the gun against my ribs. I didn't dare say anything until he withdrew it.

"Who are you?" I asked.

"Never mind who we are. Just heed the advice we are giving you," they said and left.

I never told Mielat about this, but I did tell my colleagues. We analyzed the incident in the urgent meeting we held the next day, and we saw it as the regime's last resort to make us stop our criticism.

Next, the government exploited the events of September 11, 2001 — the attacks on the World Trade Center and the Pentagon. One week later, seeing that the world was focused on the terrorist attack, President Isaias shut down all seven private newspapers — *Setit, Mekalih, Kestedebena, Tsigienay, Admas, Zemen*, and *Wintana.*

Three days after the closure of my newspaper, I was at home watching *Tom and Jerry* cartoons with my kids. Frieta sat on my left and Mussie sat on my right side. Evan was asleep, and Mielat was combing her hair in the front yard of the compound. Around seven, the bell rang. Mielat opened the door of the compound and saw the woman who had nearly destroyed her marriage and family — Nadia.

"What are you doing here?" Mielat asked in a shocked voice.

"I'm sorry to come to your home like this. But can I come in please?" she said.

"What for?" Mielat demanded.

"I need to speak with your husband. It's important," she said.

Mielat breathed heavily and let her into the compound.

"Okay, wait here; I'll call him."

Mielat burst into the living room and told me to come to the next room. Frieta clung to me playfully and tried to keep me from leaving the room.

"I will be back sweetie," I said and eased her back onto the couch.

I followed Mielat out of the room.

"Are you still seeing Nadia?" Mielat demanded.

"No, what are you talking about?"

"Then what is she doing here? She came to see you. Why? To disrespect me?"

"I don't know, Mielat. I told you I was done with her. What did she tell you?"

"She wanted to speak with you. Please don't bring her in."

I saw Nadia waiting at the entrance. She wore a matching charcoal skirt and blazer with a crisp white shirt and heels. The expression on her face was weary and sad. She regarded me as I walked toward her, and then over my shoulder at Mielat. I turned my head and saw Mielat observing us.

I greeted Nadia by kissing her on the cheeks.

"I'm sorry, Aaron," she said. "I wouldn't have come if it wasn't important." She looked at the ground to avoid eye contact.

"What's going on?" I asked.

"I'm here to warn you that they will come to arrest you," she said. "I don't know when. But it's inevitable. They asked me to give them your address. So I gave them your parents' address instead of this one."

The woman I blamed for trying to wreck my marriage had come to save my life.

"Thank you, Nadia," I said. "What do you advise?"

"Avoid going to public places, especially those you normally frequent," she said. "Protect yourself. And I hope I will see you again someday. Now I have to go." She opened the compound door and disappeared. I stood there immobile for what seemed like a long time.

"Are you okay?" Mielat clutched my hand and peered into my eyes.

Though I was always conscious of my movements and the houses I stayed in, I became more vigilant after Nadia's warning. I informed my colleagues about the perilousness of the situation and advised them to be careful as well. My warnings were of little use.

On Sunday, September 23, 2001, at 5 a.m., security agents raided the homes of multiple journalists. Most of them were caught.

Amanuel Asrat, Dawit Isaak, Matewos Habteab, Seyoum Tsehaye, Yosuf Mohammed Ali, Medhanie Haile, Said Abdelkader, and Temesgen Gebrekirstos were all arrested that day. I evaded arrest solely because, misled by Nadia, the security agents came to my parents' house. They swooped in at 4:30 a.m. and searched every room. Later in the day, they went to my Kahawta house, but I was no longer to be found there. They didn't give up. They kept hunting me, Dawit Habtemichael, and Fesseha Yohannes, who had also eluded arrest. But Dawit and Fesseha didn't elude them for long. They were arrested in the following days. And as the security forces controlled the checkpoints and circulated my photograph widely, I felt closed in from all sides. My battle for survival had begun.

CHAPTER 5

THE DRIVE TO GIRMAYKA

AT THE CHECKPOINT AT BLOKKO KEREN, THE SOLDIERS WERE CIRCLING us like hyenas around a wounded antelope. They pointed their guns at us and leaned into the open windows of our Land Cruiser.

"Tell him to get out of the car!" one shouted, the veins bulging in his face.

"Please calm down," I said. "Have you no respect for a disabled veteran?"

The soldier retreated a bit and peered at me with a puzzled expression. He knew he had to respect disabled veterans who'd liberated the country from the colonizers. That was one of the political lessons given to every national service conscript during training. Gebray wasn't a disabled veteran, but the soldier had no way of knowing that.

"He has a permit. Give him a second and he'll find it," I said in my most authoritative tone.

Gebray glanced at the soldier as he patted his pockets one after another. The soldier turned to the back seat. Before he could open his mouth, Petros held out his ID. The soldier inspected it and gave it back.

"I found it now. Here you go," Gebray said, presenting his permit to the soldier with a trembling hand. The soldier looked at the permit and turned to his companions.

"It's okay, guys," he said.

He returned the document to Gebray and I sighed with relief as the soldier went to the gate and lifted the bar.

I drove through slowly, my eyes darting everywhere, including the rearview mirror. The soldiers had already forgotten about us and were checking other cars. I gradually sped up to get as much distance from them as I could on the road to Keren. From the moment we passed through the gate, none of us had uttered a word. I wanted to yell at Gebray for his incompetence, but I kept silent until I felt we were safely out of range of the checkpoint. We rounded a small hill and headed toward the centre of the city.

"What happened to you?" I finally demanded of Gebray. "Why were you scared — you have a valid permit."

"I wasn't scared."

"Then why did you take forever to show your papers? How do you explain that?"

"I was just trying to find them."

"They were in your breast pocket where you put them. You weren't supposed to give them any reason to suspect us. But you did. Pull yourself together for Christ's sake, if you want us to escape safely."

"The soldier was impatient."

"Please don't blame him, blame yourself."

"Okay, that's enough," Petros finally said. "Fortunately, we made it through. For our next checkpoint, Gebray, please have your papers ready in advance."

Gebray nodded and turned to contemplate the buildings and houses of Keren. I could tell he was still shaken, so I let the matter rest and turned my attention to the people and the donkeys on the streets of Keren.

Keren is one of the largest of the five major secondary towns in Eritrea, with a population of over a hundred thousand. Though it's a diverse city — a place of Bilen, Tigre, and Tigrigna ethnic groups — a majority of its people are Muslim. The white gowns of the men and the colourful dresses of the women give a distinct Muslim feel. I knew the city for its banana plantation and dairy herds that supplied its fresh milk, butter, and cheese products.

I slowed when I saw a line of camels crossing the road. Camels and donkeys were frequently used to carry trade goods, wood for fuel, and water for household consumption or trade. They greatly outnumbered the cars. I had to drive slowly and yield the right of way as they marched in procession with their owners to market.

We followed highway P-2 through the city, past the elegant buildings in the city centre that the Italians built during their colonial period. There were other signs of Eritrea's colonial past. The Keren War Cemetery, also known as the Commonwealth War Graves, was one of them. It held the graves of 406 British soldiers who were buried at the site of the most decisive battle between Italy and Britain here, in February and March 1941. It was then the colonization by the Italians came to an end and the colonization by the British began. Keren became a symbol of defeat for Italy and a symbol of victory for Britain.

Before long we had traversed the city and were on the road to Akurdet.

"In five minutes, we'll reach the next checkpoint," Petros said.

I glanced at Gebray and he returned my look, though neither of us said anything.

"This is not a strict checkpoint," Petros said.

I knew it would take us more than five minutes to reach the checkpoint because the way ahead was clogged by men driving herds of animals. We'd pass a herd of cows, only to encounter a herd of sheep. So, I had to drive carefully to avoid hitting an animal — or a person. When I finally wove through the live obstacles, I sped up, and we bounced along the pitted asphalt road.

"Slow down, please," Petros said. "We're here."

I did as he said and drew up behind a truck. There were seven soldiers sitting on a low wall beside a shabby building near the road. One of them jumped down and approached the truck in front of us. I kept my eyes on the soldiers. They appeared to be relaxed, brushing their teeth with *mewez* — a twig from either an olive or a *tahses* tree, the traditional toothbrush for most Eritreans, particularly in the provinces. It is so effective that the people who use it are known for the uncommon whiteness of their teeth.

Once that truck left, I drove up to the gate. The soldier came around to the passenger side and asked to see our papers. Gebray and Petros handed theirs over immediately, and the soldier gave them a cursory look before passing them back.

"Have a great trip," he said.

"Thank you," Petros said. As we put the checkpoint behind us he explained that the soldiers took greater care checking vehicles entering Keren than those that were departing.

I glanced back again at those soldiers who were busy brushing their teeth with *mewez*, and remembered a conversation with my father from years ago, which now seemed to have taken place in another lifetime.

It was a few weeks after we launched *Setit*, and the whole family was in the living room watching television. The presenter spoke about dental hygiene and highlighted the importance of brushing your teeth using toothpaste. My father was reading that day's edition of *Setit* as he listened to the program. It was his habit to comment after he finished each article and I liked knowing his impressions of what I was doing.

"Excellent work, son," he said, removing his reading glasses.

My mom and Mielat were in the room with us and they looked in my direction.

"I like everything you have published here," my father said.

"Because you want to be kind to your son," I said wryly, eliciting laughter from Mielat.

"Maybe," he smiled. "But I am really proud of you, son. This enlightening content that you put in the paper informs people of their rights and duties as citizens. You should consider having a dedicated column in your newspaper for educational content. Not like what they are presenting here," he said, pointing at the TV.

"What's wrong about a program on dental hygiene?"

"Because this is a direct translation of Western media. It speaks about a Western lifestyle that has little in common with the reality experienced by most Eritreans. For instance, what percentage of our people use toothpaste to clean their teeth?"

"Probably one percent," Mielat answered.

"Right," my father said. "Maybe even less. So instead of devoting so much time to toothpaste they should speak about *mewez*, since the great majority of our people use *mewez* for dental hygiene. Just as we have been doing for generations. It is cost effective. It's better than toothpaste because it is all natural. It doesn't even require water. You could write about the benefits of *mewez*, something most Eritreans will actually understand and employ in their daily lives."

Now, leaving the checkpoint, this exchange replayed in my mind like a scene from a movie. At the time, my father was a priest in his sixties and head of Saint Georgis and Abune Gebre Menfes Kidus (*Enda Gabir*) Orthodox Churches of Gejeret District. Beginning in his early thirties, he'd become a successful contractor and housing developer. He also came to grow four hectares of sorghum, making him one of the key suppliers to the Melotti brewery, and owned a dairy farm and more than thirty apartments units that he rented out. Additionally, he served as an elected city councillor.

As he always wanted to see our independence, in the early 1970s he collaborated with the Eritrean People's Liberation Front (EPLF) that fought to liberate Eritrea from Ethiopian rule.

One early morning in April of 1976, fed up with his dissidence, the Ethiopian authorities tried to arrest him. It was around four in the morning and my father was at church leading a service. One of the deacons noted that an extraordinary number of soldiers had descended on the church's compound. He informed my father, who took off his vestments and mingled with the worshippers before the soldiers entered the sanctuary. Undetected, he was able to sneak out and evade arrest. He escaped on foot through Godaif District and later joined the EPLF.

In reprisal, the regime arrested my mother, confiscated our properties, and turned our life upside down. I was seven. My youngest sister was one, my oldest brother was fifteen, and we had to stay with our grandparents until the regime released my mother. Afterwards, my father moved me and my brothers to an area controlled by the EPLF and enrolled us in Arareb School. That was in 1978. My mother remained in Asmara with my sisters, and we were unable to reunite until 1991.

"Your mother is a brave woman," my father would say. "She hid every document I had; like lists of names of all the people who donated money to the EPLF. They tortured her but they could not break her."

I could see the pride and respect he had for her.

"She saved many lives."

And when my father was diagnosed with leukemia in 1996, I discovered just how wide his circle of friends and admirers was. He was hospitalized repeatedly and senior government officials, religious leaders, and many ordinary citizens came to visit him. Their admiration for him filled my heart with pride. They spoke about his generosity to the poor and disadvantaged, his bravery in the face of the Ethiopian colonial authorities, and his skills as a mediator in brokering a deal between the EPLF and the Eritrean Liberation Front (ELF) to divide the weapons that each faction captured from Ethiopia in the battle of Selaedaero in 1977. What stood out in my memory, though, was a story I was told by Teklay, his friend and fellow priest.

In 1974, the EPLF fighters ambushed the Ethiopian army in Adi-Hawsha, twenty kilometres south of Asmara, killing sixty soldiers. It was a humiliating loss for the regime. They brought their dead to Asmara and wanted to bury them in Saint Georgis Orthodox Church of Gejeret, my father's parish. My father refused them permission, asserting that those grounds were exclusively for the villagers. When the church's congregational committee advised him that his recalcitrance could cost him his life, he answered to the effect that the struggle for independence could only succeed if the people of Eritrea challenged the occupiers by every means at their disposal. To their surprise, the regime of Emperor Haile Selassie relented and buried their soldiers outside of Asmara.

My wife gave birth to a baby boy in October 1997, which filled my heart with happiness. But at this same time my father had been admitted to hospital, where he showed no sign of improvement. It felt like a zero-sum game. Whatever happiness I derived from the birth of my second child, Mussie, was countered by the plight of my dying father.

My father died on November 21, 1997, at the age of sixty-five. Even though I knew his death was inevitable, I was devastated. Hundreds of people gathered at my parents' home to pay their respects to my grieving mother and my siblings. So many came that it was necessary to arrange benches out in the street, outside the walls of the compound. My mother, sisters, aunts, and all our close female relatives and friends openly expressed their grief. They wept, wailed, beat their breasts and foreheads, and called for my father to return to us. Some walked around in a circle. I tried to stifle my emotions like the rest of the men, but I was unable to stop my tears.

On the second day, with throngs of visitors packing the compound, I sat beside my cousins and friends when President Isaias Afwerki, Minister of Defence General Sibhat Efriem, and Commander of the Armed Forces Major General Berhane Gerezgiher (one of the G-15) also came to honour my father's memory.

We conducted the funeral service at Asmara Patriots Cemetery with patriotic zeal. Knowing I would never speak with my father again felt unbearable. Answering my daughter's questions about her grandpa's death was excruciating. But how painful, I thought, it would be for my father to know that his son was being hunted like a criminal by the regime for which he'd sacrificed so much.

* * *

A downhill, zigzagging road brought us to Hagaz, about a third of the way to our destination. We passed the checkpoint there without incident and proceeded toward Akurdet. There was little traffic on this stretch from Hagaz to Akurdet. We saw some camels loaded with wood trudging beside the highway. A few trucks and buses rumbled in the opposite direction. Closer to Akurdet, I saw the blackened remains of several Ethiopian trucks, shunted to the side of the road, artifacts of the war.

Two minibuses were ahead of us at the checkpoint and I pulled up behind them. Three military policemen eyed the vehicles while a fourth checked the passengers' permits. It was around noon on a boiling hot day.

One of the soldiers signalled for us to come forward. I drifted to the left and drove forward to the checkpoint gate.

"*Menkesakesi wereket*," (permit paper), the military policeman said, as he glanced at Gebray and Petros. An AK-47 was slung over his right shoulder. His face gleamed with sweat, his lips were dry, and he looked very tired and hungry. His appearance and bearing made me nervous. Petros and Gebray both handed him their documents. He glanced at their papers and returned them.

"Have a great day," Gebray said. The soldier didn't respond, and went to lift the iron bar.

I drove to the middle of Akurdet. It was a modest town with several modern buildings — including the second-largest mosque in the country, built by Emperor Haile Selassie in 1963 to win the hearts of the Muslim community of the lowlands. There was also a Catholic church, a hospital, schools, and some residential areas. Either on account of the stifling heat or because most of the youth had been conscripted into the national service, there were few people on the streets. We drove on past tailor shops, retail stores, bars, and coffee shops. I saw a restaurant and pulled over so we could eat a proper meal, refresh ourselves, and stretch our legs.

As we left the car, three little boys who looked to be about eight years old rushed toward us to sell chewing gum and roasted cereals. We ignored them, entered the one-room restaurant, and decided to sit on the patio. Its floor was dirt, neatly swept. It was cozy and had a good view of the main street. There were two tables, each with four chairs. The tables had plastic tablecloths, decorated with a floral pattern.

"This is cool," I said. The shade made the patio quite comfortable.

"Do you think this is a good place to eat?" Gebray asked. "Why is no one here?"

"We don't have the luxury of choice. Let's just sit, please."

I sat down on a chair with my back against the wall. A woman in her fifties appeared and greeted us with a broad smile. There was no need for a menu, since she was able to offer only two choices: *tibsi* (marinated meat) and *fritata* (fried eggs). All of us ordered *tibsi* and soft drinks. She came back quickly with three Cokes.

"Don't you have help?" Petros asked.

"No. Since they took my daughter to the national service last year, I'm on my own," she said. "It's hard but what can we do?"

We sympathized with her and nodded our heads in agreement.

"Children, stay away from here," she warned some deprived-looking kids who were gravitating toward our table.

"While she prepares the meal," Petros said, "we'll quickly find a store and buy *shida*," (sandal-style shoes).

"*Shida*? For whom?" Then I looked at Gebray's shoes and saw he was wearing Adidas sneakers.

"Sorry, Aaron, I forgot."

"How? That's the first thing to prepare. Did you plan to cross the desert in those shoes?"

"I'm sorry," Gebray said and rose to find a store.

"I can't believe this! What if you run into someone you know?"

"I'll go with him." Petros said. "We'll be careful."

There was nothing more I could say. Past Girmayka, we would be crossing the border on foot. Walking in the desert for eight hours with running shoes wouldn't be fun. Sand would get into shoes and torture the soles of your feet. The beauty of *shida* was that they had many openings. The feet can breathe and the sand can escape.

Petros and Gebray went out through the restaurant's back door. I sipped my Coke and tried to protect it from the flies that tried to settle on the lip of the bottle.

Knowing the woman was busy in the kitchen, two of the children approached my table.

86

"This is fresh roasted cereal. Please take some, sir." A little boy put a bowl with roasted chickpeas and nuts down in front of me. He wore green shorts and a red dress shirt that was missing all its buttons. An even younger boy, who carried two packs of chewing gum, wore a white T-shirt and blue shorts. With his left hand he waved away the flies attracted to the trickle of snot running from his nose. The two boys bore a resemblance.

"Are you brothers?"

"Yes," the older boy answered. I asked them to sit and order Coke or Sprite. The younger boy smiled and licked his lips and looked at his brother for approval. The older boy scratched his head.

"Sir, is it possible that you give us cash instead? We haven't sold anything today, and my mom would be angry," he said, looking at the ground shyly. I admired the boy and was curious to learn more about him and his brother.

"How much do you sell in a day?"

"Five nakfa."

"Five?"

"But, while I was selling newspapers, I used to make fifty nakfa and sometimes, if I didn't go to school, one hundred nakfa. It was really good." He smiled nostalgically.

I was touched. My heart ached for them, partly because they made me think of my own kids. I assured the boys that they would go home with cash and asked them to order the soft drinks anyway. They both ordered Cokes and sat down at the table with me. The older boy explained that their father had gone to fulfill his duty in the national service and they hadn't seen or heard from him since 1999. Their mother was not in good health and she stayed at home with their little sister. Though I wasn't unfamiliar with such sad stories, it pained me that there was little I could now do to ease their struggles. But I gave them Nfk50 and refused to take anything from them in return. They happily finished their drinks and left just as Petros and Gebray returned.

"So you had company?" Petros said.

The woman brought us our food and apologized for the delay as she set the plates down before us.

"It smells great," I said. Gebray and Petros picked pieces of cooked meat and chewed them while the woman waited to see if we were pleased.

"It's delicious," both of them said together.

Everything had gone almost as well as planned, and we even had time to kill, but we knew we couldn't linger in Akurdet. It wasn't implausible that someone might recognize us here. We got back in the car as soon as we finished our meal.

We left Akurdet behind and drove straight west, leaving the good roadway that leads to Barentu and Teseney on the left and taking the rough Bisha-Keru road toward Forto. There were soldiers and checkpoints in every small camp we encountered on our way, but they weren't strict. After all, it was unlikely that any civilian would travel this route. The military police at each of the checkpoints leading to Forto assumed we were somehow affiliated with them. They waved us through not even bothering to check our papers or ask the purpose of our trip or our destination. Since we were able to travel practically unimpeded, we neared Forto around four in the afternoon. We didn't want to go through Forto too early and get into Girmayka before dusk, as we needed the cover of darkness to steal across the border. So we stopped shy of Forto in what could legitimately be described as the middle of nowhere.

I parked the car beside the dusty road, next to a small hill. We all got out to stretch our legs.

"The next checkpoint is the toughest one," Petros said as he descended into the roadside ditch to pee. "They will ask to see our permits and the reason for our trip."

"So let's rehearse our answers again," I said.

"Yes, but not only our answers but also how to stay composed. There may be people there from the National Security who are trained to read every movement of your face."

"That's scary," Gebray said.

"Don't worry too much," Petros said. "At this time of year most of them aren't happy to be there."

We brainstormed every question they could ask and the plausible responses we could give. We lingered for over an hour, waiting until the sun set. We were an hour away from the checkpoint at Forto. I felt apprehensive. It would be the last checkpoint we had to cross.

"Are you ready, Gebray?" I asked.

"Yes, sir!" he laughed and looked more confident. I was happy to see that his spirits were up and that he seemed eager to confront this next hurdle. Both Petros and Gebray resumed their seats. I kicked the tires to make sure they were sound and got back behind the wheel. I pulled out into the middle of the road and accelerated. A Toyota Land Cruiser raced toward us from the opposite direction. A huge plume of dust followed in its wake. I slowed down to give it room to go by. The driver never slowed but continued to hurtle toward us despite the narrowness of the road.

"This driver is crazy. I'll pull over to let him pass."

I edged the car to the side of the road and stopped. The driver flew past, billowing dust.

"Idiot," I said. "Is he running from someone?"

"No, I think he's afraid," Petros said. "He probably wants to get to Keru before dark. Sometimes the terrorist groups sneak in from Sudan to ambush cars."

There had indeed been three incidents in the past year. All of them occurred on the Akurdet-Keru-Forto route.

I steered the car back onto the road and we made our way unimpeded to Forto. Forto was a military zone. No civilians lived in the area. As it was close to Sawa military training centre, the soldiers had been instructed to be aggressive and strict. When I slowed down before the wooden barrier blocking the road, I saw some thirty soldiers congregated by the huts. Two soldiers in their twenties approached us, one on either side of our vehicle. The sun had already set, but there was enough light to discern the expressions on their faces and to interpret their body language. Only one of them was armed with an AK-47; he stood at my side and placed his hand on the door handle. Both soldiers eyed us grimly and spoke tersely and authoritatively.

"*Menkesakesi*," (permit), the short soldier said, and leaned into the passenger side, menacing Gebray. He thrust his hand into the car and Gebray deposited his permit into the waiting palm. The soldier inspected the document closely, rubbing the pages between his fingers to test its authenticity.

"So what brought you here?"

"My sister. She lives in Girmayka," Gebray said.

"How long are you going to stay?"

"Just two days. I'll be back after the holiday," Gebray said woodenly, as if reciting from a script. Before the soldier could ask any further questions, Petros offered his ID and volunteered his story. He was coming to visit his brother who was at the Sawa military training centre. On the way he would buy butter and firewood for the wedding of his other brother from Girmayka. He'd heard about the quality and affordability of the butter in Girmayka. So he wished to sample it while he was there.

"When will you be back?"

"Tomorrow."

The soldier kept staring at the papers, which he kept toying with in his hand. He seemed to have run out of questions, but didn't want to let us go just yet. We all felt uneasy and wondered what he was waiting for.

"By the way, is Wedi-Haile around?" I asked, in an attempt to distract him.

"No, he left last week to celebrate Christmas with his family," he said.

"Lucky boy. Please extend my greetings. My name is Samuel."

"Sure, I will." He turned to his companion and ordered him to lift the bar as he returned Petros's and Gebray's documents.

"Have a great evening," I said.

He waved his hand. I crossed the last checkpoint proudly.

"Wow! We made it!" I laughed euphorically.

Petros and Gebray both cheered. I checked the rearview mirror and gunned the engine toward Girmayka.

"Who is Wedi-Haile?" Petros asked.

"I have no idea," I laughed. "I just made it up."

"What if Wedi-Haile was around and he called him?" Petros asked.

"Well, I would have said, the other Wedi-Haile."

He and Gebray both laughed. For the moment we felt invincible.

CHAPTER 6

THE BORDER

DRIVING ON SEMI-DESERT WESTERN LOWLANDS IN THE DUSK WAS FUN. FOR the first time, I could appreciate the beauty of my surroundings without worrying about what I would face in the next checkpoint. I could see above the acacia trees small fires in several locations, left and right — signs there was life. The nomads who lived in *agnets* (tent-like structures), the herds of goats dozing by thorny bushes under the grey sky that abutted the flat land.

"Speed up, Aaron, though we have enough time," Petros said.

I checked the time and sped ahead. Our plan was to meet the smuggler at 7 p.m., before we entered Girmayka. There were no villages along the road between Forto and Girmayka, only the scattered agnets of the nomads. I wondered if the smuggler would be at the meeting location.

"Slow down over here," Petros said. "Here is where we'll pick him up." It was an overgrown area near a small valley. I drifted off the road and stopped the car. We watched the bushes for several minutes but no one emerged.

"Are you sure this is the place?"

"Yes, I am."

"It looks like the middle of nowhere," Gebray said.

"It's five minutes' drive from here to Girmayka."

The time was 7:05. The smuggler was five minutes late.

"Just wait," Petros said. "I'm sure he's watching us."

"Let's stretch our legs then," I said. I turned off the engine and hopped out of the car. Petros and Gebray followed my lead and stood by the car. As we discussed how the smuggler would get us there, a short, skinny man with a moustache, wearing grey trousers and a light blue shirt, stepped out of the bushes.

"Hello, comrades," he said.

Petros shook his hand. He wasn't a stranger to Petros and me. He was a relative of ours, but he hadn't known in advance that I was to be his client.

"I heard you had fled the country," he said.

"That was the rumour, now we'll make it reality," I said as I embraced him.

"Well played!" he laughed.

After the security forces failed to arrest me at my home, they dangled the promise of a reward to any disgruntled former employees and freelancers from the paper who could find me and turn me in. One of the most determined was a freelance cartoonist known by his nickname, Snake. He carried my picture in his pocket and asked openly about me in coffeeshops, bars, and lounges. Eventually Snake and his ilk gave up, and the search had gradually died out.

Gebray said, "What's your name?"

"Best not," said the man, scrutinizing Gebray from head to toe.

"Tell us more now about Girmayka, the border, and the army that patrols the area," I asked.

Our smuggler was a member of the National Intelligence based in Gash-Barka — one of the six geographical divisions of Eritrea's administration. He was in his thirties, but his thinness and short stature made him seem younger. He spoke both Tigre and Arabic fluently. He knew Girmayka and its surroundings like the back of his hand.

There was no fence or other barrier between Eritrea and Sudan. Division 37 patrolled the border in the Girmayka region. Sometimes they would stay out a whole night, sometimes they would leave their patrol area around eleven or midnight.

"It's crucial to get the latest information," said the man, "because the shoot-to-kill policy has been in place for a while now."

"Yes, we know that," I said.

"What do you mean?" Gebray asked.

"If the patrolling army orders you to stop and you refuse, they can shoot you on the spot. But don't worry about that, we will cross the border after they leave the area," he said.

He tapped Gebray's shoulder to assure him the crossing would go as planned.

"It's better to be captured than dead, though," Gebray said, and laughed nervously.

"You don't even need to try if that's the way you are thinking," I said.

"I'm just joking," Gebray said. "What time are they leaving the border tonight?"

"Eleven. According to the latest information."

The smuggler also told us that the government required all hotels to submit the list of their guests' names to the Eritrean National Security (ENS) as soon as a room was booked. So he advised us to avoid doing that. And also not to trust anyone. Business owners or waiters directly or indirectly worked for the ENS.

We drove together to Girmayka and the smuggler got out when we reached the outskirts. He was not supposed to be seen with us at all to avoid any suspicion.

"So, I will see you at the Sahel Hotel around ten p.m."

"See you later, Samson," Petros said. I could feel Petros's immediate regret for speaking the man's name. I pretended I didn't hear or it was not a big deal. Samson stopped for a second, then moved off.

Girmayka was a small town of about a hundred houses clustered in one area. There were no streetlights or electricity. A few bars and hotels had their own generators. There were no modern buildings, everything was built from mud and wood. Most of the people were Tigrigna speakers who came from other parts of Eritrea to run the retail stores, bars, and hotels that served the army deployed near the border, and the pastoral nomadic groups who lived in the region.

We drove straight to the Sahel restaurant and hotel, which was located at the end of town. It consisted of two mud and straw huts and a dining place with a thatched roof. Gebray and I climbed out of the car with our bags and Petros moved to the driver's seat and drove the car about two hundred metres away from the hotel.

For the first time in my journey I thought about the bag I held in my hand. It was a cheap-looking bag but it contained US$1,500 that I'd sewed into the handle. Inside the bag I had two pairs of underwear, a white robe of traditional Sudanese style, and a small hat. I intended to change into the clothes once in Sudan. I also had five hundred U.S. dollars in my pocket.

I kept the bag close to me as we entered the restaurant and I looked for a place to sit. There were four tables, each with four wooden chairs, but all of them were occupied by men in uniform. All the tables but one were covered by empty beer bottles. The waitress approached and tried to take us inside the hut.

"There is no vacant place here?" I asked as I swept my eyes across the tables. One table was occupied by only two men, and two of the chairs were empty.

"Hello guys," I said. "Would you mind if we join you here?"

"No problem. We're leaving anyway." They both rose from their seats.

We thanked them and sat on the wooden chairs as the waitress accompanied them inside to pay their bill.

We made ourselves comfortable and primed our ears to listen to the conversation of the soldiers. The waitress showed up and diverted my attention. She looked to be in her thirties. Her hair was covered with a red scarf that matched her dress. She moved gracefully and had a pretty smile.

"What can I get you?" she asked.

"What do you have?" Gebray inquired.

"Anything you want," she laughed.

Gebray and I both ordered beer, and she spun around to place our orders. I watched her go and then let my eyes roam toward the rumble of the generator. There was a small valley behind it, and there were no houses or businesses out there. When the time came, we could disappear into the bushes, attracting no one. It was a great location.

The waitress returned with two beers and set them down in front of us.

"Would you like to book a room at the hotel?"

"We will, but later," I said. "Our friends are coming. Tell us, what do you have for dinner?"

"*Tibsi*, *zigni* (spicy beef stew), and pasta." Behind her, Petros appeared and she glanced back at the sound of his footsteps.

"For me, *tibsi* and beer," Petros said as he pulled one of the chairs toward him.

"Me too," Gebray said.

I ordered spaghetti. She came back quickly with a beer and opened it in front of Petros.

"By the way, how long would it take our food to arrive? I am starved," Petros said.

"Not long."

We all sat in a relaxed mood, chatting about everything but the trip. We were careful to behave in a way that wouldn't cause anyone to deduce why we were there. Five minutes after Petros came, the soldiers left one after the other, and two men in civilian clothes entered and sat down at the table across from us. One of them was bald and the other wore sunglasses. They greeted us as they sat. It was common to greet people even if you didn't know them, but I didn't want to take that too lightly, especially since one of them was wearing sunglasses at night. I strained to listen to their conversation. The bald man was trying to comfort the other man. I could make out only snatches of their conversation and wasn't sure if what I heard was genuine. It seemed that the man in the sunglasses had tried to smuggle two sacks of charcoal into Asmara with his business partner, a bus driver, but the military police found out. The bus driver was arrested and the man feared for his fate if he returned to Asmara. He seemed to be contemplating escaping to Sudan. I said to myself, *talking like that, either these people are naive or it's a trick to lure us into their conversation.*

We ordered more beers, pretending that we had no plans to go anywhere. Before our food arrived, our table sported six empty bottles. The waitress wouldn't be removing the bottles until we'd paid, so we pushed the bottles into the centre of the table as she returned with yet more beers.

It took about forty-five minutes for our food to arrive and in that time I saw three different men enter the hotel and quickly come out again. I didn't know exactly the purpose of their visits but I could guess, based on what Samson (the smuggler) had told us. They were likely members of the ENS, coming to gather the names of the guests booked in the hotel. I prayed for time to pass quickly so it would be ten o'clock already and Samson would return: I felt the ponderous slowness of time. We filled the time eating our meal, discussing practically every topic under the sun — soccer, movies, books — but time crept like a snail. I made every effort to appear at ease, but I couldn't stop myself from repeatedly checking my watch.

The bald man and his friend in sunglasses put cash on the table and gestured for the waitress to collect it. Once they left, we were the only remaining customers. I signalled for the waitress to bring us more beers.

"I think it's enough," Gebray said. "I haven't even finished this one."

"It's still only nine thirty. We can pour it on the floor. We'll pretend we have no other plans but to drink."

The waitress arrived with more beers and asked us again if we wanted to book into the hotel. We gave her the same answer we had given her before, and kept drinking.

Samson showed up at 9:50 p.m. and greeted us as if he'd just met us. We invited him to join us while the waitress approached him from behind. He sat down and ordered a beer. Once the waitress served him and left our table, he told us that the plan hadn't changed and the army would leave their patrolling area at eleven. My excitement spiked.

"So, we will leave at eleven from here," he said. I didn't like the idea of waiting a full hour more while the waitress asked us again and again if we were going to book.

"Let's leave at ten thirty before we get questioned and we can waste more time in the forest," I said. Samson checked his surroundings and turned to me.

"That is not a good idea," he said. "It is only a half-hour or forty-five minutes' walk from here to the border. So it's better to waste the time here than in a more suspicious area."

We agreed to meet Samson at eleven outside the hotel in the valley, and he poured his beer into his mouth like it was water and left.

When the time to go neared, I couldn't miss the opportunity to express my gratitude to Petros for everything he had done over the past months and until this very day. Nothing would have happened without him.

"I owe you for life," I said.

"Me too," Gebray added.

"Hold on, the mission isn't over yet," Petros said. "You can say that after you cross the border."

"If something goes wrong from here, it's on us," I said. "But don't worry, we are in good hands. I will call you once we reach Kassala, Sudan."

We told the waitress that our friend had already booked a room in the other hotel and took our leave. We gave her a handsome tip to dispel whatever suspicions she might have harboured about us.

It was a moonless night. Gebray and I walked out through the main entrance and turned right to go to the valley while Petros continued straight to go to the car. Petros would go back to Asmara with the car the following day, and we would cross the desert to Sudan, travelling in the other direction. I felt a gnawing pain in my stomach that I might never see Petros again. I wanted to embrace him and express openly what I felt, but I couldn't. The risk of attracting unwelcome attention was too great. So in the end we parted as if it were nothing at all.

Gebray and I walked to the valley to meet Samson, who was dressed in long pants and a long-sleeved dress shirt to protect him from the sharp thorns of the bushes and acacia trees. It was so dark we could see only two or three metres ahead of us. So we proceeded close to one another, single-file, like a camel caravan.

I'd prepared for months for this journey while I was in my hiding place. Every morning I woke up, ran for forty minutes, did two hundred push-ups, and stretched my legs and my back in the living room that served me as my gym. Those exercises, apart from keeping me fit, helped me to battle my stress and calm my thoughts. Like an Olympic athlete, now I was ready for the event — or believed I was.

Ahead of us, the terrain was flat, and we could see the light of Kassala, Sudan. No compass would be needed once we crossed the border. Had it been possible to drive, the trip would have taken an hour. But it was more like eight on foot across the desert, through yielding sand that made the trip tougher: it let your feet sink in instead of bouncing back. The desert was also full of acacia trees with half-inch, needle-sharp thorns that could poke you while they were on the tree, and stab into your feet when you stepped on them on the ground. Therefore, a careful guide was important if you were going to make it through.

Samson led the way, I walked second, and Gebray followed me. Right away, the bushes near the valley were so thick we had to squeeze between them to get through. Sometimes the thorns would catch onto our clothing so badly that it would take time to extricate ourselves. It was worse, of course, when they snagged on our skin. We couldn't cry out in pain or make any sounds, but rather had to struggle with the thorns as quietly as we could. Samson stopped us whenever he detected any hint of movement. Most of it was wild animals — rabbits, snakes, foxes, hyenas. We were on their turf and we couldn't complain when they startled us by darting out of their cover. But my biggest fear wasn't the animals.

After we walked for about thirty-five minutes, Samson stopped. He told us quietly to show more caution as we got closer to the border. I emptied the sand from my *shida*, and adjusted them on my feet. Despite all my efforts to break in my *shida* while I was in my hiding place, they were already causing me discomfort.

Samson waited until both of us cleared the sand from our shoes. He pulled up the sleeves on his shirt and checked his watch.

"It's almost eleven thirty, the army must have left by now, but you can never be too careful."

He stepped forward. Gebray and I followed him. We penetrated the bushes one after the other, clearing the spiderwebs that clung to our eyes and mouths. Sometimes, we had to contort ourselves sideways to find a path through the dense, prickly growth. Since the bushes were only a few feet high, we also had to hunch down as we neared the border. I trusted Samson and his knowledge of the region, so I felt confident that he was leading us in the right direction. Eventually we reached the border and Samson stopped beside a thicket of acacia trees that stood about five feet high.

"This is it," he said.

There was no border fence. The line of the border was represented by small hills that we could see from afar. While he was explaining to us what was Sudan and what was Eritrea, harsh voices roared at us from seemingly every direction.

"Stop where you are!" I heard the clatter of guns being cocked mixed in with their shouting.

They were only a few steps away from us. I couldn't believe everything had fallen apart so drastically. Samson had done his best to get the latest information but, unfortunately, he'd been wrong. The army hadn't left the area at the appointed time, and we were trapped.

I didn't see any option but to make a mad dash toward Sudan. I charged ahead into the thick acacia. Adrenalin suffused my body and I ran like a man possessed, with a speed I'd never thought myself capable of. Gebray and Samson charged along behind me. When the soldiers realized we weren't going to surrender, they started firing their guns. I thought my life would end right there, bloodied by bullets and thorns on the flat land of the border. The border of life and death.

The shooting broke open the silent night. Rabbits jumped out of their holes, foxes out of the bushes. By scattering in all directions, they drew some of the soldiers' fire away from me. We were all running to save our lives. The shooting kept up and bullets whistled over my head, but it never occurred to me to surrender. I knew that if I was captured it would be the end for me anyway. So I forced myself to run, to prolong my life for even one second more.

The night was pitch dark and it was nearly impossible to see what lay before me. I weaved in and out of the bushes. I had to break the branches that barred my path, wrench myself out of the thorny bushes that seized my skin and clothes. But nothing could stop me. Mortal fear made me superhuman. I flew on until I stumbled over a downed tree and dropped to the ground. My body and my bag went in opposite directions. I didn't bother collecting my bag but just kept going, leaving my belongings behind. I needed to get away and stay alive. I heard Mielat's words in my head. "You have to survive for your children, for us. I don't want to be a widow. I don't want to raise our children by myself. Remember the dream we had to get old together; to see our children grow, graduate, and start lives of their own."

I felt my mother's prayer too. She petitioned all the saints and God himself to protect me from those who would wish to take my life.

I ran this way for over an hour. I was deep into Sudan by then. I had escaped. I finally slowed down and took my bearings and gathered my thoughts. I kept hearing gunfire from where I had last seen Gebray and Samson. I checked myself. It felt like there was no part of my body that hadn't been torn. My face, arms, legs, and my belly were stained with blood and sweat. There was blood on my right leg, and below my T-shirt something felt like a more serious injury. I might have been shot, though I didn't feel any grave pain. But the blood that flowed from my leg worried me. I carefully diagnosed my injury.

I'm all right. It's only a scratch.

I scooped some soil from the ground and sprinkled it onto the wound to staunch the bleeding. I stretched my back and looked around. I heard the barking of dogs ahead of me and gunfire in the distance behind me. Finally, the shooting stopped. I didn't know what that meant, but I hoped both Gebray and Samson had also managed to get away. I felt a hollow, lonely pang in my stomach. I kept going toward Kassala, Sudan, hoping that Gebray and I would find each other there.

CHAPTER 7

ANGELS AND DEVILS

UP AHEAD, DOGS KEPT BARKING. THEY WEREN'T WILD DOGS, BUT DO-mesticated dogs used by the nomads to protect their encamp-ments. They alerted their masters when they detected a threat, whether from a wild animal or a human. I worried that the dogs might be reacting to Eritrean army men waiting to ambush me if I headed for the agnets. I veered widely around the agnets. But even after I'd moved far beyond, dogs kept barking. I did my best to put them out of my thoughts and focused instead on reaching Kassala.

Ahead, the lights of Kassala grew brighter as I jogged faster and faster toward them, my morale lifting with the diminishing dis-tance. Despite the pain in my feet from the rubbing of sand in the sole of my *shida*, I didn't slacken my pace. I knew it was imperative that I reach the city before the sun rose and the Sudanese military police awoke. They would secure the checkpoint starting at 5 a.m. to monitor the cars and people coming in from Eritrea. At night, nobody would stop you if you avoided the main road. But even if I stayed far from the main road, once the sun was up the Sudanese police would spot me from kilometres away on the flat land. There was no place to hide. They could be upon me in a matter of min-utes in their four-wheel-drive cars. According to Samson, they had captured several Eritreans this way and had handed them over to the Eritrean army. I forced myself to keep running.

Like an Olympic long-distance runner, I jogged for about two hours, keeping a pace somewhere between walking and running. For long stretches I avoided looking at the lights of Kassala, hoping that when I did look up the city would be near at hand. But if I looked, it seemed I hadn't closed the distance at all. It was as if someone kept moving the city farther away and I was jogging in place. I'd been told that if I actually ran for about four hours from the border I would reach Kassala. I slackened my pace from jogging to walking, but forced myself to keep moving. I was exhausted, thirsty, and in pain, and it seemed my misery would never end, but I forced myself to keep going.

The night was still, without so much as a breeze. I was the only moving object, vainly trying to reach the city. After a time, the pain and sense of futility cracked my resolve. Now, the more I focused on the lights of the city, the more I wanted to give up. I checked my watch. It was 3:50 a.m. I panicked. I wanted to go faster, but I had no energy. My legs moved mechanically under me. I knew if I sat down to rest, I wouldn't get up. It was then that I prayed sincerely for the first time in my life. Desperately, naively, I expected an instant result. I looked at stars in the sky and tried to will some connection. *Please God, give me more energy to march farther and enter Kassala. You got me this far and you have to let me finish the journey.* Nothing happened. My mother always said that God answered her prayers because she prayed regularly, not like me, out of desperation. But I knew that she was praying for me, even at that moment. I hoped He would grant her prayer if not mine.

God helps those who help themselves. Keep moving. I heard my mother's voice echoing in my head and I stepped forward as if propelled by an outside force. In fact, I was. A wind had picked up at my back and was blowing me in the direction of Kassala. It was like a miracle. A constant gust that bore me forward. My legs moved faster. The hopeless feeling vanished. Now I strode with great confidence and hope. In half an hour I found myself behind a small hill that blocked the lights of Kassala. When I sped up and went around the hill, I saw hundreds of huts. I had reached a satellite village of Kassala, Krama.

"Thank you, God," I said under my breath.

Once in the village, I felt a sense of relief. Most people who lived in Kassala and its outskirt districts were Eritreans from the ethnic group of Tigre known as the Bini-amir tribe. Everything was quiet. I avoided the huts on the exposed perimeter, looking for one deeper inside the settlement. I saw three huts surrounded by a one-metre-high wooden fence. I pushed open the wooden gate and, once inside the compound, lay down on the ground intending to rest until the residents awoke at five for prayers. My watch read 4:30, and I didn't intend to sleep, but I drifted off almost immediately.

"*Alah ilalah!*" the loud voice of a man shouting in Arabic resounded in my head. At first I thought it was a dream but as he kept shouting, I opened my eyes and saw a tall man in a white robe gripping a stick in one hand ready to strike.

I raised both my hands to show him that I wasn't armed.

"*Ana shakhs masalim,*" (I am a peaceful person), I said in Arabic. He stepped back, and I raised myself to a sitting position. He kept speaking in Arabic, which I didn't understand. I told him in a Tigre language that I didn't speak Arabic well. My knowledge of Tigre was also rusty, but I could speak it well enough to convey the basics.

"Are you Muslim or Christian?" he asked.

I wasn't surprised to hear the question, in fact I expected it, like a student who has prepared well for an exam. While I was in

107

my hiding place, I had rehearsed answers to a variety of questions or scenarios that I might face in Sudan. My name, religion, the place I grew up, and the school I enrolled in, etc. Beside that I had a fair knowledge of the Sudanese culture. The majority of the people mistrusted Christians unfamiliar to them, but they trusted Muslims even if they were strangers. I had to lie.

"I am Muslim. Jeberti," I said. "My name is Aman Abdu. I hope you know the Jeberti. We are Muslim Tigrigna speakers."

"I know the Jeberti. I know a few people from the Jeberti community here."

"I need your help. Can you introduce me to them, please?"

He stared at my bleeding feet sympathetically and furrowed his brow in thought.

"What's your name?" I asked.

"Yasin," he said, and shook my hand. "You're injured. Your pants are full of blood."

"No, I'm all right, but I'm very thirsty. Can I have water, please?"

"You have to come inside before the police see-you," he said, glancing at the huts across the road. The police station was located about 150 metres from his hut. I felt a surge of panic when he told me that, but there was nothing that I could do except to rely on his help.

Yasin led me inside his hut and gave me water. He told me to rest while he went to the mosque for morning prayers. The hut was very spare. Its sole decorations were pictures of camels and mosques. There was one small rope bed, without a mattress or even a blanket. I lay down on the bed and slept like a corpse until he returned. He let me sleep for several hours but I roused when I heard him speaking to some other men, his cousins, outside the hut.

"*Enta mejnun*," (you are crazy), I heard one of them say.

I listened, keeping utterly still. The men tried to convince Yasin to report me to the police since they believed he'd made a huge mistake by letting me stay in his place. They questioned if I was really a Muslim. Wouldn't a Muslim have come along to prayers? Yasin defended me and described me as a peaceful person who just needed their help. He told them of my injured legs and how exhausted I was.

Finally, they decided to wake me and question me themselves. Three of them entered the hut and woke me up. I pretended to be asleep and opened my eyes slowly.

"Have you rested well?" Yasin asked.

"Yes, thank you," I nodded.

"Where is your gun?" a bearded older man asked aggressively.

"I don't have a gun."

"If you are in the national service, of course you have a gun," he barked. "Where did you hide it?"

"No, I'm not in the national service. I'm a teacher," I said.

"Why did you run away then?"

"I received a scholarship to study in South Africa, but the government refused to give me an exit visa. So I fled to pursue my education in South Africa." I told them that I'd lost my documents crossing the border. Their suspicions of me seemed to ease. They nodded their heads and exchanged cautious looks with one another.

"Where did you learn how to speak Tigre?" The bearded man asked, now with more curiosity than suspicion.

"Tigre is a widely spoken language in Eritrea, but I learned from my friends at school who speak Tigre."

"Impressive!" he smiled and shook my hand. "We will help you."

They brought me a gauze bandage and rubbing alcohol to clean my wounds. They trimmed my beard in a Sudanese style and dressed me in a white robe just like them. They served me porridge for breakfast, extending me the hospitality of a family member. Finally, Yasin accompanied me to the centre of town and helped me to exchange one hundred U.S. dollars to Sudanese gunaih. He also introduced me to the Jeberti Association, a group that advocated for the rights of the Jeberti people in Eritrea.

Yasin was a God-sent angel for me. He missed work to take me around, show me the city, the bus station where I could start to Khartoum, and the telephone booth. He gave me his white robe, sandals, and hat. And he refused to accept money from me.

"God sent you to me," Yasin said, "and it is my honour to fulfill His wishes."

His generosity and compassion touched me deeply.

"Now you look Sudanese, so no one will bother you," he said. Then he wished me luck and left me.

I bought an Arabic newspaper and sat in a tea shop near the bus station to observe my surroundings. It was sunny and hot despite being winter. Some people shopped at the vegetable stores, some went to the bus station. Most seemed involved in their daily routine, except for two men who stood idly near a convenience store that also provided phone service. I had agreed with Mielat that I would call her at two, if I made it safely to Kassala. I kept an eye on the two men and wondered what they were waiting for.

The Eritrean intelligence agencies did whatever they wanted in Sudan. They often kidnapped people from Kassala, either with the collusion of corrupt Sudanese police or simply of their own accord. The Al-Bashir regime was thoroughly corrupt and the Eritrean intelligence agencies exploited it easily. I kept eyeing the two men and wondering if they were indeed Eritrean agents. There was no way I could know. So, rather than take a chance, I decided not to place my call from that convenience store. I paid for the tea and crossed the road and walked further from the main street under the palm trees. I saw a small convenience store and entered there.

A young man in his twenties greeted me from behind the counter. The store was about twenty-five square metres in total. I was the sole customer. Behind the young man, I observed a room that evidently served as a residence. I could hear a muffled voice coming from within.

"*Alekum weselam*," I said in Tigre. "I would like to make a call to Eritrea."

"I am sorry, we don't provide calling service here," the young man replied and looked behind him at the closed door.

"Why not?" I asked.

"My father decided it wasn't profitable. But I can tell you where to go."

I didn't want to go anywhere, but hoped I could convince him to let me call from there.

"How much do they charge?"

"I think it is 1.5 gunaih for a minute," he said while checking his watch.

I offered to pay double if he allowed me to place the call.

He seemed tempted, but once again looked behind him at the door.

"You know, my father —"

I interrupted him and asked him his name.

"Ameer."

"Ameer, please," I said. "I will pay triple the price and only need it for two minutes."

Ameer brought the phone toward me reluctantly and I wrote the number for him on a piece of paper. He dialed and handed me the handset. After a few rings, Mielat answered. When she heard my voice, and that I was out, she shouted with excitement.

"Thank God! You made it!" she screamed with happiness and didn't realize how loud she was until she was interrupted by my daughter. "It's nothing sweetie, stay in the other room. I will tell you soon."

"Look, Mielat, I don't have much time now. Is Petros back?" I asked.

"Not yet." She wanted to talk more, but I knew I had to end the call.

"I will call you in a few days when I'm sitting on the sofa," I said. *Sofa* was our code word for Khartoum. My heart hammered in my chest as I hung up the phone. I would have loved to hear the voices of my kids, but I decided to let that wait. I paid Ameer what I'd promised and left the store.

According to the plan, Petros was supposed to have been in Asmara by noon, waiting with Mielat for my call. I took it as a bad sign that he wasn't there. I felt that I needed to leave Kassala immediately for Khartoum, and hoped to learn there what had happened to him.

I returned to the Jeberti Association, hoping that the senior person there might be able to assist me. The association was housed in a compound of wood slats woven together. About fifteen people were inside, taking refuge in the shade. Some played checkers while others whiled away the time in conversation. I passed through them toward the hut that served as the centre's office.

"*Selamat*," I said, standing in the doorless entrance.

A bald older man returned my greeting. He was a man I'd met when Yasin brought me around the first time.

"You're back," he said. "After prayer I will introduce you to Sheik Osman."

He smiled and left the room to prepare himself for prayer. I followed him. About twenty people had lined up in three rows in the yard, and I tried to join the line. But when I saw a man I guessed might be Sheik Osman, I moved toward him. I watched him wash his hands and face in preparation for prayer and imitated his actions. Afterwards, I joined the lineup while Sheik Osman stood before everyone to lead the prayers.

Salah (prayer) is the most important ritual of the Islamic faith, performed five times daily. Everyone there knew how to conduct themselves, except for me. Hoping to be least conspicuous, I chose a spot in the rearmost line, so that nobody would observe me from behind. Unfortunately, once the prayers started, three new people arrived and formed a fourth row. Now there were people who could notice if I failed to properly mimic the actions of the man in front of me. At one point, when all the others rested their foreheads on the ground and prayed, I prematurely stood up. I hoped that nobody noticed my mistakes or paid attention to the sounds emanating from my mouth, since I was merely humming in some approximation of what I heard around me. Unfortunately, as soon as the prayers were over, a man with a lazy eye grabbed me by the hand.

"Are you really a Muslim or are you here for papers?" He still held my hand as he questioned me. I realized they were used to having visitors like me come for help in getting papers for travel to Khartoum, but I didn't want to admit it.

"Yes, I am a Muslim." I stared at him. "Are you?"

"I don't believe you, come," he pulled me toward Sheik Osman. I pulled my hand free and told him I would go voluntarily. I remembered a conversation I had with Petros while we were working through different scenarios that could help me on my journey. Petros hadn't liked it when I told him I might present myself as a Jeberti Muslim.

"That would be a big mistake," Petros had said. "What if they ask you to pray in front of them?" His question struck me, and I hadn't known how to respond. I had picked up the Arabic-Tigrigna phrase book he had brought me and flipped through the pages.

"That book can only teach you basic conversational Arabic, not the Islamic prayers," Petros had said. I might learn how to pray by reading, but I still might mess it up under pressure.

"Come," the man barked. Like a child rushing to his father to report the misdeeds of his brother, the man ran to Sheik Osman and, in a flurry, told on me in detail.

Sheik Osman, a man in his sixties, short, portly, and grey-bearded, nevertheless greeted me warmly.

"What a blessing Allah brought you to your brothers," he said as he sat on a rope chair. He invited me to sit beside him and gestured for the other man to go.

"We are all human, we all make mistakes," he said and asked me my name.

"Aman Abdu," I replied.

While I expected him to subject me to a line of questioning to establish my identity, he instead expounded about the history of the Jeberti and their persecution at the hands of the Orthodox Christians of Eritrea. How they became a nation of merchants, tailors, shopkeepers, and urban dwellers because their land rights were denied. How their existence as a distinct ethnicity was rejected by the Eritrean government, who suspected them of being a fifth column for Ethiopia.

Sheik Osman also claimed to know the roots of every Jeberti family in Eritrea.

"What we need to do is to extend that network even in exile to fight for our rights," he said.

He sounded very knowledgeable and erudite. I suspected that he might indeed know the ancestors of every Jeberti family in Eritrea and consequently could catch me in my lie and hand me over to the Sudanese police. I badly needed him to believe me and connect me with someone who could get me a document for travel from Kassala to Khartoum. No Eritrean could transit from one city to another in Sudan without such a pass. Through regular channels this request could take a month or more, but brokers could be hired to bribe officials who could issue a pass right away.

"Now, tell me your story," he said, leaning back in his chair.

I told him that I was from Nefasit and that my father was named Abdu Hassen. In fact, I did have a Jeberti friend from Nefasit and had been the best man at his wedding. I knew his family very well, so it was easy for me to impersonate him.

"You are Abdu's son?" Sheik Osman asked with a puzzled face. I nodded.

"Abdu is a short man like me, and he has three children, two boys and one girl," he said, looking at me from head to toe. I was shocked that he knew the family as well as I did. "The one son is —" I cut him off.

"Yes, Semir is living in Saudi Arabia, and Yasin in Massawa, and Nejat got married and is living in Asmara. We don't have the same mother," I said.

"*Ya ilalalah.*"

"My mother is Christian. I was raised by my mother in Asmara and I don't think many family members on my father's side know of my existence," I said. I told him that my knowledge of the Islamic religion was weak and that I was eager to learn more.

"My poor son!" he cried, and promised to help me. He looked over to where the man who had suspected me loitered with his friends. Sheik Osman rose from his seat and beckoned the man. I also rose.

"He is our brother," Sheik Osman said to the man, who nodded his head but didn't apologize. He then moved on to speak to two other congregants.

The centre was a quiet place to relax. There were two pots of cold water for any thirsty person to drink, and mats for people to rest on, and checkers for entertainment. People came there to pray and discuss current events, politics, and business. Several men approached me to offer greetings and ask after news from Eritrea. They told me most of them came to Sudan a long time ago to live in an Islamic country instead of a Christian one. They spoke about the constant harassment Muslims faced in Eritrea and how the Orthodox Christians were trying to eradicate them. I felt like they were speaking about a country I didn't know and tried to correct their impressions.

The population of Eritrea was 50 percent Muslim and relations between Christians and Muslims were mostly harmonious, unlike in Sudan or Ethiopia. The Christians celebrated Eid with their Muslim neighbours, and the Muslims celebrated Christmas with their Christian ones. I saw several intermarriages too. Even when Emperor Haile Selassie ordered his soldiers to kill Muslims in the 1960s in Hazomo, the southern part of Eritrea, Christian villages like Seree and Kelaibaaltiet gave them refuge by letting them wear a wooden cross around their necks. It seemed to me that some radicals spread propaganda to recruit Muslims to their organizations. I said that the Eritrean government harassed Christians and Muslims alike. But I didn't think my words convinced them.

I saw that Sheik Osman had concluded his conversation with the two men and I went to him. He'd had a man named Omar in mind, a man who could serve as a broker.

"No luck, my son," Sheik Osman said. "Omar hasn't come back yet. He will be back after tomorrow and he will get your pass then. If you have a place to stay tonight that would be good. Tomorrow I will connect you with one of our members and you can stay with him until you get your papers in order."

I was devastated. I'd pinned my hopes on this for lack of any other alternative. There was no way I could wait that long, but I didn't want to shut that door forever. I thanked Sheik Osman and left the centre, promising to come back the next day.

I decided to go back to the only other person who had shown me any kindness. I found Ameer still at the counter of his convenience store where he had been earlier that afternoon and asked if he might know someone who could help me get a pass to Khartoum so I could catch my flight to South Africa. Ameer said he'd never been involved in such dealings and didn't know where to start. But as I felt I had no other choice but to convince him to do a miracle for me, I promised to pay him handsomely if he could do it. Whether it was the money or his generous nature, Ameer said he would try. I watched as he called several people and spoke to them in Arabic. I didn't understand a single word, but his body language was telling. He grimaced and struck the table with his fist each time he hung up his Nokia phone. Finally he reached a low-ranking Sudanese police officer who had gone to high school with him.

"Come," he smiled and looked at me. "My police friend is coming over to discuss it, but he hasn't done it before either."

Ten minutes later, Ameer's friend showed up. A tall, dark man dressed in civilian clothes stretched his hand out to greet me. He looked more like a merchant than a policeman. He pulled out a small plastic pouch full of tobacco from the pocket of his white robe, pinched a small amount with his index and thumb, and dipped it between his gums and lips. He offered some to each of us, but we declined. Ameer quickly went through the introductions and explained the urgency of my situation and the one hundred U.S. dollars I had offered to pay for the document. The sum clearly made an impression on the policeman, and he left the room with a broad smile on his face.

"He will speak with his superior and let us know soon," Ameer said, his voice full of excitement. He sounded optimistic, as if he'd found the key that would unlock my problem.

"For a Sudanese policeman, one hundred American dollars is six months' salary."

The store didn't seem to be busy; only three customers came to buy cigarettes and tobacco while I was there.

"Is it slow today because it's Sunday?" I asked and immediately realized my mistake for assuming Sunday was their holiday.

"Sunday is like any other day, Friday is the holiday of the week here," he said while locking the door of the shop for the day. He invited me to follow him out the back door of the shop into a courtyard where there were three plastic chairs and a small table beside a *mim* tree. He bade me to sit there while he went back to get us tea and bread.

Ameer was a great host and a friendly person. While we sat together, he told me briefly about his life.

He lived with his mother, father, and sister. His father, currently in Dubai, had an import-export business. His ultimate goal was to become like his father and import electronic items to Eritrea. His biggest regret was he had never been to Eritrea, though it was his family's ancestral home. But his father forbade him to go because he didn't want him to be conscripted into the national service.

Though I tried to listen attentively, my mind wandered, anxious about the pass. The more time passed, the more restless I became.

Two hours later, Ameer's phone rang.

He spoke briefly and hung up. "It was my sister," he said.

"Can you check on your friend, please?" I asked. "He was supposed to call back by now, right?"

"Let's give him a few minutes, he will call." Ameer stood up and collected the cups to return to the house. I looked up at the sky and saw countless bright stars. I tried to spot a falling star that could bless me with luck. I wasn't superstitious, but I was willing to grasp at anything. I watched to see if a star might fall on my right and bring good news from Ameer's friend. But no such thing happened, and Ameer showed up with a bowl of rice and placed it before me. He poured sugar on the rice.

"Let's have dinner," he said. He scooped the rice with a spoon and put it on the two plates. I was overwhelmed with his generosity. Though I wasn't hungry and didn't like eating rice mixed with sugar, I ate out of respect for him. Before we finished our plates, the phone rang.

"It's him," Ameer said to me. He listened quietly, spoke a few words, and hung up.

"What did he say?"

"His boss is in, and his boss is calling his superior, but he said they may ask for more money," Ameer looked at me to gauge my reaction. "But don't worry, we will convince them to accept the terms. A hundred dollars is a lot of money for them." I nodded my head and kept eating.

The good news arrived one hour later. Ameer answered the phone and leaped up with happiness. "It's done! Let's go. They are waiting near the office."

We walked to the main street and took a taxi to get there. While Ameer expressed his excitement by saying the paper had already been signed by one officer, I resisted becoming excited until the other person in charge signed as well, since the pass had to be signed by two senior officials. The taxi stopped near an old building surrounded by trees. Ameer called to inform his friend that we'd arrived. I gave him US$150 and told him to check the document and negotiate on my behalf.

"I trust you," I said.

Five minutes later, Ameer's friend showed up with the paper. I looked on as they engaged in a cordial discussion in Arabic while I tested the paper's authenticity with my fingers. There was no way I could know whether it was valid or not, but I had to trust them.

"They are asking for one hundred and twenty-five dollars," Ameer said.

"It's all up to you. That's your money now."

I put the paper in my pocket and waited for Ameer to finish his negotiation and contemplated my next challenge — finding somewhere to spend the night. Ameer showed up with a broad smile and jumped in the taxi.

"If you want, you can stay with me tonight," Ameer said, "and I will take you to the bus station tomorrow morning. It's outside the city."

Most people were sleeping outdoors on account of the heat. I slept in a hammock in Ameer's backyard. He gave me two blankets in case I got cold. I lay on my back and looked at the stars the whole night. Thinking about my angels — Yasin and Ameer — who sheltered me, fed me, and assisted me, while the devils — Eritrean intelligence agencies — were searching for me in every hotel in Kassala to burn me in their fires.

"The Angel always wins," my mother would say. Indeed, my angels had won.

In the morning, Ameer accompanied me to the bus station and wished me luck.

"I hope *Rebi* (God) will compensate you for your good deeds, Ameer." I hugged him like an old friend.

There were nine buses at the station. I carefully monitored my surroundings before I boarded mine. All the other travellers seemed preoccupied with their own affairs — loading their baggage or scanning for their buses — and paid me no mind. I was the only one without luggage, carrying only a newspaper. I followed the line of passengers and took a window seat at the middle of the bus. It was a cozy bus, with comfortable seats, two video screens, and even an air conditioner.

Once everyone had boarded, some sixty passengers, I gazed about and identified ten Eritreans who, despite their best efforts, had not convincingly disguised themselves. Some of them spoke Tigrigna, and some of them didn't wear the small round hats of the Sudanese. Silently, in my heart, I wished them the luck they'd need to pass successfully through the four checkpoints on our way.

The bus started its 625-kilometre journey from Kassala to Khartoum at 5:30 a.m. The minute I sat down, I resolved to behave like a deaf person. The passenger who sat beside me was convinced, and left me to enjoy my solitude for the nine-hour journey. I pretended to read my Arabic newspaper. Some passengers started chatting with their neighbours. Others dozed off. The morning sun filtered in through the windows on the eastern side of the bus.

Coming from a mountainous country, I marvelled at the uninterrupted flatness that stretched ahead for hundreds of kilometres. The bus drove smoothly on the well-maintained road. There was hardly a bump. I felt like I was flying.

Around ten, we reached the first checkpoint. Two police officers entered the bus and walked down the aisle asking for the passes of those they suspected of being Eritrean. They did not give me a second glance. At the second checkpoint, some hours later, this procedure was repeated with the same results. After that check, the bus stopped at the roadside to give us passengers a chance to stretch our legs or eat lunch. After ten minutes, we resumed our journey.

At around three in the afternoon, we reached the third checkpoint, and here the approach was different. Two officers entered the bus, and asked anyone they suspected of being Eritrean to disembark. Of the ten I had spotted, they selected five. Each of them

121

had a pass, but it was known that sometimes corrupt officers would shake down passengers anyway for bribes. Ten minutes elapsed, then fifteen, then twenty. I heard passengers start to grumble about the delay. Finally, the police allowed three of the five to return but detained the other two. I heard one of the Eritreans say, in Tigrigna, to a girl as he passed, "They wanted a bribe." I felt very sorry for my two countrymen who had been detained. I imagined that their fate could not be a good one. I thought about them all the way to the final checkpoint. This last one passed without incident and I fell asleep.

One hour later, the bus stopped, and I was awakened by a passenger who shouted in Arabic, "We have arrived in Khartoum!"

CHAPTER 8

TRAVEL DOCUMENT: KHARTOUM

SINCE I HAD CONTACTS, IT WAS EASY TO NAVIGATE KHARTOUM. A RELA-
tive of my sister's husband offered me a place in his three-room
house in the Giref neighbourhood. It was round, with mud walls
and a conical straw roof. Each room housed a different Eritrean
family; they had been there for fifteen years. They told me most
Eritrean immigrants lived in the Giref or Tsehafa neighbourhoods,
working with the Eritrean Embassy in Khartoum to raise funds
for orphaned children of war, doing voluntary activities on national holidays, etc. I didn't sleep well that night, worried that
the neighbours might tell other neighbours about my presence,
and that word would reach Khartoum's Eritrean Embassy, which
infiltrated community networks to gather information. So the
next day I moved out in search of a place to rent in a Sudanese
neighbourhood.

As I walked Giref's main street in search of its internet café,
I noticed a small group of Eritrean youths passing, wearing the
same sort of jeans and shirts as youths did in Asmara. Seeing their
hesitancy, I guessed they were also new to Khartoum and also
looking for an internet café. However, we were heading in different

directions. As I wondered which way I should go, another group of men came toward me. Among them, I saw a former classmate at the University of Asmara: Alexander Teame. He was a tall, thin, and very compassionate man. After graduation he had landed a job at the Ministry of Information but, as I soon found out, he had later fled the country. It was a great relief to find someone I could trust, and whom I could ask for information.

"Hey, Alex!" I called. Alex, confused, stared at me. My clothes and beard made me look Sudanese. I had long whiskers all over my face but left very little on the upper part of my lip. He knew me when I had had a simple moustache. "It is me, Aaron Berhane," I had to say as I approached him. When he could see my eyes clearly, he laughed.

"Oh my God, indeed it is you," he said, hugging me. We stepped away from the others to share our stories. Alex had fled to Sudan a year earlier and now ran an internet café with a friend, just a hundred metres from where we stood. He gave me a brief introductory lesson on Khartoum and its Eritrean refugees, and on the Eritrean government's activities in the city. I told him to keep my identity secret, even from his friends, but he assured me they could all be trusted, except for one acquaintance who frequented the Eritrean Embassy.

Getting money was my first big challenge in Khartoum, and Alex quickly solved that. He introduced me to his two friends, Yonas and Tesfom, and they both helped me transfer money and showed me around the city while I was there. I needed my wife to send me money, but it could not be via regular channels. Yonas ran several businesses with his uncle in Sudan, so we arranged that my wife would deliver the money to Yonas's sister living in Asmara, and I would take the same amount of money from Yonas. My biggest initial problem had been solved instantly, in one phone call.

Finding a secure place to stay was my next challenge.

Most Eritrean migrants lived in houses subdivided by mud walls into small rental units. A group of five, six, or more would occupy a single room. Since it was easier to join an existing group than to rent a new place, the group might grow to ten. No one cared about comfort: most slept on the floor with their heads on the ground. They considered their accommodation only temporary, a place to stay until they left for Libya or somewhere else.

Four days later, as I walked to Alex's internet café to ask him to help me find a place to rent within the Sudanese Arkawit neighbourhood, I met a man I had known while teaching in Mendefera. He was a relative of a colleague, and his name was Misgina. He had been living in Khartoum for about two years with his two friends Fanus and Sulieman. Like other Eritrean youths, they had fled to Sudan at the end of the Eritrean-Ethiopian border conflict, after the Eritrean government refused their request to be demobilized from national service. They lived in the very neighbourhood where I wanted to stay, and I didn't hesitate to say yes when they suggested I share their room, rather than renting one of my own.

Their home was comfortable and secure: a huge room of fifty-six square metres with a conical awning made of straw for shade, a shower, and a huge tree, all surrounded by a compound fence. Moreover, they refused to let me pay my share of the rent once they learned my plan. My plan was to stay until I acquired proper papers that would not jeopardize my future, and then leave to another country. It might take weeks or months, I didn't have a clue. From day one, they assiduously supported and protected me during my four-month stay in Khartoum. They made it possible for me to move around the city undetected; they provided the information and protection I needed to be able to visit the office of the United Nations High Commissioner for Refugees (UNHCR), meet the right people, or visit internet cafés.

Once I found a new home to stay in, with the help of these amazing people, four days after my arrival in Khartoum, I initiated email and telephone contact with my wife, Mielat, with friends in Eritrea, and with journalist-advocacy organizations. It was then I learned the terrible news: Gebray had been captured; my cousin Petros, my brother Amanuel, and my fixer Samson were arrested; my wife and mother had been questioned at the police station in Asmara. I also learned that four National Security agents had been sent to Khartoum to kidnap me. I was devastated. I had so many questions, but no answers. The situation was volatile, and my wife's phone was tapped, which made it harder to touch base with her easily. So, I had to depend on my accountant friend to arrange phone calls with my wife. I would email him to set up a call at a specific date and time, and he would arrange it. Mielat would then go to a friend's house to receive the call.

I remember the last time I called Asmara from Khartoum, on January 20, 2002. I asked who had betrayed us. "You have to leave Sofa immediately." (*Sofa* was our code name for Khartoum.) "It is not safe" was all Mielat told me, her voice trembling. "Let's not talk again until you get out of Sofa." For her safety, and for that of my friends, I immediately cut all phone communication with her.

Suddenly, the insecurity that I had already felt in Khartoum had become far greater, I no longer felt safe walking around in the city, even in disguise. Since no one knew who the Eritrean government agents were, or what they looked like, I began avoiding areas where Eritrean immigrants congregated, and where the agents might mingle. I stopped communicating with all but a few individuals whom I could trust, and attended only meetings I organized myself.

I created a sort of routine for myself to avoid boredom. I woke up at 10 a.m.; read the *Sudan Tribune*, the Sudanese English newspaper, for an hour; ate breakfast at eleven; read whatever book I found in the house until 4:30; ate lunch around five, and went out around seven, either to an internet café or to meet people who could help me leave the city.

I sent one email after another to Dr. Asefaw Tekekste, a former senior official of the Eritrean government who had defected after the crackdown, and other influential individuals who now lived in Europe and the U.S.A., asking them to send me an invitation letter that could allow me to enter the country where they lived. They were supportive in principle but didn't promise anything concrete. I soon realized I would have to pursue another path.

One afternoon, I asked my roommate Fanus to arrange a meeting with Robel, a former journalist from the independent *Wintana* newspaper in Eritrea. According to my friends, he had fled Eritrea before all the independent newspapers were closed, after being conscripted into the national service to fulfill his duty. He had been in Khartoum only a year or so, but he had built a good network and also started working at a retail store in the city centre.

"You are really lucky, Aaron," Robel said when we met in a coffee shop near his workplace. He was a gentle soul and eager to help however he could. He told me about Milkias and Semere, journalists from *Kestedebena* who had fled Eritrea a few weeks before their newspaper's closure, about the threats they received in Sudan from Eritrean government agents, and about their escape from Sudan to Ethiopia. Both journalists had taken refuge in the Ethiopian Embassy in Khartoum before flying to Addis Ababa.

Asking asylum in Khartoum's Ethiopian Embassy was not an option for me. First, I didn't want to justify my accusers' false accusations that my friends and I were collaborating with Ethiopia. Second, I never trusted the Ethiopian regime. I saw Ethiopian Prime Minister Meles's and President Isaias's regimes as two sides of the same coin. Immediately after Eritrea's independence, I had begun to believe Meles and Isaias had certain agendas to see

Eritrean patriotism and pride weakened in my country and gradually to shape the region's future geopolitics to their whims.

The first question I had discussed repeatedly with my friends and my cohort generally at the University of Asmara was this: Why was the border not yet demarcated? I even asked Eritrea's president that question in 1995, when he invited citizens to ask him any question they wanted. Unfortunately, my question was not selected for an answer, and I could not go with those whose questions had been selected to hear the president answer them in person at the Cinema Capitol's theatre hall. The president did, however, answer that question on another occasion: "We should think beyond the border," he had said, emphasizing that a border shouldn't be necessary, or even be an issue. So, who knew how the Ethiopian regime would respond if the Eritrean regime asked them to arrest me? I never wanted to take that risk.

All I thought about was flying to Kenya. I needed a passport to fly there, and I didn't want to buy a fake one. A false passport might complicate any future refugee process, so I decided to approach UNHCR for help despite the possible danger. I had been told the UNHCR was unsafe, that some interpreters or staff there were on the local Eritrean Embassy's payroll. I had no option but to go there two weeks after my arrival in Khartoum.

I left my house that morning around eight. The buildings in my neighbourhood were stunning, but many of the streets were either unpaved gravel or in bad repair. As I walked along them toward the main street in search of a taxi, I noticed pots boiling in front of several convenience or grocery stores, right next to the street. Later I learned that the shopkeepers were boiling beans for breakfast, to be eaten around ten thirty or eleven. Sudanese took their breakfast tradition very seriously: many store owners or employees wouldn't serve you around that time, inviting you instead to join them for breakfast. Breakfast was superb: they would put *ful* (boiled beans) into a bowl, smash them up, and then mix in sesame oil, feta cheese, tomatoes, and onions before offering them with bread. Locals would sit on the ground around the bowl and eat together. Neighbours or strangers who approached would be invited to join in. The generosity fascinated me. "No one goes hungry," a shopkeeper told me once, when I expressed my fascination.

I took a three-wheel taxi, or *raksha*, to the UNHCR office that day. The driver was young, probably in his twenties, and he drove like crazy, speeding and honking all the way, ignoring the traffic rules. He drove through stop signs, cut corners, squeezed between other cars. I yelled at him several times to drive carefully. "*Maalesh*," (it's okay, sorry), he'd reply, and carry on. I didn't know how to convey to him that my Arabic was limited. He turned from the main road onto a dusty unpaved road without slowing, almost overturning us as his right rear tire left the road and I bounced up and down like an inflated ball. I was outraged: I'd survived gunfire at the border only to have a reckless driver end my life on the streets of Khartoum. "*Qaf*," (stop), I roared. He slowed, muttered something, and pointed ahead of him. I told him again to stop, and he did. I grabbed his neck and twisted his face toward me, staring at him for a few seconds before telling him to drive slowly. He understood my expression, if not my words. He nodded in agreement, trembling, then drove on carefully in silence. For the first time, I could pay attention to the buildings I was passing and noticed there were countless plastic garbage bags along the streets. Suddenly, we arrived at the UNHCR office. I paid my fare and jumped out of the *raksha*.

The offices were inside a modern building surrounded by a long compound. Though it was only 8:30 a.m., about fifty people were lined up outside. Most were young Eritreans. They teased one another in Tigrigna, laughed loudly, and glanced at the gate now and then. I felt I was watching high school students on their break.

They were twenty metres away from the entrance. I went straight to the security guard there, ignoring the line.

"*Eud*," (Go back), the security guard said. Ignoring his order, I approached him. "*Eud!*" he said again, standing up.

"*Lahzat wahida*," (One moment), I replied.

A skinny translator popped out from the gate and told me in a Tigre language to get into the line. Presumably he had assumed I was Tigre, given my dress.

"I have an urgent case," I said.

"Do you have an appointment?"

"No, but my case is urgent."

"Yeah, that's what I hear every day," he said in Tigrigna, apparently recognizing my accent.

"This is different, sir. I have to speak with a protection officer, now."

"It is not going to happen. Line up to book an appointment," he said as he moved inside the gate. Although I called him repeatedly, he disappeared inside the compound. I stood there like a statue, not knowing what to do. My anger was boiling at being denied the immediate help I needed before it was too late. The security guard pushed me back when I didn't obey his order to move.

I left the premises immediately. I needed to work out how to get into the building without waiting in line or being stopped by the guard. Walking back to the main road, I hailed a taxi to take me to the nearest internet café. The driver could have led me a merry chase, since I was new to the city, but instead he drove for about five minutes and dropped me in front of the building.

Entering the café, I saw five young Eritreans waiting for the seven computers already in use. It felt like I was still in Asmara, this running into Eritreans wherever I went. I stood near the door scanning the street for trouble. Not recognizing me as Eritrean, the youths chatted freely about their travel plans and their travel brokers, their attention captivated by one youth in their group who seemed the most knowledgeable.

"If you pay five thousand American dollars, he can take you to Europe using a Schengen visa," he said. "The visa lets you go to any European country you want. If you want to go to America, it costs you ten thousand dollars, and he takes you there via Hong Kong to Mexico, from where you can sneak into America. If you want to go to South Africa …"

The café's owner called "Next!" when someone left the computer. Since the boys remained engrossed in their conversation about how to get out of Sudan, I slipped through the small counter door to occupy the now-free computer. There I searched the contact information for the UNHCR protection officer in Khartoum, writing down every phone number I saw on the screen. The boys were still talking about the broker and how to get smuggled out of Sudan when I left the café.

I couldn't stop thinking about the youths' conversation as I went to find a telephone. Some brokers prey on desperate Eritrean refugees, taking their money but not delivering any service. My roommates told me many stories about people scammed out of five or ten thousand dollars by brokers or smugglers who take the money, then disappear. In the end, it's the family members living in Europe or North America who bear the financial cost for their young brothers' and sisters' escapes.

Reaching the right person at the UNHCR office via phone was challenging: I was transferred from one person to another like a pinball. At one point, someone flatly told me to book an appointment in person, then hung up. It was frustrating, but I didn't give up. Finally, after calling again and again at least fifteen times, I found someone who seemed ready to hear my request on the phone.

"I know you called earlier; the protection officer is right here. I can translate for you," the male voice said in Tigrigna.

"Thank you, sir. Can I speak with the officer directly, please? I may not need a translator," I said.

Ignoring my request, he kept asking questions in Tigrigna.

"What is your name?" he asked.

"My name is Aman Abdu, but I would really appreciate it if you connect me with the officer to discuss my issues," I said. I heard him translating my statements into English for someone.

"Hello, this is Janet, how can I help you?" a female voice said.

"Thank you for speaking with me. I have a very serious issue, but I would like to speak to someone in person. Can I meet you in your office today, please?" I heard them speaking to each other but couldn't make out what they said.

"Can you tell me what is going on?"

"I am scared for my life, but I can't say much on the phone. I can't wait in line with the rest of the refugees, because my case is not the same as others. Please give me five minutes of your time."

She paused for a while, probably checking her schedule. Finally, she agreed to meet me the next day at 11 a.m. in her office, giving me explicit instructions on how to find it. I was thrilled and left the phone booth smiling from ear to ear. Anyone seeing me at that moment might assume I'd discovered the ultimate solution to the human condition. I walked with confidence, a big grin on my face, feeling the air fill my lungs. Everything looked perfect for me, even the burning sun.

I had learned from experience how to celebrate each victory without losing the momentum to continue moving forward. My celebration ceremony was simple: I smiled and greeted people warmly whether I knew them or not. For an hour, I thought only about the delightful news, refusing to think about my other problems.

The next day, I went to the UNHCR office around 10 a.m., as agreed the day before. Ignoring the long line I went straight to the guard and asked him to call Efriem for me, as arranged. The tall guard stood up, spat out his *toombak* (a special Sudanese snuff) and with his big boot covered it with dirt. He hadn't understood me, either because I had mispronounced the Arabic words, or because my grammar had been wrong. Instead of asking me, he turned to his colleague and asked him what I had said. I repeated the name again, Efriem, and added that I had an appointment. They told me to wait there. After a few minutes, a tall Eritrean man wearing a grey suit but no tie came to ask my name. I gave him the same false name as earlier: "Aman." He immediately allowed me in and let me sit in a corner with some refugees. Before I could ask his name, one of his colleagues called "Efriem," and asked him in Arabic to come with him. I understood the action, though not the language.

"Stay here. I will call you at eleven," he said as he left.

I sat there looking through a newspaper, but I hardly read a word. I checked everyone passing in the corridor, especially if they looked like Eritreans. I knew Eritrean Embassy spies worked there as interpreters or staff, but I didn't know who they were. My only option was to distrust any Eritrean who worked there.

A few minutes later, Efriem returned and escorted me to the office of Janet, the protection officer with whom I had my appointment. As we walked along the long, wide corridor, past a long line of offices, Efriem described how many people like me he had helped, his extensive experience, and how well connected he was to senior UN administrators. I nodded silently in agreement. Finally, we reached Janet's office, and knocked on the door.

"Please come in," a voice requested. I followed Efriem inside.

A tall, well-dressed Black woman in her thirties rose from her desk and came toward me. She wore a red jacket, black trousers, and high heels.

She greeted me warmly.

"Welcome, my name is Janet Mugai," she said, stretching out her hand.

"Good morning, Janet," I replied, shaking her hand. Looking closely at her, I saw a friendly face and a beautiful smile, and I instantly felt her compassion and concern for her clients.

Returning to her desk, she invited me to sit on one of the three chairs against the wall of the twenty-square-metre office. Efriem was already seated on one of them. I pulled another chair close to her desk, on which sat a computer, a telephone set, and a tray of papers.

"Thank you for taking the time to see me," I said, adjusting my seat for what I hoped would be a lengthy conversation.

"It is my pleasure. What can I do for you?" she said, switching her eyes from the computer to me.

"You have a Kenyan accent, are you from Kenya?"

"That's a good guess. Yes, I am. Tell me your story and how I can help."

Not wanting to speak in front of Efriem, I showed my discomfort with his presence by staring pointedly at him.

"I would prefer to share my story with you only. If that's okay," I said. Janet nodded her head and looked at Efriem who, clearly unhappy with this, did not move.

"I'm just an interpreter," he responded.

"Yes, I know, but I may not need one," I replied. With a wave of her hand, Janet immediately ordered him out of the room. Efriem complied reluctantly, dragging his long legs to the door.

Once he'd gone, I confided to Janet my concerns about Eritreans working in the Khartoum UN office, and why I wanted my information kept private from them.

"My name is not Aman Abdu, my actual name is Aaron Berhane. I am co-founder and editor-in-chief of the first and largest independent newspaper in Eritrea — *Setit*," I said, monitoring her expression. She stared at me with enormous eyes that seemed both surprised and to be examining me closely at the same time. As she took notes, I recounted to her what had happened to my newspaper, my colleagues, and my family members, how I had escaped, events at the border, and how I came to lose my documents. I left out no details and underlined the risk I faced from the local Eritrean Intelligence Agency's efforts to kidnap me.

Janet listened attentively and with great compassion. I could feel she had already felt my pain: her breathing quickened and she became emotional when I described the gunfire at the border. She listened to my story without interruption, jotting notes in her logbook and then googling my name in her computer. In a few seconds she found my name among a list of jailed Eritrean journalists in a BBC report. She was well-informed about Eritrea, and expressed sadness that Eritrea was now heading down a dangerous path after the enormous sacrifice its people had paid for their liberation. After chatting for a few minutes about recent events, she turned directly to my situation.

"Do you have ID?" she asked.

"No. As I told you, I lost everything at the border."

"How do I know you're actually Aaron Berhane, then, if you don't have ID to prove it," she said politely. "Anyone can come and claim to be Aaron, and this report says Aaron is in jail."

I explained that the Eritrean government does not release the names of those individuals actually in custody, so the BBC reporter would have reported the list as provided to him by his sources.

"I am glad you are safe now," Janet replied. "However, while I'm not saying I don't believe you, I will need proof of your identity before I can help you."

"But Janet, it's impossible to get an ID from the government that is trying to arrest me, even kill me."

"It doesn't have to be from the government. Find anything that can prove your identity." With that, Janet closed her logbook and laid her pen across the top of it.

Though I understood her position, I was very angry that I hadn't gotten what I wanted straight away. No matter how I presented the dangers I would face after leaving her office, she made it very clear that she could do nothing without proof of ID. However, she did give me her phone number and email address to make it easier to contact her.

I thanked her and left the office defeated.

Earlier that morning, I had travelled to the UNHCR office excited and smiling, hoping and expecting to accomplish my plan. Just a few hours later, I walked back along the same streets crestfallen and despairing; I had no idea how to get documents that would prove my identity. The streets suddenly looked ugly, the air dustier, the sun more burning. Walking along, I noticed that many people walking ahead of me wore slippers so small that their heels flapped on the ground. I didn't get it: were these slippers some fashion, or something else? Whether because of the dry ground, or the dusty wind, their soles were rough and deeply cracked, the cracks deep enough to hold coins comfortably. The Arabic speech flowing around me, which until now I had loved as musical, seemed suddenly harsh and ugly. I badly wanted the people around me to shut up. Indeed, the entire outer world now seemed to take on the same dark cast as my inner turmoil.

I hired a *raksha* to drive me to the city centre with no clear destination in mind. After paying my fare, I went to the first restaurant I found. It was packed with people eating lunch and drinking juice. Seeing one empty spot in the corner, I rushed to occupy it. Sipping a mango juice — I had no appetite — I grabbed my pen and notebook and concentrated on what identity documents I might acquire. Two possibilities came to mind: academic credentials and letters of support. The first possibility I eventually ruled out because it would put at serious risk those people still in Eritrea who could help me get them, and even then such documents might not be accepted. Besides, it would take forever to get mail from Asmara that evaded government scrutiny. Finally, I decided to request a supporting letter from the organizations that advocate for journalists.

Unlike Asmara, Khartoum had several internet cafés, and people could browse the internet free of the covert government scrutiny that Eritreans faced. The waiter directed me to the nearest internet café where, to my surprise, half the seats were empty. Unusual. And no Eritreans either. That seemed odd. Later I found out the café had just opened and wasn't yet well known.

On the computer I typed the draft letter I'd written in my notebook. I described what had happened to my colleagues and to all independent press in Eritrea, how I had escaped the country, the incident at the border and the capture of Gebray, my current situation — including the threat from Eritrean security agents in Khartoum — and, finally, the risk I faced because of lack of documents. I told them what I needed from them. I explained it all as if my life depended on their help, because it did. I had nowhere else to turn. After double-checking the text, I typed in the email's To line: "The Committee to Protect Journalists (CPJ)" and "Reporters Without Borders (RSF)." Then I pressed Send. I imagined my message flying across the ocean, reaching its destination in an instant. Blessed technology! I felt good, though I had no idea what to expect from the email, or whether those organizations would even care about the problems of someone they had never met.

I checked my email morning and evening for three days. No response. I became restless. Had they gotten my email? If so, why hadn't they replied? Should I write them again, just in case the email had landed in their spam boxes? Or were they just researching me and my claims before responding? I wrestled with these negative and positive thoughts for about four days before receiving an email from Dixe Wills at PEN International. I hadn't contacted PEN, but they seemed to have already done due diligence to verify my identity. Dixe expressed his happiness that I'd escaped from Eritrea and promised to help me as soon as possible. Just three days later, he sent me a wonderful supporting letter, which he also faxed directly to the UNHCR office. Later on, CPJ and RSF also sent letters to the UNHCR case officer.

To my delight, whatever suspicions Janet had had now evaporated after she received the letters from these prestigious organizations. She treated me as a hero and offered me whatever help I needed during a cordial meeting in her office.

As I walked home down a quiet street, I kept thinking about the organizations that advocate for journalists, about the writers and human rights activists all over the world, about the people in these organizations who dedicate their lives to the defence of others' rights, and to solving others' problems, putting their own lives at risk to advocate for these victims. It is noble work. I imagined their great compassion, their outstanding personalities. Dixe Wills of PEN International, Elisabeth Witchel of CPJ, Ambroise Pierre of RSF might not realize how big a deal it was that their prompt actions changed the trajectory of my situation, how they saved my life. In that moment, I saw them as angels who had given me entry through a door to safety.

Once the case officer became involved in my case, it was as if she worked only for me. She gave me her full attention, working diligently to protect me and to promote my case to countries that could provide asylum. Although my final goal was to resettle in a peaceful democratic country, I didn't want to arrive there directly from Sudan. So, I asked her for an ICAO convention travel document (CTD) in order to travel to Kenya. The Sudanese government issued CTDs at the recommendation of the UNHCR, but in Sudan the corruption of Al-Bashir's government meant it would take forever to get the document. In the end, the Sudanese Government's Commissioner for Refugees (COR) did issue the CTD: Janet knew how to navigate the system.

Janet wrote the request letter and CTD application on February 9, 2002. I took it to the COR office immediately, but for some reason the COR officer was absent for what turned out to be two weeks, and nothing could happen until his return. It was an enormously frustrating time: my four to five calls a day to COR went unanswered until finally, on March 2, he picked up the phone.

Within an hour I was in Haider's office. He was a tall, smiling man in his fifties, dressed like a soldier in brown khaki pants and shirt. "Yeah, it is you. Good to see you. I was just on the phone with Janet," he said, shaking my hand brusquely. "Please sit, we will finish everything quickly." He printed some papers, sorted them, and then put them in a large envelope. He asked me to walk with him, dropping off the envelope with the woman at the reception desk before taking me to a tea house nearby.

"She will get the senior officials to sign your application," he said. "Hopefully, you will have it by tomorrow." He spoke very good English and liked to joke. I felt comfortable chatting with him.

"What did you find funny in Sudan?" he asked as he sipped his tea.

I reflected and said, "Well, I wouldn't call it funny, but I wondered a lot when I saw several people wearing slippers too small for their feet. They must hurt their feet, because their heels are hitting the ground. Why do they do that? Is that a fashion?" I asked.

He exploded with laughter.

"This is funny, really funny," he laughed heartily. "A Norwegian man asked me the same question a few months ago. Here, some people don't care about the clothes or shoes they wear, they care only about the food," he continued, before breaking into more laughter. It was an icebreaker. He told me how peaceful and peace-loving the people were, how corrupt and poor the government was, how a few individuals controlled the country's wealth and ran their businesses without paying tax. He went on and on, and I sensed his resentment and anger with his country. I had to change the conversation.

"I think you are right. That's what they call the curse of African countries," I said. "We will change that curse to a blessing, one day. But while we're on the subject, tell me what you found funny in Asmara."

He sipped his tea and smiled before he answered.

"A woman with a short mini-skirt," he laughed. "My two col-leagues and I walked out of Khartoum Hotel the day we arrived in Asmara and immediately saw her. You have to know I had never visited a non-Muslim country before. There she was: a beautiful woman walking past the gate wearing nothing but a piece of cloth that covered her butt and her chest. I felt like I was watching a movie; I have never seen someone dressed like that in the middle of the street, in the middle of the day, and walking with such con-fidence. We laughed for hours on that. Of course, we learned later that most prostitutes dress that way to attract customers."

I laughed with him.

"I loved Asmara, though; it is not boring like Khartoum. To tell you the truth, I hate sharia law. It's designed to control the low-er classes and women." Haider returned to his earlier theme, and dissected the Sudanese government to its heart, explaining how the rich and the politicians drank alcohol every day with impun-ity, in violation of sharia law. He kept on and on until his friend arrived in a car to pick him up. He told me to check up with him the next day and left.

Over the next five days I returned repeatedly to his office to check the status of my application. He had no news. Once he and his superior had signed the paper, it had been sent to the Passport Division of the Ministry of Immigration, where it now sat despite the urgency of the application and additional UNHCR comments. I knew government employees very often demanded extra payments for services that refugees were legally entitled to. Like me, Haider was frustrated because he also knew what was happening, and could do nothing. However, he didn't say anything until I broached the subject directly.

"I know this head of the Passport Division could be busy, but do you think he could work overtime to finalize my application if we paid him one hundred American dollars?" I asked gently, trying not to make it sound like a bribe.

Haider scrutinized my face.

"You are a smart man. You know exactly what he wants," he said. I pulled out US$150 from my wallet and put it on the table. He picked up the money immediately and put it in his pocket. He seemed nervous. In theory, facilitating active or passive briberies like gifts is prohibited for public sector workers, according to Sudanese law. However, enforcement is weak, as in many developing countries. I stood up.

"It would be good if you can take me with you," I said.

"I will go myself this afternoon and you can pick up your document tomorrow."

"You seem certain?"

"You bet I am."

I left his office, promising to return the next day at noon. I wasn't sure whether to believe him until I had that travel document in my hand. But I had to believe it would happen.

"*Raksha!*" I called, for a ride. I headed to the internet café, where I found three recent emails, two from people I knew wanting

141

to know where I was, and one from someone called "Zero." I had a rule not to communicate with anyone not involved in my escape plans. I opened the email from Zero.

"Hi Aaron, Sorry for my late response. Since they think you're planning to fly out of Sudan they're monitoring the airport. Don't leave the country that way. That's the only info I have for now. Your friend."

I froze. How did Eritrean National Security know I was planning to fly? I had told no one, not even my roommates. But once I had figured out Zero was really Goitom, my former source in the Interior Ministry, I knew the information was credible. I'd emailed him nearly four weeks earlier to tell me more about the agents sent to kidnap me.

Immediately, I emailed my UNHCR case officer, Janet, to tell her that I hadn't received the travel document yet and to ask her to prod the head of the Passport Division to sign my documents quickly.

The next morning I went to Haider's office around nine. I had been visiting his Ministry every other day for three weeks, so often that some people probably thought I worked there. I only ever sat or stood in the corridor, but my behaviour wasn't all that different from many of the workers, who often spent hours chatting and laughing in the corridor outside their offices, sometimes even longer than inside their offices. I used to wonder when they did their actual work. Immediately I saw Haider coming along the corridor to his office, and I hoped fervently he would get there before someone stopped him to chat.

"Good morning, Haroon, did you sleep here?" he laughed as he entered his office. "Do you know, your name in Sudan is Haroon? It's from the Koran. Haroon was the brother of Musa. I was bad at this. I just learned yesterday." He went on and on about how different cultures spelled and pronounced the names in the religious books differently. I couldn't listen; I wanted to know about my travel document.

Trying to change the conversation, I interjected.

"Interesting, Haider. Did he sign the document?"

Haider, however, was not to be interrupted, responding that I had yet to hear the most interesting part. Though I tried to listen patiently as he continued on his theme, it seemed to me that he didn't understand the direness of my situation, and that I was the only one who could impress it upon him.

"Haider," I said, "why don't you first tell me about the document, and then we can chat about this more over lunch?" Clearly, he was not happy with my interruption; he pulled some files out of his drawer, put them on his desk, and began reading them without saying a word.

"Haroon, I see you are in a rush," he finally said. "In Sudan, it's the custom to chat socially for a half hour or so before proceeding to the main agenda. That's what I have been doing. How do you do things in Eritrea?

"It is the same, Haider," I replied, even though it wasn't. "I'm just in a rush now because I have another appointment this afternoon. Sorry if I'm rushing you.'

He took some papers from his bag and inserted them into the files on the desk, before returning these to the drawer.

"Your travel document is signed. It's ready," he said, as he returned the files.

"Thank you," I said. "Can I have it?"

But Haider said he did not have it.

"What do you mean? I thought you would bring it with you after it was signed."

"No, that's not how it works" he said. "You have to sign the document at the Passport Division before they can give it to you.

But everything is in order." Haider stood up to pick another dusty file from the shelf at his left. I felt myself getting angry at his words; I thought he'd said I would be able to get it from him. I wondered if it would take another bribe for me to finally get the document.

"Can you go with me to get it," I pleaded. "Just in case there are further obstacles."

"Sure, if you can wait an hour," Haider promised. "But you'll have to buy me lunch," he added, laughing.

"Sure. That's the least I can do."

"I thought you were in a rush," he laughed again, as he saw my acquiescence.

"I am, but you are a busy man, and I have to respect that," I replied, laughing in return as I stood up to leave.

"Wait! I am just joking. We can go right now. You are a busy man, too."

The Passport Division was a twenty-minute drive from Haider's office, and his office's driver drove us there. The whole time Haider never stopped laughing and talking either to me or to the driver. Preoccupied with getting the document, I had no appetite to chat or laugh, so I just kept nodding my head whether he was speaking Arabic or English. The traffic was heavy, and wild, so the driver had to drive slowly and carefully among the hundreds of small cars on the lineless arterial road, honking often. I noticed a collision on the opposite side of the road. But before I had time to really register what I was seeing, somebody rear-ended our car, jolting us all forward. Fortunately, no one was hurt. The driver stopped, and we all jumped out to see the damage.

"What's wrong with you?" our driver yelled. Both our back bumper and the front bumper of the other car were broken and trailing on the ground.

The other driver apologized immediately and forced himself out of his car. "*Maalesh, maalesh*," (sorry), he said instantly. Our driver barked like a dog for two minutes and then calmed down quickly. He dismantled the bumper and put it in the trunk. I thought the incident would go on forever, but after exchanging a few words each driver went back to his car — we passengers following — and both cars drove off. No one called the police or asked to exchange insurance information.

"So how is your driver going to find the other driver later?" I asked Haider, surprised by the lack of exchange.

"Why would he?"

"So he can pay for the damage he caused."

"He said '*Maalesh*,'" Haider responded. "So that's enough. It wasn't deliberate. It's an accident." Haider explained at length that Sudanese very often resolved such problems with forgiveness, since they believed that whatever happened during their daily travel was God's will. I was impressed; our driver had genuinely forgiven him and didn't even mention the incident again until he dropped us off.

Haider and I entered the immense government building along a path through a small gate. After passing the security guards at the entrance, we took the stairs to the passport division office on the second floor. Haider went off to meet someone, while I sat on a bench to wait. The office was crowded with people either submitting their passport applications or signing the completed document and collecting their passport. I felt joy for the latter; that was what I wanted too. Haider conversed behind the counter with a bald man for a few minutes, then called me to the counter.

"Everything is in order; you just need to sign here and here," said Haider, pointing to lines on the paper that the bald man handed to me. I grabbed the pen he held out and scratched my signatures on them quickly, my heart beating faster and faster. Immediately, the man handed me the travel document and took the papers back from me. By this time my heart was pumping rapidly.

"Please check if there is any error," he said in Arabic. Haider translated. No errors. It was March 18, 2002, and my travel document was in my hands. In Eritrea, when people receive a passport — a privilege and not a right in my country — they invite friends over to celebrate with them. The Eritrean government denies everyone under forty a passport unless they satisfy endless constantly changing criteria. I was denied twice, in 1997 and again in 2000, when I planned to take part in the World Association of Newspapers' conference. The government never gave a reason for refusing Eritreans passports; applications were just returned with the stamp "Deny."

This was my very first passport, one that would allow me to travel to any country. Neither Haider nor the bald man could possibly understand my happiness and relief at having this document in my pocket.

I shared the wonderful news with Janet, my UNHCR protection officer, and with PEN International's Dixe Wills, Elizabeth at CPJ, and with RSF. Once they learned of my plan to fly to Kenya for my own safety, Dixe Wills sent me contact information for a nonprofit organization there called Goal Kenya. Amha Domenico, an Eritrean activist, also sent me contact information for Elias Habteselassie, an activist in Kenya. Though a relative in Nairobi would pick me up at the airport, such support from established individuals and organizations was crucial.

Nearly forty days later, I had an entry visa from the Kenyan Embassy. Then it was time to fly to Nairobi. I didn't tell my roommates until the evening I left, because they hadn't been involved in my plans. At 10 p.m. on the night I was to leave I arrived home and found them lying on their beds scattered about the room, chatting and laughing enthusiastically as they did every evening. Each had experienced war, hunger, and a tiring journey to get to Sudan, but they didn't talk about their misery. Instead they talked of hope, fun, and their dreams of reuniting with their girlfriends still in Eritrea. Despite the unfinished business they had on their plates, they were always happy and optimistic.

"Hi, guys," I said as I entered the room.

"Hey, you are late today," Fanus said, raising his head from the bed. Fanus acted like a responsible father and wanted to check everyone's situation.

"Yes, you are right Fanus. I had a busy day, and I have news to share. I hope you will understand," I said.

"If it is good news, I'd love to hear it," Sulieman said as he laughed at his own statement, and we all laughed with him.

"I am flying tonight."

"What?" All three of them sat bolt upright and looked me in the eye. I was still standing near the door.

"I am sorry I didn't tell you in advance."

"I thought you trusted us. Why didn't you tell us?" Misgina asked angrily.

"I trust you all. That's why I have stayed here for all these months. You have done a great job of protecting me and comforting me. I am very grateful for that. The reason I didn't tell you is because I was not sure myself until I held in my hand the papers I needed. So, Misgina, please don't misinterpret my intention," I said.

"That's okay, Aaron. It's understandable," Fanus said. "What time is your flight?"

"One thirty in the morning."

"That's not an early flight, that's late night," Sulieman said.

"Yeah, you are right, but it's less likely that Eritrean security agents will be waiting for me at the airport. They won't stay around that long."

"That's a smart plan, we will accompany you to the airport," Fanus said, stepping out of his bed. Fanus and Sulieman accepted my reasoning fully and focused their discussion on my future plans, but Misgina was stuck on why I hadn't told them.

"If you told us at least yesterday, we could have thrown a farewell party. What you did is totally wrong." He felt betrayed and he was not able to understand, whatever I said. He lay on his bed while Fanus and Sulieman got ready to go with me.

"I am sorry, Misgina. Now it is time for me to go. Thank you for everything." I approached his bed and he stood up and hugged me.

"Have a great flight," he said, while sitting on his bed.

The only luggage I had was the *Sudan Tribune* newspaper in my hand. We arrived at the airport by taxi at midnight.

Fanus and Sulieman drove around the airport to see if anyone Eritrean-looking was parked outside. There was no one. Once I got their assurance, I entered the airport with them. The airport looked abandoned. Except for the security guards, nobody was around.

I passed through security and comforted myself on the hard chair until my flight arrived. As I had dreamt and planned, I flew out from Khartoum on May 6, 2002.

CHAPTER 9
LIFE IN THE SAFE HOUSE: KENYA

IT WAS MAY 6, 2002. THE PLANE FOR KENYA TOOK OFF AT 3:15 A.M.

There was an actual flight attendant standing beside me. I could hardly believe it.

"Sir, what would you like to drink?" she asked. It took me a few moments to reply, but I stared at her with a big smile. She smiled back.

"Coke, Sprite, Fanta, water?" she asked again, still with her contagious smile.

"Coke, please," I said. She served me Coke and crackers. The taste of that Coke felt different, not like the Coke I used to drink in Asmara or Khartoum. This one tasted like freedom and joy. I enjoyed every sip.

At 5:50 a.m. we landed at Jomo Kenyatta International Airport in Nairobi, one of the busiest airports in Africa. It's named after the first president of Kenya. Jomo Kenyatta played a significant role in bringing together his country after Kenya got its independence from Britain. He deserved the honour. I couldn't imagine Asmara International Airport being named after Isaias Afwerki, the first president of Eritrea, who deliberately tried to incite conflict between religions and different regions to prolong his power. That man deserved nothing. I said to myself that if I had the power I would not even name a small street after him if I ever came back to Eritrea again.

Since I didn't have luggage, I went straight to the immigration officer who checked every passenger's passport. I handed my travel document to him. He looked at it as if he were studying for a test.

"Where is your vaccination card for yellow fever?"

His question surprised me. When I spoke to the Kenyan consul in Khartoum about the documents I needed he never mentioned that. I suspected this official just wanted to make an extra buck by playing the vaccination card.

"I don't have one," I said, thinking how much it could cost for him to let me pass.

"Well, you have a big problem, so I am afraid we will have to send you back," he said, staring at my eyes to observe my reaction. I remembered what Nadia used to tell me about her upbringing in Kenya and the corrupt culture of police and immigration officers.

"Do you have somewhere I can get a vaccination?"

"No. The only option you have is to go back to Khartoum." He smiled, his tiny teeth showing. He seemed like a picture painted by a child.

"That will not happen," I said firmly. "If this vaccination is mandatory, your embassy in Khartoum would have told me, but they never mentioned it. Let's talk about something else. Let me pay my fee here and get the vaccination when I enter Nairobi."

"Come with me," he said. I followed him, looking left and right. Everyone seemed occupied with their own business. He stopped me and checked that no one watched him.

"If you pay me fifty U.S. dollars I will let you pass," he said, looking away from me. I never hesitated. I just paid him and he let me pass to the next immigration officer. He said something in Swahili and turned to me. "No one will ask you about a vaccination card now."

I walked a few metres with an immigration officer. He told me to wait my turn and left. As I wondered what other obstacles I could face before I could leave the airport, the officer signalled me to approach his counter.

I gave him the passport and he read it carefully.

"You are Eritrean, right?" he asked.

"Yes." I wondered why he asked. The passport stated I was.

"You wouldn't have needed a visa if you used your Eritrean passport. But you seem to have an issue with your government." It was a statement rather than a question, but I nodded. He asked me to follow him. We went upstairs to his boss's office. He let me wait outside the office while he spoke with a man inside in Swahili.

"Please come. He will verify the authenticity of your visa and he will let you go," he said. He rushed out of the room. I looked at the man who sat behind the desk. His hair was uncombed and his eyes were red. It seemed that he had spent the night working.

"Please sit," he said, after flipping through every page of my passport. "What brought you to Kenya?"

"To visit my relative."

"How long are you planning to stay here?"

"One or two months."

"How much money do you have?"

I remembered what Nadia used to say: many Kenyan officers would ask you how much money you had before asking the reason of your visit. What they cared about was what percentage of the money would end up in their pockets. I told him a lower figure.

"Five hundred dollars."

"How are you going to live on five hundred dollars for two months? Please tell me the truth," he barked.

"I will stay with my relative. That's enough for me. You need not worry about that," I said with a smile, but he was not in the mood to smile. He stared at me, motionless.

"I don't think you understand. There is some issue with your visa, and I am trying to help you here, but you have to tell me the truth."

It's tricky to deal with corrupt officials. If you first suggest to pay them before you hear their request, it would cost you more. They could arrest you for trying to bribe them, and then once they have you, they might ask you to pay more before they transfer your case to their superior, which might lead you to prison or cost you even more. Thanks to Nadia I was familiar with their game, and chose not to put myself in the trap.

"Listen, officer, my visa is legitimate and there is no issue about that. I have already wasted too much time for nothing. Please let me go now or pass me to your boss," I said confidently. He looked at me without saying a word.

"Look, I will consult with my senior officer, but you better think to tell the truth by the time I come back." He left the office.

A few minutes later someone in his early thirties showed up and greeted me warmly. Like a hyena that saw meat, he seemed happy to see me. With a broad smile, he introduced himself as Joseph and told me to be patient as the officer tried to resolve the issue of my visa with his superior.

"What I don't understand is why he is trying to create an issue when I have a legitimate entry visa," I said loudly.

"I am sorry to hear that. But I think I can help. You have already waited long. How much money are you willing to pay? He will not ask you that because he doesn't want trouble, but I can arrange it," Joseph said, moving back and forth in the door to look if anyone was coming. I didn't answer but stared at him quietly.

"How much money do you have?" he asked. He already knew that. He was working with his colleague to get a bribe.

"Five hundred dollars."

"How much of this would you like to pay to get your passport back and go to your relative in Nairobi?" He spoke fast. He seemed as if he wanted to close the deal quickly.

"I think I can afford to pay one hundred," I said reluctantly.

"That's too low. Understand, they can return you back to Eritrea. I am sure you don't want that."

I was angry but smiled at him sarcastically: "How much are you suggesting?" I asked.

"Three hundred," he said instantly.

"No. Just take one hundred before it's too late. If I don't show at the meeting with the UN officials at nine o'clock, they will check with your minister, and they'll know exactly where I am."

"Okay, make it two hundred."

"One-fifty," I said, pulling out my wallet.

"No, no, that's too low, make it two hundred," he said impatiently. "This is your chance if you need my help." He stepped toward the door. I saw his desperation and felt strong enough to stick to my offer.

"Listen, Joseph, I can't afford more than one-fifty. Let's close the deal before it's too late."

He left the room without agreeing or disagreeing. I forced myself to keep quiet. Five minutes later, he and the other officer showed up.

"Sorry for keeping you waiting," the officer said. "I think everything is good. But I have the other meeting to catch, so Joseph will take it from here. Good luck!" he said as he left.

Soon after the officer left, Joseph tried to increase the bribe to $200, but I just pulled out $150 and stretched my hand to give it to him. He could see the three paper fifties. He accepted them with a smile and gave me my passport.

"It's good to do business with you," he said. I nodded and left. As I walked toward the exit, I heard someone calling my name. It was Yoel, the relative who had been waiting for me for almost two hours. We hugged each other, then I briefed him on what took me so long. But he was not surprised, as he had lived in Kenya for ten years. "There are always corrupt officers wherever you go," he said, leading me to his car.

Instantly I felt that Kenya was different from Eritrea or Sudan. The traffic rules were different. Kenya is one of the countries that have left-hand traffic. The steering wheel was on the right and the gear change on the left, and he drove on the left side of the road. It took me a few minutes to adjust and stop panicking whenever I saw vehicles coming on the right side of the road.

As we drove into Nairobi, Yoel told me about the huge number of Eritreans who lived in Nairobi and the strong affiliation they had with the Eritrean government, and how critical they were of the G-15 (the senior officials who had criticized the president), and of journalists and anyone else who opposed the Eritrean government. I thought to myself that the regime's propaganda machine was working nicely.

Before we got to his home, I asked him to stop for a few minutes so I could call Annette Ludeking, the Director of Goal Kenya, a nonprofit organization. I called from his cellphone. I told her that I got her number from Dixe Wills of PEN International. She agreed to meet me the next day. I would have loved to go straight there before any Eritrean saw me or learned of my arrival, but it was not possible.

Yoel took me to his apartment where he lived with his wife and six-year-old son. It was in a neighbourhood where many Eritreans lived. They offered to accommodate me until I got my things in order, but I didn't trust their neighbours or the friends who might be dropping by. I needed to leave quickly, for both Yoel's family's safety and my own.

I asked Yoel to drive me to Goal Kenya. On our way, we went to an internet café, and I sent emails to update my advocates and supporters and thank everyone who helped me to survive and flee Sudan. I got an email from Amha Domenico with details about Elias Habteselassie, who lived in Nairobi. Elias would be glad to meet me immediately.

Nairobi is a beautiful city. We passed several stunning modern buildings and came onto a major street that was packed with countless minibuses that provided taxi service. I worried I would be late, but Yoel did his best to get us out of the heavy traffic.

An enormous gate was watched by two security guards. Yoel parked outside the gate and waited for me as I walked toward the gate.

"Good morning," I said. "I am here to see Annette."

"Do you have an appointment?" The guard asked while looking at me intently.

"Yes. She is expecting me." One guard walked toward the building to deliver my message. As I looked around, internally admiring the beauty of the place, I heard a woman's voice. I turned around and saw a white woman in her thirties with a big smile coming toward me.

"Hello," she said as she stretched her hand to greet me. "My name is Annette Ludeking."

Instantly, I felt like I knew her from before. She was friendly and warm, and seemed to understand the pain of people in distress and how to comfort them.

"My name is Aaron Berhane."

"Welcome to Goal Kenya," she said. We headed to her office.

"I know it can be exhausting to give your story to anyone you meet, but it's important," she said with a smile. I gave her my story: my family's condition, my colleagues, the journey to the border, my contact with UNHCR in Khartoum, and the fear I felt there and even in Kenya because of the vast clandestine networks within the Eritrean community. She was a brilliant listener, and that encouraged me to pour out my story like water from a pipe.

"I am glad you are safe now," she said. She didn't want to give me false hope; her organization had limitations. She told me about Goal Kenya's mandate and how it assisted UNHCR, but it didn't provide resettlement to any third country. She explained UNHCR helped resettle refugees if they were eligible. She didn't hide a powerful feeling that they would accept my case, but she didn't want to confirm it until I did my interview with the UNHCR officer.

"Do you have a place to stay for a while?"

"It is temporary, and it is not safe," I said. "I would really appreciate it if you can help me on that, too." She nodded and stepped out of her office with her cellphone. I didn't want to go back to Yoel's neighbourhood since it would be just a matter of time before the Eritrean Embassy in Kenya found out where I was. I waited patiently until Annette came back. A few minutes later she returned, with a phone number.

"His name is Julian, Professor Julian. Give him a call, he would be happy to find you accommodation," she said. "But make sure to come here tomorrow at nine to complete the application. We will get the form from UNHCR for you."

I called Professor Julian right away. I told him about how badly I wanted to be accommodated in a safe place.

"How long can you wait?" he asked.

"Maybe one day. It is not safe here," I said. I imagined I might be caught by Eritrea's security agents and taken back, or end up dead in the streets of Nairobi. He promised to do something and hung up. But I didn't want to put all my hopes and burdens on him, so I phoned Elias Habteselassie.

Since Amha had told me about Elias, I trusted him immediately. We met at a coffee shop. For about two hours we talked about what should be done to bring Eritrea back on track. He promised help if I needed it. His eagerness pumped up my optimism. Finally, he dropped me off around 6 p.m. at Yoel's place.

Knowing there were people on my side who would like to help gave me hope.

Professor Julian had phoned, wanting me to call him. He asked again how long I could stay in Yoel's place. I told him only that night and explained how active the agents of the Eritrean Embassy were in kidnapping people.

"Don't worry, we will get you somewhere safe by tomorrow," he said enthusiastically. "We will talk tomorrow."

The next day Yoel drove me to Goal Kenya's office to meet Annette. Professor Julian called to tell me to come with all my stuff. He had indeed resolved one of my biggest problems.

Annette introduced me to Bhavna, her colleague. "She will assist you in filling out these forms." She told me that the head of the UNHCR would come to interview me that morning. I was happy to hear that Annette was driving my case fast.

Bhavna took me to another office. She interviewed me and filled out the forms before Sergio, the head of UNHCR in Kenya, arrived. I never imagined it would take us over two hours to fill out the forms. I had to write a detailed profile of my upbringing, the place I grew up, the school I studied at, the challenges I faced as an editor, the situation of my family, the arrest of my family members. Bhavna double-checked the story and asked questions whenever she found any missing link or I failed to elaborate an event. Once I completed the forms, she took them to Annette. After about fifteen minutes, she came back and took me to Annette's office where

Sergio awaited. I was nervous but was relieved to see Annette's smiling face. Sergio shook my hand firmly.

"You are very brave, I am glad you are safe," he said. He had a thick accent, but I couldn't guess his first language.

"Where are your wife and your children now?" he asked.

"In Asmara, Eritrea."

"Do you want them to join you?"

Immediately, I knew he had accepted my case. I felt an enormous relief.

"Eventually, yes, but not right now. My wife is under constant scrutiny by the regime. It's risky to flee with children."

"That's okay, they can join you later," he said. "Thank you for sharing your story. We will assist you with all your needs."

My lungs filled with happiness, my blood shared the victory with every cell of my body.

While they discussed my case in private. I thought about the hassle I had had to go through to meet the UNHCR officers in Khartoum, and how smoothly it went in Kenya because of Dixe Wills. If he hadn't connected me with Annette, I wouldn't have been able to meet with the UNHCR officer in such a short time. I owed many people.

Annette joined me and said, "We are lucky. The U.S.A., Australia, Canada, or the U.K. could accept your case. Where do you want to go?"

I was touched when she said, "We are lucky." I could feel to what extent she worked hard to find a solution for my problem, as if it was her own. I knew I found another angel and never hesitated to follow her advice and suggestions afterward. I could see that purity of purpose in her eyes to help others; it was in her DNA to advocate for her clients as if she were doing it for herself.

My first option was to go to the U.S.A. I had many cousins and friends there who could help until I familiarized myself with the country. But when I was told it would take about seven months to resettle me there, I was concerned. I didn't know what might happen if I stayed a day longer than I had to in Kenya.

"What about Canada? How long would it take?"

"Since you have a high-profile case, they may process it in three months," Annette said. In a heartbeat I said I would like to go to Canada — even though I had no relative or even a friend who lived there.

"Bring your luggage and we will put you in a safe house." She advised me not to share my information with anyone, or to communicate with anyone. I didn't have luggage except an extra pair of pants and a shirt. But I had to go back to the car to grab them and say goodbye to Yoel.

The safe-house was in Limuru, about forty kilometres northwest of Nairobi. I was the only passenger in the minibus. It was around 5 p.m.

"I thought I was done for the day," the driver said. "You must be an important person."

"Not as important as you."

"I am just a driver."

"I am just a passenger," I smiled.

He laughed and started the engine.

I couldn't stop admiring the beauty of every hill we passed and the villages we went through. I wondered if I might visit as a tourist one day. We went up and down the small hills. After about an hour, he turned onto a village road. There were several farms, but no buildings except a sizable one in a compound. It seemed we were in the middle of nowhere.

"We are here," the driver said, in a tired voice. He stopped in front of the gate. I jumped out and we walked toward the guards. The driver handed them a piece of paper and went back to his minibus. He waved his hand to say goodbye to me. I waved back.

Across at the main building some people were standing and far away some others were playing tennis. I saw a volleyball net, a soccer field.

This looked like a great place to be!

The person in charge, who looked in his fifties, said, "Welcome sir, you will stay with us for a while. There are certain rules here, and we expect all our residents to follow them." I nodded.

"Communication with the outside world is not allowed. It is not allowed to go outside of this compound. You have to protect yourself from anyone who tries to hurt you. I am sure if you don't communicate with anyone, you will be okay. No one will know you are here. If you have any questions or concerns, please come to speak with me. I know you are tired now, so let me take you to your room."

As we walked down the corridor, several people waved a hand to say hi. Though most of them were in their thirties and forties, there were also children with some of them. Remembering my own kids, I thought to myself how lucky they were to have their families with them.

"This is your room," he said, opening a door with his key.

The room was cozy, with a beautiful view of the farm.

"Breakfast starts at seven, and the cafeteria is downstairs. Enjoy your stay." He handed me the keys and left.

My eyes roamed the room. It was about twelve square metres. There was a bed for one person, neatly made, a table light, and a small chest with a drawer. I pulled out the drawer. There was nothing inside. I lay down without taking off my shoes. I stared at the white paint on the ceiling, thinking how safe this place could be for me. The more I stared at the ceiling, the more it felt like I was in my hideout in Asmara. I imagined the freedom of the sky and stars.

I remembered one of my wife's visits to my hideout. Mielat laid her head on my chest while I stared at the ceiling and held her head softly and played with her hair. She played with the hair of my chest.

"Do you think we will have a normal life again?" she asked, in a low voice. I didn't reply but kept staring at the ceiling as if I would find an answer there.

"I miss our old life." She kept talking, though I didn't respond. "Your children miss you very much. Frieta never stops asking when you will be back. Mussie always runs to the gate whenever he hears the sound of the car, and yells 'Baba.' Lucky Evan, he doesn't know what's going on. He smiles and stares at the ceiling. He is not actually suffering like Frieta and Mussie. Sometimes I get frustrated because I don't see the end game of this; the happy ending. But you always seem to be sure of that. How is that?" Her tears dropped on my chest. I said nothing. I was *not* sure, but I never showed my uncertainty to my wife, because it wouldn't help. I had to act as if I had a solution for any problem that could arise. Lost in my thoughts, missing the touch of my wife while lying on a bed by myself in a foreign country, I imagined the smell of her body, her beautiful face, her warm heart, her radiant smile.

A knock on the door interrupted this.

"Sir, sir," a man's voice reached me through the door. I stood up and opened the door.

"Hello, my name is Seifu, an Ethiopian journalist," a short bald man said in Amharic while stretching his hand to greet me.

"*Eendiet neh?*" (How are you?)

"It is dinner time. I saw you coming earlier. I know you are new," he said, standing in the corridor. I pulled the door closed behind me and followed him.

The big cafeteria could accommodate fifty or more people. About ten people were dining as we entered.

"How many refugees live here?" I asked.

"I think about twenty or thirty. You will see them tomorrow. Most of them have already eaten their dinner," Seifu said. He handed me a plate and grabbed one for himself. It was a buffet: a dish of mashed potatoes, rice, porridge, and lentils beside a big gallon of water. I was not hungry, so I only took a little and sat beside Seifu at an isolated table.

Seifu seemed to be happy to find a companion. He never stopped talking. He told me how lonely he felt because most of the Ethiopian refugees in the safe house were from the Oromo region.

"I am the only person from Amhara. Unfortunately, those Oromo journalists see me as the enemy because of tension in the past," he said, chewing his rice. I didn't want him to get into that topic, so I interrupted him.

"Are there any Eritreans here?"

"No, you are the first person from Eritrea. There are people from Rwanda, Somalia, Uganda, Congo, and Ethiopia. That's it."

"How long have you been here?"

"Fourteen months."

"Wow!" I couldn't hide my surprise, as I couldn't imagine myself staying that long.

"There are people who have been here for more than two years," he said, sticking his spoon in the mashed potatoes. "I finished my interviews to go to Canada, but I am still waiting for medical exams. Once they ask you to do your medical exam, it doesn't take long, just a few months. What about you? Have you finished your interview? Do you know where you will be settled?"

"This tastes good." I never intended to finish what was on my plate, but once I tried I didn't stop.

After dinner, Seifu gave me a tour, introducing me to anyone that we met on our way. We passed the volleyball court and reached the soccer field. He wanted to chat more and learn more about me, but I was not ready to share everything, and besides, I was tired.

"I have to go to sleep," I said, turning myself from the field toward the building.

"It's only eight o'clock."

"Yes, but I am really exhausted. We will chat tomorrow."

I went to my room. The bed was comfy, the room temperature was good, my surroundings were quiet, but my eyes refused to close. I didn't feel safe. I lay on my back. The minute I closed my eyes, I found myself running at the border, bullets flying over my head, soldiers knocking at my door. I was wide awake, so it was not a dream, but I couldn't shake the disturbing thoughts. Finally, I gave up. I let my eyes open wide and stared at the ceiling, forcing myself to think about my future and what kind of preparation I should make in case things didn't work out as planned. Unfortunately, I could not think of anything that could give me peace. I didn't get to sleep until 3 a.m. Then it felt like I slept for five minutes before someone knocked on my door.

"Endemin aderk," (Good morning), Seifu said behind the door. I checked the time, it was 7 a.m.

"It's breakfast time," Seifu yelled.

I forced myself to get up. I didn't want to leave the room, but I didn't want to disappoint him either. I washed my face and joined him for breakfast. I grabbed bread, fried eggs, and tea. It felt like a hotel, not a camp that accommodated refugees. The administration, the cleanliness of the building, the taste of the food were far better than I expected. I was prepared to experience the worst and couldn't believe what I encountered. The people who entered and left the cafeteria were full of smiles. What I read in the faces of most of the refugees was optimism and hope. It was a great feeling. The only gloomy face at that moment was mine. I was occupied in figuring out how life would unfold in that camp.

"Can we play tennis?" I asked.

"Sure," Seifu said, picking our empty plates to shelve them with the dirty dishes.

We headed straight to the tennis court. Five people stood around. Seifu introduced me to them and we waited our turn.

"Do you see this man? He is from Rwanda," Seifu said. "He lost his wife and all his family members during the genocide." My heart sank. I felt terrible on his behalf. I had read about the Rwanda genocide of 1994, but I had never met anyone from that country. I tried to read his grief, though seven years had passed. He seemed cheerful. He laughed when the players missed the ball or fell. I tried to put myself in his shoes and my eyes filled up with tears. I couldn't imagine what it would feel like. I tried to shake the idea from my head and concentrate on the game but failed. I kept thinking about the pain every refugee carried, the trauma they experienced, and the hope they had to overcome their challenges. The thoughts kept coming again and again until I started to play.

Around lunch time, a Goal Kenya car showed up in the camp with two individuals. One of them was Martin from Amnesty International London. He had come to interview me to gather information about the names and activities of my colleagues who were in jail, and Eritrea's political environment.

The day went fast, playing, listening to the painful stories that drove the people to land in the refugee camp; the sacrifices they had made to do their jobs as journalists or activists. We were targeted because of our work. The whole evening until I fell asleep, I kept going over the stories I had heard, to inject myself with hope. I reminded myself how lucky I was to be resting on that bed right then. I slept like a baby.

The next day, I chatted with four Ethiopian journalists that Seifu had introduced me to. We analyzed the border conflict. The similarity of our ideas amazed me. We all blamed the politicians for choosing war over dialogue; we agreed how prosperous the Horn of Africa could be if there were peace between Eritrea and Ethiopia. Around eleven, while I was playing tennis, someone came to tell me I had a telephone call.

It was Professor Julian. He told me Yoel's apartment had been visited by two Eritreans and two Kenyan security agents on Friday and Saturday. I froze. I voiced the first thought that jumped to my head. "What did they do to Yoel and his family?"

"Yoel and his family are okay, they are out of the city for a while," he said. He calmed me down, but reminded me to be careful until they moved me to a safer location. He told me to be ready. A car was on its way to pick me up.

I felt guilty for disrupting Yoel's family life. Before I showed up at his apartment, he was leading a simple life as a regular person. Now he was a fugitive, just because of me. He would have to stop working and his son would have to stop going to school. These things were my fault.

A few minutes later, the car showed up. Seifu and three others were coming toward the car to learn what was going on, but there was not much time, I just jumped in the car and left without a proper farewell.

Even here, I hadn't been entirely safe. I wondered if I would ever find a haven at all unless I left for Europe or North America. And for that I had to depend on Goal Kenya and UNHCR.

Where were we heading now?

Driving at noon was much better than it would have been in the afternoon. There was no heavy traffic that could slow the driver. Before I knew it, he cut away from the main road and headed east. He drove for about five minutes and stopped in front of the iron gate of the Benedictine monastery Prince of Peace in Tigoni. The driver jumped out of the car and spoke to the guards. We drove inside the compound. Despite the vast acreage the monastery occupied, there were only two main buildings: the church and the retreat house of about thirty rooms. The driver stopped the car beside the church. We both jumped out and went in through the side door to meet with the person in charge. He introduced me to another monk

"This is Brother Joseph," he said. I was surprised to hear the name *Joseph* yet again. It seemed like half the men in Kenya were named Joseph. That officer I bribed at the airport was a Joseph, there was one at my former accommodation, and now here.

"Welcome to the Benedictine monastery," he said.

"Brother Joseph will help you settle in your room," the senior monk added.

Since it was lunchtime, Brother Joseph suggested taking me to the cafeteria first.

There were about twenty people there, all of them were monks in their thirties or forties. I could feel their discipline and intention to serve God as they murmured and ate. They nodded. The only person not wearing a monk's robe was me. I felt awkward, and my appetite disappeared despite the aromas of the rice and mashed potatoes on my plate.

The rules were the same here as at the safe house. No communication with the outside world, no travelling outside of the compound. The retreat house was a beautiful building, both outside and inside. The rooms were just like a hotel's, neat and furnished with everything I needed. My room got cleaned every day, the towels got changed; there was a lounge room with a TV and video player. Nature surrounded the building: green grass, tall trees, birds, a view that could allow you to get lost in your thoughts.

"Do you have any questions?" Brother Joseph asked while handing me my room keys.

"Where is my monk's robe?" I asked.

He smiled, thinking I was joking. I smiled back, remembering he knew nothing about my case or why I was there. After all, the retreat was open to anyone who wanted some quiet time, if they could afford it. Lucky for me, I didn't have to think about that.

"Every Sunday, there's a service for the general public, so you are always welcome to join us," he said.

I spent the whole afternoon walking around the vast compound. I visited the barn and watched while a man milked the cows; I saw men digging the soil. I would have loved to strike a conversation and learn about their life, but I thought it was inappropriate to interrupt them at their work. I headed to the valley and walked around for about an hour and sat under the trees on top of the hill. The landscape reminded me of a trip I took with my family in early 2001 to Bar Durfo, the eastern escarpment of Eritrea.

Every Sunday, my wife and I would take our children to different recreation centres: Kelete Hotel, Mai Serwa, Biet Giorgis, Expo, and Bar Durfo. Most of them are no farther than a twenty-minute drive from Asmara. My daughter, Frieta, was the boss in our house, so we had to go where she chose if we wanted to see her smile. Mussie didn't care, he was just happy to go anywhere that he could have fun. We went to Biet Giorgis, Asmara's zoo, based on her choice, but we found it too crowded.

"What if we go to Bar Durfo now and come back here later?" I suggested. Frieta and Mussie cheered. Bar Durfo offered a spectacular view, especially if you climbed up the hill. It was 2,400 metres above sea level. If there was no fog you could look out to the sea. I collected stones and allowed Frieta and Mussie to throw them from the cliff.

"This is for the hyena," Frieta said as she threw a stone.

"Why do you want to hit the hyena?" Mielat asked, handing her a stone.

"Because it eats the farmer's sheep," she said. "This is for the other hyena." She kept yelling about hyenas while she threw one stone after another. Mussie tried to imitate his sister.

"Hyena, eat this." He threw a stone, that landed ten metres away from him. We all laughed.

"Give me more, Dad," he said. I supplied him with another stone and he threw it, yelling the same mantra.

Once they finished tossing their piles of stones, we sat on a rock and admired the view.

"What is out there, Dad?" Frieta asked. She was curious to know everything.

"That's Nefasit."

"Do people live there?"

"Yes."

"What about after that?"

"Yes, sweetie?"

"What about that farthest place … ?"

My body was in Tigoni, Kenya, but my thoughts were in the cliffs of Durfo with my family, replaying in my head the joyful memories. Was I going to see them again? Tears rolled down my cheeks unchecked. I didn't resist them.

The next morning, I woke up rested. I washed my face, brushed my teeth, and left the room to watch the sun rise. My father used to say, "If you catch the sunrise in the morning, you are in control of your day." He used to urge me and my brothers to wake up for the sunrise, whether we had something to do or not. I didn't enjoy it then. Waking up early wasn't my strong suit, probably because I was not the captain of my life then. But now I really wanted to control my day and my life, if it was possible. I was a refugee, a person who couldn't protect himself, and who didn't know what would happen in the afternoon or even after the next hour. I watched several birds chirping, chasing one another on the trees. It was peaceful and relaxing. The rays of the sun reached me. I felt great and smiled like I had made it happen. I sat for a while absorbing the mild heat of the sun on my body before I went to eat breakfast.

"Good morning, sir," Brother Joseph said as he approached my table with a broad friendly smile.

"Good morning."

"Did you sleep well?"

"Yes, thank you," I said, by now sipping the last drop of my tea. "Please sit, I can wait for you."

"Oh, I already had my breakfast. The driver is waiting for you outside." I looked outside. It was the Goal Kenya car.

I jumped in the car. The driver started.

"Where are we heading? What is the plan of the day?"

"You have an appointment at the Canadian Embassy," the driver said. My heart swelled with joy. I didn't ask him any further questions, but watched the beautiful landscape, the passing cars, the people working on the farms.

It was Wednesday; the driver dropped me at the Canadian High Commissioner's office around 9 a.m. Someone from Goal Kenya took me upstairs.

Five people in the waiting room sat quietly with their thoughts. I sat on the first empty chair I found. Life has so many important turnings, and this for me was the most significant one. To live or die. I was a stateless person, my journalistic profession had put my life at risk, and the Eritrean government was hunting me like an antelope either inside the country or outside it. I had nowhere to go. For good or bad, my life would depend on the Canadian officer I was about to meet.

My brain raced. I didn't notice the picture hanging in front of me or the people sitting beside me; I was just lost in thought, reshuffling one plan after the other. *If I am not granted asylum*

169

instantly, how many days am I going to survive the Eritrean security agents in Kenya? What is going to happen to my wife and my kids? My brain was overwhelmed with scary thoughts.

It had been almost five months since I had fled Eritrea under gunfire. My colleagues were languishing in jail without charge. My wife was interrogated constantly. My children were left without a father. I didn't know what would happen to my brother, to my cousin, to Nadia, to Samson, or to the many more who had risked their lives to save mine.

"Aaron Berhane!"

I was slow to respond. There is a proverb in Tigrigna that says, "It is the heart that sees, not the eyes." I saw a woman standing in front of us calling my name, but never heard her.

"Are you Aaron Berhane?" the woman asked, staring at me.

"Yes. Yes, I am," I said, like a person woken from sleep.

I followed her. A counsellor put down a phone. She was a tall, beautiful woman in her forties, I guessed, and she greeted me with a big smile.

"You must be a brave journalist; you have terrific supporting letters. Please sit down." She seemed already convinced after having read my case file, and the supporting letters of PEN International, the Committee to Protect Journalists (CPJ), and Reporters Without Borders (RSF.)

"Thank you! I was just doing my job," I said. I looked around the cozy, elegant office.

"Yeah, it still needs courage to stand up for truth. Do you need anything to drink?"

I never imagined seeing a caring and sensitive visa officer, probably because I heard so many negative things about visa officers from friends. A friend who was twice denied visas to enter the U.S.A. described them as soulless creatures. Another friend who applied to go to Britain three times described them as emotionless robots who were programmed to say only "No." This Canadian counsellor was totally different. I could see she had already put herself in my shoes and worried about my family. I guessed she was a mother.

"Where are your wife and your children?"

"Asmara."

"What about your father?"

"He passed away."

"I'm sorry. Do you have any health issue, or is there anyone in your family who has any kind of illness?"

"No."

Since I expected hard questions, I didn't think the interview had started. But within ten minutes everything wrapped up. Particularly, when she asked me if I wanted my family to join me, I knew I had passed.

"We are happy to have you. Where do you want to go?" she said with a smile.

It sounded like a dream, a message you might receive when you were in a deep sleep. All the tension that I had in my shoulders, the scary noises that I heard in my head disappeared, and I breathed easily.

"So where do you want to go?" She smiled again.

"I have no one in Canada, so take me wherever you want," I said smiling up to my ears. She made notes and congratulated me. I thanked her for giving me a safe haven.

I came back to the monastery at Tigoni with great news, but I had no one to share with or cheer with. However, that didn't stop me from celebrating by dancing alone in my room without music. I played my favourite singer, Abraham Afewerki, in my head, twisted my body right and left, jumped up and down, again and again. I am a horrible dancer, but who cared, if no one was watching. I didn't think I would care even if somebody did see me through the window. I felt that joy in my bones, my mind, and my soul.

Now, the biggest hurdle was behind me. I was accepted by the Canadian government and I would settle in Canada. In order to see that finalized I just needed to have a medical exam. I didn't know when it would take place or how long it would take, so till then I went back to a routine. I woke up early each morning, walked around the compound, chatted a bit with the monks during mealtimes, and read the newspaper, the *Nation*.

I wouldn't go far from my room before 11 a.m. I hung out around the gate or in my room, reading the newspaper or the Bible. In the afternoons, I walked in the valley and sat under the trees with the Bible. That was the only available book to read, and I used to read it like fiction.

Six days passed and no car showed up to take me to do my medical exam. I was anxious to give my mind the peace it needed to focus on something else.

On the morning of May 22, the Goal Kenya driver known as Mike showed up in the compound around nine thirty. I ended up at Nairobi Hospital. A light-skinned doctor checked my vital signs, blood pressure, breathing rate, pulse rate, temperature, height, and weight. At the end she sent me for a chest exam. Then a nurse, Rose, took me to a clinic known as Accident House, that specialized in internal exams. The lab technicians took samples of my blood and saliva. They knew what they were doing. I saw my blood moving through the tube into tiny bottles one after the other. The nurse took the needle out of my arm and covered the spot with cotton. She asked me to hold it tight.

"How are you feeling?" Rose asked.

"I am good," I said. "What now?"

"Now, we have to wait until we get the result from the doctor," she said, walking to the other room. I sat in front of her on a metal chair. We were the only people there.

"How long will it take to get the result?"

"Maybe twenty minutes," she said. "I think you must be an urgent case, that's why they are doing it right away. Usually, it takes two weeks."

I kept quiet. I picked up a newspaper from the table and forced myself to get lost in whatever news article I found on the front page. I was not able to focus; my mind was with the doctors examining my blood, my saliva, the image of my chest. I had never had a thorough health examination like this in my life. The only illness I could remember having was malaria. Even then I only spent three days in the hospital. Was I healthy? Would they find an illness I was not aware of?

A doctor popped in at the door and smiled at me. I stood up, putting the newspaper on the table.

"You did great," she said, with a friendly smile, but she didn't hand over any documents, either to my nurse or to me. Confused, I stood where I was, staring at the doctor.

"Let's go," Rose said, walking toward the exit.

"So ..." I said, not sure how to frame my question, but the doctor was quick to read the expression on my face.

"You are as healthy as a horse," she smiled again. "You are done now, we will send the documents."

"Thank you," I said, striding to catch Rose, who was already waiting for me at the door. Then we had to head to the offices of the International Organization of Migration (IOM) for a physical exam there. The whole day, they moved me from one clinic to another, from one examination to another, physical to internal.

Once I finished my interviews, medical exams, and other screenings, I had to wait for the last part of the process, the flight to be arranged by the IOM. Since Goal Kenya was handling my case with them, my role was just to sit and wait in my solitary place. I kept myself busy by following my established routine. I woke up early each morning, watched the sunrise, took a walk, and read the day-old newspaper before breakfast. Then I chatted for a few minutes with some monks. I would always love to hear more about their histories, what motivated them to become monks but, due to their tight schedule of attending prayer and working in the different departments of the monastery, I was usually out of luck on that. I had to go to the valley and sit underneath the trees for hours with my thoughts. In the evenings, I watched TV.

"Today is Sunday; you can join us in church," Brother Joseph said one day, as I headed out of the cafeteria after breakfast. I saw several well-dressed people in the compound and walked to the church.

"What is going on? Who are those people?"

"They come from the neighbourhood villages to worship," Brother Joseph said. "They do that every Sunday."

I stood there and watched the people going to the church. I contemplated whether I should go in. I had never been to any church other than the Orthodox Tewahdo Church that I used to go to on special occasion like the baptism of my kids or at Christmas. Finally, I went in.

I walked down the aisle under the high ceiling of the enormous church. It was packed. Framed pictures of saints and Jesus's crucifixion hung on the wall. The sanctuary where the priests delivered the sermon had a stand where the Bible was read from, a table where the bread and wine were blessed during the Eucharist, and a crucifix. What surprised me most was what was on that cross of Jesus. It was a Black man. It was not the image I had known from my childhood. However, I knelt when the congregation knelt, and I stood up when they did. When they lined up to receive the blessing of bread and wine, I lined up to receive the blessing too. I didn't know what I was doing.

Right after church was over, I approached the priest to ask about that image of Jesus Christ. "If Jesus was born in Israel, in a white community, why is He depicted as a Black man here?"

"No one saw Jesus as Black or white," he said without hesitation. I could tell he had been asked this question often. "Jesus is the son of God. They painted Him based on their imagination, and we do it based on our imagination. When we think of Jesus, that's the image we see."

That morning the priest gave me lots to think about. I had never read the Bible before I came to the monastery and didn't know what Christianity was all about, despite having been born in a Christian family. I was determined to finish reading the Bible, both the Old and the New Testaments, before I left the monastery. In one month, I finished it all from the first page to the last. Though I couldn't say I understood everything I read, I found grounds to question why I and many others found belief in a book that only tells a history of the people who live in Israel and its surroundings.

I did my best to keep myself busy by walking, reading, and watching TV, but time went slowly. Sometimes even walking was not possible, because of the constant rain. On Sundays, I would go to church and pray whole-heartedly that I might land in Canada before the Eritrean agents located me. This was my new normal and I accepted it, even watching the World Cup by myself. That made me nostalgic. I remembered the bets we used to make in my family during the 1998 World Cup before every game. I used to support the underdog teams, and my daughter Frieta always cheered with me.

Now, in 2002, as Senegal played France I felt the presence of my family. I imagined how we would behave. My wife would side with France and I would side with Senegal. Frieta would cheer with me, and Mussie would cheer with everyone since he was too young to understand the game. Evan slept in the arms of his mother. Though I was by myself in this TV room, I didn't feel lonely. I yelled, cheered, and laughed as if I had companions. Senegal beat France 1-0. No one expected that to happen.

Late on the sixth day after the World Cup started, the Goal Kenya driver showed up. I was surprised to see him coming so late; if I had an appointment, they usually came in the morning. Three men in their early twenties got out of the car. They were Ethiopians from the Oromo community. Their father was an Ethiopian cabinet minister but he had to flee when the Ethiopian regime came to arrest him. When they failed to catch him, they came after his children. Luckily, they had escaped and here they were in the safe house with me. I really enjoyed their company. We watched the World Cup, we walked in the valley, we dined in the cafeteria together.

One morning, around six, I clearly heard the gurgling of a baby. I jumped out of bed to look through the window. No one was there. I dressed quickly and walked along the long corridor to the lounge. No one there, either. When I went out of the building, I saw one of the three Ethiopians enjoying the fresh morning air.

"*Endiet aderk*," (Good morning), I said. "Do we have new guests?"

"What guests?"

"Refugees. A few minutes ago I heard the gurgling of a baby."

"I don't think so," he said. "I couldn't sleep much last night, and I've been up since four. I heard nothing, saw nothing."

It must have been in my head. I nodded and walked to the soccer field, thinking about my children. Suddenly, it hit me. Today, June 22, was the first birthday of my son, Evan. I felt a wave of emotions: euphoria, anger, a burning fire in my stomach, pain in my chest. My eyes filled with tears. I felt guilty for not being there. That whole day I kept hearing his gurgling voice, the laughter of children, the nieces, the nephews. I could feel the burden of my wife, my mother, and my sisters. They couldn't talk about the elephant in the room — my absence.

Then, the day that I had waited so long for finally arrived. The Canadian Embassy issued my visa, IOM arranged my flight, and

I was booked to fly on August 20, 2002. Two people would fly together to Canada, Seifu and me. (To where in Canada? I really didn't know.) Seifu was the Ethiopian journalist that I'd met in the first safe house. The people of Goal Kenya congratulated us and smiled all day until we finally departed from their office at 4:30 p.m. They had helped hundreds of political refugees like me and they might not remember my name now, but I still remember theirs. Annette Ludeking, Dr. Malik, Dr. Bhavna, Mr. Allen, Professor Julian, I remember them and I always include them in my prayers. They are my heroes.

My plane took off from Nairobi at 12:07 a.m. to London, then we transferred to Toronto with Air Canada on flight number AC869. After a two-hour break, they flew us in another plane to Regina, Saskatchewan. We arrived in Canada on August 21. The coincidence surprised me. I had published the first copy of my newspaper on August 21, and I landed at my new country on August 21. This is my luckiest number if there is one.

"Welcome to Canada!"

CHAPTER 10

MY FIRST EXPERIENCES IN EXILE: REGINA

TWO EMPLOYEES OF THE REGINA OPEN DOOR SOCIETY (RODS), A NON-profit organization that provides settlement and integration servi-ces to newcomers, welcomed us at Regina International Airport. They waited at the arrival gate, holding up our names on sheets of paper in big letters. It was around three in the afternoon. Seifu and I walked toward them in a swarm of passengers. It took us a minute to reach them. As we got closer, I could see how cheerful they were.

"Hello, my name is Aaron," I said to the lady who was holding up my name.

"Welcome to Canada, Aaron. My name is Mellina." She shook my hand. "And this is Nora, my colleague." They were warm and very welcoming. We chatted a bit about our trip, and then they led us to their car.

Both of them were children of immigrants. They now called Canada their home, and they worked with RODS to assist people like me to settle here. As we drove from the airport to the city, they briefed us on how RODS assists newcomers by offering them temporary accommodation, language training, and settlement services. They said they would take us to the guest house where we would stay for a few days until they found us an apartment to rent. As I listened to the conversation, I looked at the marvellous, endlessly flat and green land. I expected to find a hill or perhaps even a mountain as we drove into the city and toward Saskatchewan Drive, but we encountered none.

"Wow! This is really beautiful, full of green plants and fancy houses, and I haven't seen a single hill yet," I said, staring at the limitless straight lines of the roads that we drove on or crossed.

"Yes, it's green in the summer, and we don't have mountains here," Mellina said. I thought she was joking, but when she went on to describe the landscape of Saskatchewan in detail and how different it was from Alberta or British Colombia, I was stunned. In my head, I started to compare the landscape she was describing with the mountainous areas of my country — Eritrea. Not in the lowlands, but in the highlands, it was impossible to drive straight for a single kilometre. You had to turn again and again, around the many hills and mountains.

Ten minutes later we arrived at our destination, 1610 Toronto Street.

"Here we are," Mellina said as she stopped the car near a two-storey detached house. I jumped out and looked around, taking in my new neighbourhood, its houses and streets. Green trees, green grass, and the streets were all straight with perpendicular intersecting roads as if drawn with a ruler.

"This is beautiful!" I said.

"Indeed!" Seifu added in Amharic.

They led us into the house. It had five bedrooms. We went upstairs, and they had a room for each of us. The rooms were all the same in size. My room was at the corner of the house, and fully furnished with a bed, drawers, and cupboards. I dropped my bag on the bed.

"This is cozy!" I said, looking through the window to the quiet streets.

"Let me also show you the kitchen."

We walked downstairs, and they showed us a fully equipped kitchen. The cabinet was full of plates, mugs, and drinking glasses. I opened the fridge, which was packed with lots of groceries.

"Does anyone live here?" I asked with surprise.

"No, that's all for you," she said.

I went upstairs to my room and closed the door to let my new reality sink in. Finally, I was in a safe haven. *The Eritrean regime can't come after me anymore*, I thought with a smile, looking through the window of my room.

* * *

The next day I woke up feeling fully rested. I felt even more joy than the previous day when I opened the curtain on the window. It was sunny and about twenty-five degrees Celsius. Everything that I watched through the window, the trees, the grass, the cars, brought me more joy. Just watching the branches of the big trees swaying back and forth with the wind, and hearing the gentle sounds of the passing cars, smelling the freshness of the air, I felt alive.

As I walked downstairs to the kitchen, I heard Seifu chatting in Amharic with a man in the kitchen.

"Good morning!" I said.

"Good morning. My name is Getachew; I am your case-worker."

His name sounded like an Ethiopian name, but he spoke fluent Tigrigna. I couldn't tell if he was Eritrean or Ethiopian. Before I dropped my question, he said that he belonged to both countries. He had come to Canada in the 1980s, and it had been his home ever since.

"How big is the Eritrean population here?" I asked.

"It's small, forty or fifty families. I'm not sure," he said.

As our case worker, Getachew helped us to rent a two-bedroom apartment, drove us around to shop in stores, to open a bank account, to apply for social and health insurance, and to deal with the Immigration Canada application to bring our wives and children over. He explained to us that, as government-sponsored persons, we were eligible for one year of financial assistance.

Since Seifu had started the application process for his wife and his two children while he was in Kenya, he learned that they would join him in three or four months. So he was eager to find a job before their arrival, despite the language barrier he faced.

A few weeks after we moved into the two-bedroom apartment, he came to tell me that he had found a job.

"Are you joking?" I asked.

"I am serious. It is in Alberta. I am moving next week," he said. "My friend told me there are lots of job vacancies in Alberta, unlike here."

"What kind of job? You don't even speak the language," I said. I still couldn't believe him.

"It's in meatpacking. I don't need language for that."

Seifu moved out to Brooks, Alberta, to work at a meatpacking plant before the arrival of his family. I couldn't afford the two-room apartment on my own, so I had no choice but, with RODS's help, to move to a one-bedroom.

As parents take their children to school for the first time to register and make sure the teachers treat them well, the RODS employees were always available, whether I was going to school, to banks, or to stores, or had an issue with a landlord. They were there at every step to help me navigate my way and restart my life.

For the first two months, I visited the RODS office almost every day. I had nowhere else to go. I attended workshops, browsed the internet, and arranged for driving lessons there. I tried to hang out there with the other newcomers who had arrived before me, from Sudan, Ethiopia, Afghanistan. I tried to learn from their experience, but language barriers made it difficult to communicate smoothly. I didn't spend over ten minutes with any of them. We all spoke broken English and could barely understand what the other person was trying to say. So, our engagement was bound to be mostly superficial, with a few exceptions. It was much easier to connect with the employees of RODS.

The first time I visited the RODS office, I was introduced to Haile Berhe, an intelligent man in his late forties, a gentle soul. He was of Eritrean descent and had come to Canada in the 1980s. He worked as an accountant at RODS. He said that, since the crackdown in Eritrea on the press and the arrest of the reformers, the Eritrean community here in Canada had split into pro- and anti-Eritrean government. He advised me to keep quiet about bringing my family over, to avoid obstacles the supporters of the regime might throw up. He introduced me to his brother Tesfay, his friend Futsum, and his wife and children. All of them treated me like family, inviting me to their homes and offering any help they could. Whenever we met at a coffee shop or in their houses, we discussed Eritrean politics. No matter how hard we tried to talk about other issues, that topic never left us.

The other Eritrean that Haile introduced me to, and I enjoyed spending time with, was Million. He was a young man in his twenties, who had arrived in Canada two years before. He was soft-spoken and, having been raised in Ethiopia, spoke Tigrigna with an Amharic accent. As a religious person he didn't particularly enjoy talking about politics, preferring other issues like work, religion, and ethics. Unlike my other friends — Tedros, in his late thirties, Michael and Mewael, in their twenties — he didn't go much to bars or nightclubs, and if he ever did, he didn't drink any alcohol.

183

Every day, he would call to check on me. One morning, the call went like this.

"Good morning." I instantly recognized the voice on the other end of the line.

"Good morning, Million."

"What are you up to today?"

"Nothing. I just got up."

"It's Sunday today, I am going to church. Would you like to accompany me?"

"Sure." Everything was an adventure for me then, and, besides, I needed to get out of my apartment.

He picked me up at 8:30 a.m., and we drove for about ten minutes from downtown Regina where I lived to the east side of Regina along Victoria Avenue. The streets were quiet; I saw very few cars on the road.

"This is our church," Million said as he turned right from Victoria Avenue onto Edgar Street. I saw a church just a few metres away from us, and a diverse crowd walking toward it from the parking lot. Million parked the car, and we walked in. I stopped to read the name of the church, Saint George Orthodox Cathedral.

It's a Romanian Church but it serves Eritreans, Romanians, Egyptians, Croatians, Ukranians, and others from Eastern European countries. The priest preached in English and everyone was quiet for his sermon, but I was on a different mission. I was counting how many Eritreans were sitting in that church with me, how many men, women, etc. I felt like a distracted high school student. There were about thirty.

After the mass was over, we went downstairs to the cafeteria to mingle and eat snacks. To my surprise, all the Eritreans that I met there already knew about me.

"So, you are the freshman; we heard a lot about you." That was the standard sentence I got to hear when Million introduced me. I could sense they were being a bit reserved, from the expression of their faces. I guessed they didn't quite know how to interact with me, but there was one woman who was eager to talk. She pulled me aside, to give us some privacy.

"Is it true that you are hanging out with Haile Berhe and his friends?" She breathed heavily, adjusting her *netsela*, a traditional two-layered white cotton scarf, around her neck and head. She was in her forties and looked like one of those people who like to intervene in people's lives and enjoy providing unsolicited advice. Her weird question made me grin. I noticed an older man who must have been in his fifties was trying to eavesdrop on our conversation.

"What is your name again?" I asked her before I answered her question.

"Stay away from them; they are *Jebha*," she said, in an authoritative voice, as a mother might speak to her son. I burst into laughter. Jebha is the nickname of the Eritrean Liberation Front. The woman meant my friend Haile was a dangerous rebel.

The older man got closer to us. He seemed to suspect things might escalate, and apparently wanted to intervene before it was too late.

"I am serious," she barked. "They are against our government. They always say bad things about our country. I don't want you to be like them."

"What do they say?" I asked.

"President Isaias is a dictator, there is no democracy in our country. So many stupid things," she said with a distasteful tone.

"Are they wrong?"

She gasped, opened her mouth, and widened her eyes before she managed to regain her voice to puff out some words.

"Are you crazy? Of course they are wrong."

"They are not wrong," I said. "I just came from there, you know. There is no constitution, no democracy, no freedom of speech." As I said this, the older man whispered something into her ear and tried to pull her away.

"Really?" she answered loudly to the man's whisper. He nodded his head and she stepped back abruptly, as if from a scary animal.

"Is that you, the journalist who was insulting our government on Asmarino?" she asked. Asmarino was a popular website for the Eritrean diaspora. She must have seen an interview I had done with Tesfalem Meharena, the publisher of that website, a few days before.

I nodded my head with a smile. She spun away without saying goodbye, an expression of defeat in her face.

"He will be a problem. We have to tell Million to stay away from him," she told the man, but I could hear what she was saying.

It was an eventful Sunday. Seeing most of the Eritrean Canadians who lived in Regina in that church gave me an impression of the tight network they had. It was easy to identify the die-hard supporters of the government and the neutral. One by one, many of them left, including the woman with the big mouth. I chatted with the priest and the others for a few minutes, and then I stepped out of the basement myself.

It was a sunny day and warm. As I looked around, I noticed an Egyptian man who was trying to convince his five-year-old son to get in the car. The boy didn't seem ready to go home. The father was yelling in Arabic. As if in a cinema, I watched the argument unfold and waited for the climax, observing the father and the son attentively to see how it would end. It didn't last long, but, in the process, I got lost in my own thoughts, about a memorable struggle I had with my own son, Mussie.

The last time I took my kids to the playground was a week before the closure of my newspaper. Mussie was three and a half years old. While Mielat stayed home with Evan, who was three months old, I took Frieta, Mussie, and my niece Bietu to a recreation centre a dozen kilometres south of Asmara. The centre had a full complement of recreational equipment — a seesaw, a merry-go-round, a swing set, a slide, a jungle gym, chin-up bars, and a spring rider. After the kids had played for over an hour, I wanted to take them home. But Mussie refused to go. He begged for one more round on the swing set, then one on the slide, then one more on the seesaw. Usually, when he wouldn't leave a place easily, news of something better to do after that would convince him. Ice cream was my usual trick, but it didn't work that time. I spent another half hour playing with him, then had to actually lift him into the car.

Standing by the church, I remembered how Mussie ran around the playground equipment with me trying to catch him. Suddenly I felt jealous of the man who was trying to catch his son and get him into the car. *Does he know how lucky he is? His family is here. Mine isn't*, I thought to myself.

I felt both anxiety and anger. My mood changed quickly every time I thought of my family, about the situation I had put them in, the trouble I caused my kids and my wife. I had to recall another memory to create inner balance — I reminded myself how lucky I was that I could still chat with my family on the phone, unlike some of my colleagues who languished in prison. How painful would that be? But that relative happiness didn't last long, since here I was, in a different country, in different circumstances, and I could see the joyful hugs and routine struggles of parents and kids in front of me physically. I know life is about perspective and relativity: what's good for one can be bad for the other. But I had to remind myself constantly not to compare myself to others, but only to myself in my previous state, remembering how far I had travelled, both internally and externally. The minute I managed to turn my thinking in that direction, I could feel the anxiety and anger gradually evaporate from my bones. Even that, though, needed a constant inner effort, which exhausted me sometimes.

* * *

Meeting members of my community at RODS or at church was a great help. I had several standard questions that I used to ask whenever I was introduced to any immigrant, particularly if they were Eritrean or Ethiopian. "What was the biggest challenge you faced in the first year of your arrival?" "What was your first job?" "How did you find your first job?" "What path did you follow to get to where you are now?" Most of them answered me genuinely, proud of the progress they had made in their lives, but some were not. They evaded my questions, or got upset.

I remember vividly the interaction I had with an Ethiopian man who was the husband of an Eritrean woman. She introduced me to her husband when we met at the mall in Regina one afternoon. They had been living in Canada for about seven years. We sat down for a coffee while his wife went shopping. After having chatted about back home politics for a few minutes, I changed the topic to inquire about his experience in Canada. He seemed reluctant to share his experience, but I couldn't read him well. I kept asking one question after another. Finally, he barked, *"Mindenow yihe?"* (What is this?) He leaned back in his chair. "What are you doing? It sounds like an interrogation."

"I am just trying to learn from the experience of anyone who came before me," I said in a very gentle tone.

"Do you ask these questions of everyone?"

"Yes, I do."

He observed me for a few seconds.

"You are a strange man, not the same as the other Eritreans I have met here," he finally said, nodding.

"How so?"

"Maybe another time. But I am not proud of my job. I became a cleaner when I arrived, and I am still a cleaner, and I will be a cleaner tomorrow, too. That's the fate we have here. I think I should go now," he said, standing up from his chair.

"Thank you! It was nice meeting you," I said.

He nodded and left.

This was a particularly draining experience, and my mood changed to contain a good portion of pessimism. I had heard similar stories before, from other immigrants who did odd jobs, but most of them were at least optimistic about the future. They believed they would eventually land a better job if they got a better education or a better opportunity came around.

* * *

While waiting for my English classes to start, I passed the written and the driving test, and got my driving licence. As usual, I tried to create a routine for myself to avoid boredom. I woke up in the morning, visited the RODS office for updates, attended various orientation seminars, and tried to gather whatever information I needed. Then I headed to the public library close to the RODS office. I would spend three or four hours there, reading the Regina *Leader Post* and browsing the internet for news from Eritrea before going home to cook my usual meal — a fried egg.

I was tired of eating fried egg twice a day. I tried cooking other meals. But whatever else I tried — meat, fish, or lentils — turned out quite badly.

One Sunday, after finishing chatting with my kids, I told my wife that the biggest challenge I faced so far was cooking. She couldn't stop laughing.

"What are you cooking?" she asked.

189

"I tried to cook fish, meat, lentils, but it all tasted bad."

She kept laughing.

"Okay, Mielat," I said. "Give me a quick lesson. How should I start if I would like to cook meat?"

"Okay," she said, "fry the onion with oil first."

"No, I don't use onion."

"Why?"

"It makes me cry when I chop it. Can I do it without onion?"

Mielat couldn't stop laughing, and I didn't want to interrupt. I laughed with her, imagining my beautiful wife was beside me. Her laughter was like therapy for me; it gave me joy and energy. Luckily, I knew how to make her laugh. We had been together since we were teens. But I hadn't intended the bit about the onions as a joke, I really did try to avoid onions and didn't even buy them anymore.

"You can't make ... ha ha ha ha ... a tasty dish without onion," she managed to say, still laughing. "You will get used to it."

I had never questioned the culture I grew up in before, but then I did. Why is cooking considered women's work? Why doesn't Eritrean culture teach boys how to cook? This is an essential skill; how could they not see that? I was frustrated because I didn't know how to cook other dishes. Every day, I simply stuck to the one I knew best — fried eggs.

One afternoon, I decided to cook pasta, which I assumed would be reasonably easy to handle. What could go wrong? You boil the pasta and mix it up with the ready-made tomato sauce. At least that's what I thought. I put water in the pot and dumped the spaghetti in it, and let the pot sit on the hot stove. Waiting for the pasta to cook, I started to watch a horse race on TV, but after just a few minutes, I heard the water boiling over. When I went to check, I found the pasta sunk to the bottom of the pot, sticking together like a giant piece of gum. I couldn't even pick out one piece of pasta to taste if it was cooked or not. While I tried to figure out whether I could separate the mass by adding cold water, my phone rang. It was Million.

"I found you a calling card for five dollars," Million said. The calling card that I had been using to make calls to Asmara was relatively expensive in comparison to the minutes it allowed.

"Thank you, Million, let me get a pen," I said. "I hope this one is better."

"Yes, way better than the one you have been using," he said. "It will allow you to speak for ten minutes or more."

"By the way, I tried to cook pasta, but it got stuck together. How can I separate it?"

He exploded into laughter and didn't stop laughing to answer me. I couldn't help but join in.

"Tell me, how did you cook it?" He didn't stop laughing as I explained. He told me to get the water boiling first, and then put the pasta in.

"Is that it?"

"Yeah. You shouldn't put them in together right from the beginning."

"What about this lot? Are you saying I have to start from scratch?"

"Yes. That's useless now, dump it in the garbage."

It was tough to remove the pasta from the bottom of the pot. Finally, I did get the pot clean, filled it with water, and waited until it started to boil. Once the water boiled, I put the spaghetti in, pushing it around with a spoon until I could put the lid on. I reduced the heat a bit and went back to continue to watch the horse race on TV. A few minutes later the pot boiled over again, pushing the lid up. I removed the lid completely, set my alarm to go off after ten minutes, and relaxed on my seat. Whether because I was so hungry or just impatient, the ten minutes seemed like eternity. At one point I assumed there was something wrong with my watch, thinking that the ten minutes had passed though they hadn't. I checked the pot. I didn't like what I saw. The pasta had stuck together again.

I turned off the stove and left everything as it was and went to a fast-food restaurant.

For the first time, I realized that I had a serious problem. I lacked the basic skill to cook for myself. If I kept eating out every day, I would be out of money in three weeks. Besides, I didn't really enjoy the taste of the hotdogs, or the sandwiches I occasionally had for dinner. I thought seriously about how to find a solution for my problem.

The next day I went to RODS to attend the orientation event for newcomers. The centre provided orientation about an impressive range of services — settlement, school registration, driving lessons, and more. We were about thirteen newcomers, all eager to devour any information that could help us settle quickly. Nicole, an energetic woman in her twenties, had us gathered in a room to lead us in that day's activities. But before diving in, she asked us if we had encountered any particular challenges. Everyone was quiet. I raised my hand.

"Okay, Aaron, please go ahead," she said.

"I don't know how to cook, and I am having a hard time feeding myself," I said with a self-conscious grin.

This made everybody laugh. Among us were some men from South Sudan who loved to joke around; we chatted frequently when we met at the centre.

"So, do you want RODS to cook for you?" Elijah, a tall, skinny man said, and they all laughed again. I liked to joke around, too, and I teased them a lot when I got a chance. So this was payback. But even though I enjoyed the jovial atmosphere, I really needed a solution to my problem. Most of the others had come with their wives. Otherwise, they would have faced the same challenge, since they came from patriarchal societies, just as I did. A kitchen was not their territory, any more than it was mine.

"I am serious. I would like to learn how to cook. Do you offer cooking workshops, by any chance?"

"There are none at the moment, but we can certainly do something about that," Nicole said, decisively.

Three days later, the cooking workshop was set up. I was impressed. RODS had found a professional chef, Deborah Stevens, who volunteered to teach us every Wednesday for two hours for about two months. She taught us basic cookery and knife skills; how to utilize simple cooking equipment; recipes that catered to nutritional needs; how to cook pasta, meat, and vegetables; and how to use the key spices like black pepper, red pepper, rosemary, and saffron. She also taught us how to do grocery shopping by taking us to the store physically. It was a revelation for me. I learned what important and difficult work it is to prepare a meal. I felt guilty for recognizing this only so late in my life, and for never having fully appreciated the work of my mother, my wife, and my sisters.

That was the best workshop any newcomer could have had. It turned my perspective upside down. It taught me exactly the skill that I so desperately needed. I didn't become a superb cook, but at least I didn't have to go to bed hungry anymore. I even managed to cook my favourite dish — pasta.

Although I enjoyed spending time with the members of my community, I didn't feel I was learning much about the "authentic" Canada. I really wanted to go beyond what I knew and interact with "real" Canadians. However, I didn't know how. My Eritrean friends told me that this could be possible once I started working or going to school.

But I didn't want to wait that long.

* * *

One day I went to the bar at Albert Street by myself, a four-minute walk from my apartment. It was Thursday around six thirty. The bar was big with a long counter. There was a billiard table and about eight people sitting and playing inside the bar. I got closer to the counter, and a server who must have been in her twenties greeted me warmly.

"Good evening, what can I get for you?" she said.

"Good evening. Beer, please."

"What kind of beer?"

I didn't expect that question.

"What do you mean?" I asked, confused.

"What kind of beer do you want? We have Molson, Budweiser, Corona, Stella, Heineken ..." she spoke really fast. She kept going, mentioning one beer after the other. She lost me. In Eritrea, we had just one beer, which is called Melotti. You only needed to say "beer," and the beer landed in your hand, you didn't even need to say "Melotti." What else could it be? I had intended to pretend that I wasn't a foreigner, but I was quickly realizing that this wouldn't work. I knew I wouldn't learn much by trying to fake it.

"Sorry, I just arrived in Canada," I said. "I don't know the differences; I'll be happy to drink whatever you recommend."

"Cool."

"Yes, cold please," I replied.

She paused a second and looked at me.

I thought she didn't understand me, or that the way I said it wasn't the proper way to say it. So, I repeated my statement with a minor correction. "Yeah, I like cool beer."

She grinned as she opened the fridge. "Great. Where are you from?"

"Eritrea, northeast Africa."

"Cool."

"No, it's quite warm actually," I said. "The average temperature of my home city, Asmara, for example, is twenty-four degrees Celsius." I went on for a bit more about the weather in the highlands and lowlands of Eritrea.

"That's cool," she commented with a smile.

I paused, assuming that either she didn't understand me when I said it was warm, or that the meaning of this word *cool* could turn out to be something else. I produced a dictionary from my pocket to check the meaning of *cool*, as she dug to get me a cold beer, but the light wasn't strong enough. It was too dark to read in here, so I closed the dictionary and put it back in my pocket.

She served me a bottle of beer, a Budweiser. She still wore a smile.

"I don't think I understood your question," I said with a smile.

"That was not really a question," she giggled. "I said, 'cool,' which means 'great.'"

I burst into laughter and she laughed full-heartedly with me. "I thought I knew the meaning of this word a hundred percent, but I certainly didn't."

"You know it now," she said. She opened the beer bottle and handed it back to me. "You will love this one. Everyone loves it."

"Thank you." I pulled out my wallet, "How much?"

"It's on the house. Welcome to Canada!"

I was impressed and touched. Not because the beer was a big deal, but because she made me feel at home so suddenly. I didn't think there was an adequate word in my vocabulary to express the gratitude I felt toward her in that instance.

"Thank you very much! That means a lot to me." I sipped a bit and nodded my head with agreement. "Why is this beer so popular?"

She spoke fast, talked about its flavour and how it was different from other beers, but I didn't understand her very well. I thought I knew English, but that evening I realized I didn't. Unfortunately, I probably understood only 50 percent of what she was saying.

"Good evening!" She turned to some newly arrived customers.

I thanked her and walked with my beer to find a chair. There were four tables with two or three chairs around them. A few people were watching the billiards. I looked around the room and saw one empty chair at a table where two young men sat. They looked like they were in their thirties.

"Is this chair taken?" I asked.

One of the men pointed his hand to the empty chair without interrupting his conversation. I interpreted this as an invitation to sit.

"Thank you," I said, joining their table and making myself comfortable in the chair.

"How was your day?" I said.

The two men stopped talking, exchanged a look, and then stared at me with a startled expression.

"This is really an excellent beer," I continued speaking. They didn't respond to my comment.

"Do you know this man?" one of them asked his friend. His sloppy hair and his red eyes suggested he might be drunk.

"No! I don't."

"What is he doing here?"

"I don't know."

I didn't realize they were talking about me until they addressed me directly.

"Who are you?" the man with the sloppy hair asked. I thought he said "How are you?"

"I am doing fine." I smiled. "How are you?"

They looked at each other for a second, ignored my greeting, and stayed quiet.

"You know this is my first time to try this beer, and it's fantastic," I said, raising the bottle in my hand. I just wanted to have a casual conversation, but either they didn't understand my English or they were not in the mood to talk with a stranger. They remained silent. After a few seconds, they left the bar without saying goodbye.

I sensed that I had gotten it wrong somehow, but I didn't know which part, exactly. I had learned a lesson, though. The way I interacted with those two men was based on my experience back home, where it's common to go to any bar, sit on any empty chair, and strike up a conversation with anyone there. There was nothing weird about that in my culture, but for them, obviously, things were different.

* * *

The next afternoon I was in a coffee shop with Million, Tedros, and Michael. It was around four. Both Michael and Tedros loved to joke around, and they had already shared their various good or bad experiences without reservation with me. I told them about the strange interaction I had in the bar — about the free beer and warm welcome I received; and the embarrassing moment I experienced at the table. They all laughed and explained to me how weirdly that could be interpreted in Canadian culture.

"Which bar did you go to?" Michael asked.

"That bar near my building, on Albert street," I said. "It is a good bar. It even has billiards."

"Oh no!" Tedros said. "That's a redneck bar. Please don't go there."

"Who's red neck?" I asked.

"There are a few narrow-minded people who don't like Black people," he said. "They call those people rednecks. A few years

197

ago, they killed a Black man in that bar. You don't want to end up dead there." He wheezed and nodded his head like a lizard up and down, up and down. Everyone at the table turned suddenly gloomy and serious. Once I realized that Tedros wasn't joking, I felt something chilly in my stomach, and for a few moments we all kept quiet.

"When did this happen?" I asked.

"I think about ten years ago. I'm not exactly sure," he said. "When I heard about that, I stopped going to bars by myself."

"The reason they left the table when you joined them could be that they don't want you to sit beside them," Michael added.

"But that was a long time ago," I said. "I think people can change."

"Maybe."

"Have you ever been to that bar?" I asked and found out that none of them had — they had all heard about that horrible incident early on.

"You know, I was there yesterday. I watched people play billiards, and no one cared about my presence, no one looked at me differently," I said.

"Only super sick men could do such a thing. We shouldn't paint all of them with the same brush," Million said. "We shouldn't talk about this atrocity as if it were happening every day."

"Let's go there right now to play a round of billiards. And watch how they behave," I said.

"Ah, you just want another free beer and to see that girl," they laughed.

We didn't go right then, but later on, it became the place where we would hang out and play billiards.

* * *

The Language Instruction for Newcomers to Canada (LINC) class that I had awaited eagerly for weeks started at the end of September 2002. The program helped newcomers like me learn English from level one to level five. They assigned me to level four, but quickly transferred me to level five. I was excited to learn and to finally have something to do. I had to take a bus every morning to go to school, about twenty minutes away from my place. In my cohort were nine newcomers, from China, Sierra Leone, Colombia, Croatia, Afghanistan, and Sudan, who had been living in Canada for over a year.

"This looks like a United Nations meeting," I said, when they introduced themselves and told me where they came from. They all laughed.

Since they had already been going to that class for a year, they knew each other well and teased each other every chance they got. It didn't take me long to familiarize myself. During the breaks we liked to chat and share our experiences so far — how we were navigating day-to-day life and trying to fit into Canadian culture with our broken English. We exchanged ideas and laughed at our mistakes without judging each other.

One day we chatted about the awkward feelings we had experienced because of miscommunication or cultural differences in the first days or weeks of our arrival in Canada. When I told them about the silly mistake I made at the bar, the Sudanese man told us of an experience his uncle had had.

"When he first came to Regina," the Sudanese man said, "he met a nice Canadian woman. She was beautiful and a little overweight, and he instantly fell in love with her. The woman enjoyed spending time with him, but she was a bit suspicious about why he cared so much about her. One day she asked him directly.

"'Why do you care so much about me?' she asked.

"'Because I love you,' he said.

"'What do you love about me?' she asked.

"'Everything! You are beautiful, you are fat, you are —'

"'What?' she screamed. She slapped him and left," he said. "My poor uncle was totally confused as to what was happening to him."

I couldn't stop laughing with the rest of my classmates.

* * *

Although I enjoyed being enrolled at LINC and I had fun with the other newcomers, I felt I was learning little in class. The lessons were below my level. I was particularly concerned about my teacher's accent. He was a skilled teacher, knowledgeable, respectful, and fluent in English, but he had an accent because of his Asian background. I wanted to learn proper pronunciation from people who were born here and spoke the language with a standard Canadian accent.

"Could you transfer me to a higher level?" I asked him, expressing my concern. He told me that there was no higher level than that in that school and advised me to go to a university course.

"But the university will not be free," he said.

My case worker, Getachew, didn't like the idea. He tried to convince me to take advantage of the support I had from the government while I explored my situation, familiarizing myself with the culture and weather.

"If you decide to enrol in the university," Getachew said, "You will not receive financial support from the government."

"But will they pay the tuition fee?"

"No, you will have to pay it yourself," he said. "The government will give you a loan, but you will have to pay it back after graduation. Think about it and let me know by tomorrow if you really want to take this risk."

I had already made up my mind.

The fall semester was halfway through, and the only option I had was to start in the winter semester.

I had had great support from the staff at RODS and had made friends from the Eritrean community and other immigrants, but I wan't interacting as often as I wished to with Canadians. That changed when RODS found me a host "family," Chris Mansbridge.

Chris was a retired teacher in his sixties with a gentle soul. He was tall, soft-spoken, and had a kind face. We met once a week, for two hours that he would have carefully planned out. It was the day of the week I looked forward to most. I enjoyed every second I spent with him. He knew exactly what a newcomer needed to know about Canada to have a better sense of the culture. He took me to a stand-up comedy show, to museums, and to a hockey game. Wherever we went, whatever we encountered, he had a story to tell. He answered any question without reservation.

"What we did to settle here was not acceptable," he told me once, when I asked him about the history of the First Nations people. "We disrupted their livelihood. Though we have made good progress, unfortunately, that wound is still open. We are not investing enough to resolve the social problems of First Nations and other minority groups."

Meeting regularly with Chris and sometimes with his girlfriend, Sandra, I began to feel more and more connected to Canadian culture. They were like another window for me, showing me how kind Canadians were and how passionate to help immigrants and make them feel at home.

I remember the first time I saw snow. It was after I had enjoyed two warm months, from August to mid-October. It was October 25, 2002; I was running late for school. I stepped outside my building that morning, wearing a big jacket, in a rush to catch the 8 a.m. bus. The sun was on duty, but the snow didn't seem to care. It covered everything with its white ashes, and it looked like bath foam.

"Wow! What is this?" I bellowed.

The superintendent was outside smoking a cigarette.

"First time, yeah?" he said.

I put some on the palm of my hand. It was freezing. I couldn't stop admiring the snow and the sun hanging out together as friends. *How come it doesn't melt? Is this really the sun or is it another type of moon?* I missed the bus while examining the snow and speculating about the behaviour of the sun.

The snow made me think about government, too. The pedestrian paths had been cleared before I had even woken up. This country is covered in snow for about six months a year, but it still has managed to build amazing buildings, roads, and railroads, and the government functions like an efficient machine.

Eritrea, on the other hand, is blessed with beautiful weather, rich natural resources, and hard-working people. But the Eritrean government spends 25 percent of its gross domestic product (GDP) on defence. Canada's defence spending is only about 1.2 percent of its GDP.

* * *

I enrolled at the University of Regina to study English with many international students, who mostly came from Asia and Latin America. After I learned that my student loan wouldn't cover my monthly expenses, I asked my friends to help me find a job. With their help, I got one at a Mac's convenience store a five-minute walk from my apartment. The store was open twenty-four hours a day, and the manager was kind enough to accommodate my school schedule — I mostly worked at night and on the weekends. So, in total, I worked four days a week. I ran a register as a cashier, restocked inventories, and cleaned the floor during slow hours. The day shift was run by two, but the night shift by just one person. I had to stand long hours, and it was a mundane job, but I enjoyed interacting with the customers. Almost all were friendly and patient when it took me time to locate the cigarettes they requested, or to understand what they were asking for. However, every day there were a few of the sort of customers who weren't quite so understanding.

One night, a well-dressed man in his thirties entered the store while I served two women who were heading to a nightclub. They were cordial and funny. They asked me to comment on how they dressed, whether they looked attractive and sexy. The man stood there and listened. After I answered politely what I expected the women wanted to hear, they left, wishing me a joyous night.

"Why do you think she did that?" he asked me as he came closer to the counter.

"Nothing. That was just chitchat."

"I'm not talking about them."

"Who are you talking about then?"

"My girlfriend." He stared at me.

"Was that your girlfriend?"

"Not those uglies." He waved his hand. "My girlfriend is beautiful. But she left me for your brother."

I laughed, assuming he was joking. He didn't sound like a drunk.

"I don't have a brother here," I said, looking at the other customers who were entering the store. "How can I help you?"

"He is a Black man like you. He must be your brother," he banged the counter with the palm of his hand. "Get me some Marlboros."

I could see the pain in his face. The veins on his forehead seemed about to pop out of his face. I looked at him calmly and didn't comment. I just pulled the pack of cigarettes from the shelf, scanned it, and put it on the counter.

He grabbed the pack, quickly.

"You pay for this," he said, putting it in his pocket. He walked toward the exit.

"Hey, come back, pay for this," I said. He never came back. He showed me his middle finger without turning his face and left.

I was stunned. In the three weeks I had been working there so far, nobody had refused to pay. I didn't even tell my boss; I balanced the book from my own pocket.

Every day was different, every day I learned something new. One Saturday I was on duty on the afternoon shift. The store was packed, and there were about eight people in line to pay. I and my colleague were serving the customers at the two separate registers. I noticed an old man, who was holding an enormous bottle of Pepsi, standing behind a twelve- or thirteen-year-old boy who held chips in one hand and cash in the other. I kindly asked the boy to allow the old man to be served before him.

"Why?" the boy asked, squaring his shoulders. "I came first."

"Yes, but he's older than you."

"He should have come in first then," he said, putting his chips on the counter.

I served him as he wished. I thought that child was undisciplined, otherwise he wouldn't have refused to give way to the older man. But later that day, my colleague told me how common it was. "It's first come, first served. No one cares who is older or younger."

The most memorable event was on January 11, 2003, at three in the morning. Three men in their late twenties or early thirties entered the store. They were laughing as they entered. I was used by then to dealing with drunk people coming into the store after their eventful nights in bars or nightclubs.

"Good morning," I said.

"What's your name?" a man with a blue toque asked me, while the other two engaged in a conversation not far away from the counter.

"Aaron," I said, pointing at the name tag on my chest.

"Not thaaaaat," he said. "I mean your actual name."

"Well, that is my actual name." I smiled. "How can I help you?"

"Come on, give me a break," he said, pressing his face with his two palms. "What I don't understand about immigrants is, you like to change your names. Why? I know your name is Mohammed. Right?"

"No, this is my name." I pointed at the name tag again.

"You are Mohammed," he screamed.

"Okay, let me become Mohammed for a second, what is your point?"

"Don't change your name. This is Canada. We don't really care whether you are Mohammed, or Abdul, or whatever. We don't," he said, pulling out his wallet from his jacket.

"That's good to know, but still my name is —" Before I could finish the sentence, he interrupted me.

"We went over this, you are Mohammed."

"Leave him alone, prick," one of his friends said. "Just get the cigarettes and let's go."

Working at a busy convenience store felt like I was in a crash course on Canadian culture. I learned how they communicate formally or informally using slang; how they dress to go to work or to a place of entertainment, on a cold day and a warm day; the patience and the impatience of the people in the lineup; I learned about the dominant topics of the day-to-day chat with strangers — weather, sports, and entertainment; the popular items adults or children buy on weekdays or weekends; the good or bad perceptions they have about immigrants. It was overwhelming. Every day was a new day and I had to prepare myself for a surprise. I had one customer who used to visit the store every day to buy cigarettes, and she was in her thirties, and talked about her personal life as if she had known me for ages. She made common use of obscene words that didn't have an equivalent in my language. She didn't seem to mind them at all, for her they seemed to be words like *candy* or *milk*.

One afternoon, she showed up in the store as usual. It was a regular day, and I and my colleague were behind the counter. She approached the counter with a smile.

"How did your date go last night?" my co-worker asked.

"Oh, it was great," she said, getting closer to the register, staring at both of us.

"Good for you," I said, turning around to grab the cigarettes she bought every day. "Du Maurier, right?"

"So, you got laid," my colleague said, eager to know more.

"He was amazing. Every part of my body vibrated. I had an orrrgasm," she said with a smile, emphasizing this last word by stretching it slightly. "That feeling had disappeared from my life for a long time." They high-fived each other and kept talking with great excitement. I guessed that this woman had finally found the love she had been looking for. I wrote the word *orgasm* on my hand so that I could look up the meaning later. After she left, I pulled out my pocket dictionary and checked its translation. I couldn't believe that she had simply thrown this word out of her mouth in front of me as if she were referring to any item in the store. Where is this society's filter? I was judgmental, and I did try to evaluate everything in reference to my culture. This made things difficult for me.

My interactions with customers were quick and come-and-go, but the one I had with a colleague used to bother me.

She was in her late twenties and a fine-looking woman with a great sense of humour. Whenever we had a shift together, she liked to talk about her personal life — including the good and the bad times she was going through with her boyfriend. I often felt uncomfortable to listen to that, but I hid my feelings by smiling politely or nodding with surprise. What was most difficult was when she directed a question at me, and I didn't know how to answer.

"When was the last time you got laid?"

"I think I have to restock the shelf." I left the counter quickly. It felt better to do the hard work than to explain my personal life. I could see clearly that our cultures were clashing here. In Eritrea, people are more reserved and they talk about their personal life only with a very close friend or with family members. When you are at home from work or at work, you don't go into detail about how your night or your day unfolded unless there was a major incident — like an engagement, wedding, graduation, party, car collision, sickness, bomb, fight, police interrogation, or arrest. Since that was my reference, I initially felt weird when customers or colleagues started to describe how they cooked their dinner, how they played with their cat, the conversation they had with their mom, the clothes they bought, or the way they slept.

One morning, as I finished my shift at seven and left the store, I saw an Eritrean man that I vaguely knew standing beside his car. His name was Alazar. He was on the phone, but he rushed toward me as he spoke.

"Good morning, Aaron," he said. "Do you have a minute? Kidane wants to talk to you." He handed me his cellphone.

"Who is Kidane?" I asked before I talked to the man on the phone. Alazar didn't answer my question but twisted his head as if he was not sure.

"Hello, this is Aaron. Who is this?"

"Is that you, Aaron Berhane?"

"Yes."

"Aaron Berhane, the editor-in-chief of *Setit*?"

"Yes, who is this?"

"Aaron Berhane works as a cashier now, right?" He laughed loudly. "This is Kidane from California. You don't know me, but I know you very well. How does it feel like to work as a cashier now?"

"Do you intend to apply?"

"Yes." He laughed again.

"It's great. Go for it," I said, trying to laugh with him.

He laughed loudly.

"You used to work in an office with two secretaries, tea was served to you, you had respect, you were a king. That was great, but now ... Look at you now. A cashier, getting paid by the hour." He kept laughing sarcastically.

Ever since the interview with Asmarino, every now and then I got calls from unknown people at home who mocked me for my new work and tried to intimidate me. They wanted me to keep quiet. I used to ignore these calls and hang up quickly. But this guy really got on my nerves, and I sensed he was a messenger from the People's Front for Democracy and Justice (PFDJ), the ruling party. Whether because I was eager to go home at the end of this long night shift or because I was tired, I don't know, but I was pissed off. I could feel the heat in my chest boiling inside me and I tried hard to contain it.

"You are a moron," I said. "But thank you for the reminder. I have to go now."

"Wait, I have a message for you," he said in a serious tone. "A reminder, actually. The arm of our government is long, we can reach you wherever you are. So, stop attacking us, and mind your own life if you want to see your family again." He hung up before I could reply to his stupid threat.

I turned around to the man who had arranged the call.

"Tell your boss I will show you how short your arm is," I said angrily, slamming his cellphone into the palm of his open hand. Alazar didn't say a word. He quickly jumped in his car and started the engine. I stood there watching him leave and tried to memorize his plate number. I knew that PFDJ had members everywhere, doing the more or less dirty work. Without revealing the details, I asked my Eritrean friends to tell me about Alazar.

"He is one of the most loyal PFDJ members," Futsum said when we met at a coffee shop with Haile, Tesfay, and others. "He was the one who said in a meeting, 'We shouldn't attend the wedding or funeral of anyone who criticizes the Eritrean government. We shouldn't invite them to our events.'" That told me everything I needed to know at that time.

In fact, Kidane's phone call had not intimidated me. It inspired me to do more, go big, make lots of noise, even. The PFDJ members wanted to induce fear in the Eritrean community. *I'll show them how weak they are*, I said to myself. The idea of restarting a newspaper began to take shape in my mind. I wanted to tackle the Eritrean regime in a smart way. But to make that happen I needed to move to a city with a bigger Eritrean community — Toronto.

CHAPTER 11

THE PATH TO INTEGRATION: TORONTO

THE FIRST TIME I WENT TO VISIT TORONTO WAS IN MAY 2003. I CAME TO see my cousin Yordanos who had arrived in the city with a visitor visa in April, intending to claim refugee status, and to collect my visa to go to France to attend a Reporters Without Borders (RSF) event in Paris.

Yordanos was a brave young woman in her twenties who, like many Eritreans, had left her country and flown from Saudi Arabia to Canada on her own to find peace. At the beginning, the language barrier, the culture shock, and the legal process to claim refugee status overwhelmed her. She used to call me now and then to have me translate letters she received from the refugee board or Immigration Canada. Not having family members that she could trust near her was a challenge.

Family ties are very strong in Eritrean culture. It's common to treat your cousins like your brothers and sisters and to be there when they need you. Besides, Yordanos is the younger sister of Petros, the man who risked his life to save mine. I owe him and her. Visiting her was the least I could do. I needed to give her comfort, boost her courage, and assure her that I would be there for her whenever she needed me.

I flew from Regina, landing at Toronto Pearson International Airport.

Navigating my way out of that huge airport I walked slowly, reading the signs and observing my surroundings. Finally, I found my way out and looked right and left. The street was congested with cars and taxis. I walked straight to the closest taxi and jumped in.

"Good morning," I said, making myself comfortable in the back seat while handing the driver a piece of paper with Yordanos's address.

"Good morning," the driver said, turning around to look at me, and reducing the volume of the popular Somali song playing on his tape deck. I had heard it somewhere before. "No luggage?"

"No, this is the only luggage I have," I said, tapping my backpack. "I am from Regina. Not a long trip."

He nodded, took the piece of paper, entered the address into his GPS and started driving.

"Can I guess where you are originally from?" he asked.

"Sure, guess," I said, laughing.

"Eritrea."

"That's a good guess. How do you know?"

"Well, your moustache," he said laughing, "your appearance. I have many Eritrean friends here. I can tell from your accent, too."

I laughed out loud.

"Let me guess where you are from, too," I said.

"Okay, go ahead."

"You are Somalian," I said. "I can tell by your accent. What is your name, by the way?"

"Abdi."

"It's nice meeting you, Abdi. My name is Aaron. How long will it take us to get there?"

"According to the GPS, thirty-five minutes," he said, picking up speed as he turned up the volume of the music.

I settled back to take in the surroundings — the high-rise buildings, hotels, condos, houses, the compact cars and trucks. Everything was mesmerizing about Toronto.

When I first decided to visit Toronto, I asked my Regina friend Million to tell me about it, and he described the city as an enormous sea. According to him, it was not a safe place for a newcomer, but I was eager to see it for myself. If you learn to swim in a pool, you can also swim in the sea, I said to myself. Once I got there, it wasn't so much a sea as a fast-flowing river — the immense crowds I saw in the airport, in the subway, on the streets; the busy traffic all day long; the beautiful, crazy, tall buildings that seemed to want to scratch the sky overwhelmed me. I started to doubt whether the set of skills that I had for swimming in pools would serve me as well here — could I swim in this river?

"This is your destination," Abdi said, slowing his car to a full stop.

"Thank you!" I said, dropping eighty dollars in his hand. "Please keep the change."

* * *

The minute I knocked, I heard Yordanos rushing to the door to answer. When she saw me, like a child, she jumped on me. We hugged each other, and she didn't let go. I kept hugging her as her tears flowed from her eyes.

"No need to cry, Yorda," I said, pulling her away from my arm as I saw her roommate, Titi, a tall woman, approaching to greet me. Yordanos's tears were of happiness, relief, and nostalgia, and it took a few minutes for her to gather herself and start telling me news about my aunt, Petros, and the rest of her brothers as Titi set up the things to make us a traditional coffee in the living room. Their one-bedroom apartment was cozy and very neat, and they seemed to have settled in well. Since neither had close relatives in Toronto, they had bonded like sisters from the day they arrived in Canada. They managed to live happily on the little social welfare they received from the government as they studied English. Then both of them had been accepted as convention refugees and they couldn't wait to start working and support themselves and their families.

Two days later I had to go to the French counsulate to collect my visa, for which I had applied a week earlier. My appointment was at 11:30 a.m. and with the supporting letter I had from RSF, they would probably approve my visa application quickly.

Yordanos called a taxi for me.

"Good morning," I said, already trying to guess if the driver was Eritrean or Ethiopian.

"*Kemey hadirka*," (Good morning), he said in Tigrigna.

"Oh, you are Eritrean. How are you? My name is Aaron and what is your name?" I spoke in Tigrigna.

"Fessehaye."

"It's nice meeting you. I need to go to French consulate, the address is —" as I tried to find it in my notebook, he cut me off.

"Don't worry, I know it," he said, driving slowly.

"You don't want to use a GPS, just in case?"

"No, I have been in this business for over ten years now. I know the address."

"How long have you been in Canada?"

"Well, over ten years. And you?"

"Seven months."

"Ah, you are new. How is back home?"

214

"Terrible!"

He chuckled. His grey hair was sparse. He was in his early fifties, I guessed. I just let everything fly. I immediately told him how the president had destroyed our economy bit by bit, had crushed our dreams; betrayed his people, failed to deliver on his government's promises, and arrested countless innocent people. Without reservation, without finding out whether my driver himself was for or against the government, I lashed out.

"Wow! I couldn't agree more," he finally said, loudly. He explained how the Eritrean regime was messing with the Eritrean community in Toronto, and beyond. He offered a very convincing analysis of the situation and how it could be resolved.

He stopped the car near an enormous building close to Yonge and Bloor.

"Here you are," he said. "The consulate office is inside this building."

"Thank you, Fessehaye. How much do I owe you?" I said, pulling out my wallet to pay and trying to read the meter, but he hadn't even turned it on.

"That's okay. This is on me. Consider it a solidarity courtesy," he chuckled.

I thanked him and jumped out of the car.

As I came to know him later, Fessehaye was a former member of the Eritrean Liberation Front (ELF). He had joined the armed struggle in the 1970s as a young man because he couldn't stand the abuse and mistreatment of his people by the Ethiopian regime. What was happening in Eritrea had disturbed him, as it had so many others who shed their blood and sweat to defend democracy, and as it did all those who were still angry — like me.

* * *

Ten minutes later I was out of the French consulate, my travel document stamped with a French visa. I was exhilarated. I could feel the joy in my vigorously pumping heart, I felt the rapid movements of my lungs — my chest rose up and down, up and down. All together, moving in harmony, every nerve of my body wanted to dance. I stood tall, smiled, and strode confidently. I was overjoyed.

I walked along Bloor Street thinking about the state I had been in just two weeks earlier, when Amha Domenico, an Eritrean activist whom I had been in touch with since I fled to Sudan, called to tell me that RSF wanted to invite me to an event they had organized in Paris, France, for World Press Freedom Day. I had told him it would be impossible. I didn't have a passport or travel document, and I would need a visa for France. Getting those processed would take at least a month.

"It will be great if you can make it, though I understand the challenges," Amha said. "Jeff may contact you soon."

Jeff, the head of the African desk at RSF, had already emailed me a detailed description of the event and how RSF could reimburse my expenses. Immediately, that day, I had applied for a travel document with the help of my host family, Chris. I emphasized the urgency, printed out the invitation that I had received from RSF, put it together with all the necessary documents to support my application, sealed it in an envelope, and mailed it to Ottawa via Fedex on April 28, then went back to my regular life. Knowing whatever might happen to it next was beyond my control, I never thought about it after, apart from scratching notes here and there about what I would say if I did attend the event. To my absolute surprise, six days later I received the travel document. I was over the roof! Things I thought impossible, were possible. The next step was to apply for an entry visa to France, and according to the official information, processing that could also take a month, since I would have to mail my application to the French consulate in Toronto. That was a side effect of living in a small city like Regina. You had to mail everything to somewhere else, instead of dropping it off at an office in person. Not knowing whether I would get the entrance visa before May 16, I didn't want to buy a plane ticket. Jeff, however, convinced me I should buy the ticket even before I got my visa, and I did.

On May 15, I got an email from the French consulate with details of their street address in Toronto, inviting me to an interview — on May 16!

When I finally left the interview room with my visa, I felt so grateful to RSF and their work to make this happen. I couldn't help smiling with pride while I joined the busy street.

The diversity of people was remarkable — Chinese, Indians, Africans, Europeans, and Latinos. At Bloor and St. George, I saw crowds entering and exiting the subway. After a few minutes of observation, I realized I was right next to the University of Toronto. I thought about touring the University, but once I checked the time, I knew I didn't have enough left. It was already 1 p.m., and my flight to France was at seven. So, I had to go back to my cousin's and get ready for the trip. The time flew by. I had to leave my cousin's place at four when my taxi arrived.

By the appearance of my taxi driver, I guessed he could be Indian. I greeted him warmly and he did the same.

"Airport please, Terminal 1," I said.

"Okay … going on vacation?" he said.

"Not really."

He turned from Rogers Road onto Dufferin, and drove north.

"We will take Highway 401, that will be faster," he said.

"Sure, but remember my flight is at seven."

"Oh, you have plenty of time. It is only about twenty kilometres from here. Once we get on the highway, the traffic will move faster."

What surprised me about Toronto was, wherever you went, there was the traffic. Every street was full of many cars lined up one after the other. That drive to the airport was no different. From my cousin's place at Rogers and Dufferin to Pearson airport was supposed to take about twenty-five minutes, but we covered only three kilometres in twenty minutes. Finally, the taxi joined Highway 401 and moved faster.

"Now it is going to be better," the driver said with relief. The traffic was moving well. My taxi driver also picked his speed up to eighty kilometres per hour and started chatting.

"Are you Ethiopian?" he asked.

"No, I am Eritrean. What about you?"

"I am Pakistani," he said. He decelerated as the cars ahead of us suddenly slowed down.

"What is going on?" I asked with a worried voice when I saw cars ahead closing up and moving like snails.

"It could be an accident. Hopefully, they will clear it soon." The driver tried to divert my attention by bringing up different topics, but after a few minutes I stopped listening. My mind was completely occupied with coming up with alternative ways of getting to the airport quickly, none of which would work. Unless I could call a helicopter and have myself flown to the airport, getting there quickly was a wishful dream. The reality was something else, I was stuck with my taxi driver on Highway 401. In about one hour we might have covered a kilometre and a half.

"It's almost six, do you think I will catch my flight?"

"Yes, we are almost at the exit to Highway 409. That will get us away from this traffic jam on the 401."

I felt good hearing his confident statement, though I didn't stop worrying until we exited to Highway 409. He picked up his speed a bit in the long line of cars driving steadily along Highway 409. I checked my time, and it was 6:10 p.m. I sighed heavily with frustration, but said nothing, knowing he could do nothing apart from going with the speed of the cars ahead of us.

"Don't worry, from here it literally takes seven minutes," he said, driving very close to the car in front of us. I said nothing, but I felt a little bit of relief when I saw that the cars were picking up momentum. I checked my pockets for my passport, my flight ticket — everything was in order. My heart pumped quickly, I was breathing heavily, and I didn't want to say a word but focused on the traffic, as if that would help. After all, I was just a passenger who could basically do nothing else than sit and wait in the back seat. Moments later, I heard a bump, then my head hit the front seat, and I felt dizzy.

"What the fuckkkk," the taxi driver yelled.

A delivery truck had hit our car in the rear, and our car had hit the car in front of us. I couldn't believe it. It felt like I was in a bad dream.

"What is happening?" I said, covering my face with my hands.

"That idiot hit me in the back," the driver said. "Are you okay?"

I was okay, but I saw the driver's nose was bleeding. Apparently, he didn't care. He got out of his car and yelled at the driver of the truck while diagnosing the damage to his taxi. I also got out to help him check on that. The rear of the car was dented and the lights were broken.

"You smashed my car. You smashed my car," he yelled, standing in front of the truck.

"You also smashed my car," the woman driver said, pointing at the taxi driver. "Why don't you keep your distance?"

The woman driver of the small car yelled at the taxi driver, the taxi driver yelled at the truck driver, and the truck driver kept quiet and didn't even leave his seat. I stood there thinking how I could get to my destination. No one was hurt seriously. The damage to the cars was minor, a dent here, broken lights there. It wouldn't affect their ability to drive.

"What now?" I asked in frustration.

"We have to wait for the police," the woman driver said, angrily. I got closer to the taxi driver and asked him how long it would take for the police to arrive and resolve the issue.

"I don't know, my friend, twenty or thirty minutes," he said. "My insurance is going to increase, oh God!"

"How am I going to get to the airport now?"

"They will increase my insurance, oh God!"

I grabbed my bag from the taxi and started asking people in the cars driving slowly by the accident if they would give me a ride to the airport. Most of them declined because, they said, they were not heading to the airport. Finally, an elderly couple on their way to pick someone up at the airport offered me a ride. By the time I arrived at Terminal 1, it was 6:55 p.m. I was too late. The plane would depart without me. I told my problems to the airport passenger service assistant and asked her for a miracle. There was no later flight I could catch, she told me, checking her computer and all the flight connections. The whole plan that had been constructed so meticulously to get me on that plane collapsed in that instant in front of my eyes. I was devastated. It was rage that I felt, a burning turmoil inside me.

"This is very disappointing! Humiliating," I said. The assistant looked at me closely. She could clearly see that I was close to collapsing in front of her under the amount of anger I felt.

"Look, you are lucky you are alive, you could have died in that car accident," she finally said. "You'll miss your plane now, but you can go tomorrow."

There was no tomorrow. The RSF event would take place without me.

I nodded and disappeared from her sight.

* * *

After I moved to Toronto for good in June 2003, the transition was really rough. The rent was expensive, and jobs were scarce. I stayed with my cousin for a month in the one-bedroom apartment she shared with her roommate. Realizing I wouldn't find a bachelor room easily, I tried to find a roommate by visiting the Bloor-Ossington and Danforth-Greenwood areas where most Eritrean and Ethiopian businesses were, and the Eritrean community centre. At the centre, I learned about the Toronto community's long journey and how they ended up in Canada.

For decades, Eritreans have been dispersed from their home country. Colonial aggression from 1890 to 1961 and the struggle against Ethiopia from 1961 to 1991 contributed to the emigration of more than half a million of its tiny population, then 3.5 million. They resettled in different parts of the world as refugees or through sponsorship, and have become part of the social, political, and economic fabrics of the local societies. They have taken advantage of the political stability of these countries to educate their children, run businesses, and pursue their education.

Resettlement in Canada started in the early 1980s and continued to grow even after Eritrea became independent. Compared to other immigrants, the Eritreans' settlement experience was unique because their challenges didn't come only from the host society but also from the government of their home country.

The Eritrean regime has reached out its long arm to seize donations, to collect illegal taxes, to force Eritrean immigrants to attend fundraising meetings, and to try to silence them whenever they voice criticism against the government. The state's involvement in all facets of their lives aggravates friction, both in the diaspora and with people in the home country.

The Eritrean dictator controlled the population through surveillance. There were four pillars at play, checking one another — the Eritrean National Security office, the PFDJ political apparatus, the military intelligence units, and the administration units in different sectors of the government. Each of them worked separately, recruiting its own spies and informants, and following its own leads. They all reported to the president directly, bypassing the minister of interior affairs. That tight, multilayer surveillance kept the population from trusting one another. The system of spying on your neighbour, your classmate, your colleague, and your fellow soldier was implanted everywhere, including in the diaspora community.

One of the major tasks, in fact the most important task of the Consulate General of the State of Eritrea in Toronto and other cities, was to control the diaspora community through surveillance. There were, roughly speaking, three "surveillance units" abroad: The counsellor who reported to the minister of foreign affairs, the political attaché who reported to the chair of the PFDJ, and the cultural attaché who reported to certain individuals who worked directly for the president.

The political attaché managed the PFDJ chapters in Toronto and other cities. This person worked hard to recruit informants to spy on their friends and family members and to be parts of a network for disseminating disinformation and propaganda. They also raised funds for the regime, in the name of the nation's "martyrs' children," national development, or defence. The responsibility of the cultural attaché was systematically to obtain funds from the Canadian government, and also to recruit people to be spies. To do their work undetected, the spies used community centres, which they had fully under their control. Many of those spies were unpaid, but were forced to co-operate because they had no other choice, unless they wanted to risk their family members back in Eritrea, who were still in the jaws of the crocodile.

The cultural attaché in Toronto had something called the Eritrea Cultural Centre. That centre existed only on paper, but served as cover for the person who was in charge of recruiting spies in the community — Estifanos Neguse. He had arrived in Canada as a refugee in the eighties and drove taxis before he got a job at the Eritrean consulate office in the 1990s. After that he immersed himself in the business of the Eritrean regime and served as a good soldier. He had agents in the Toronto community's administration and churches, running restaurants, or driving taxis. Through those secret agents, he gathered information on anyone who opposed the Eritrean regime: "Where does that person live?" "Who are their family members, their friends, and colleagues?" "Where do they work?" "What does their daily or weekly schedule look like?" "What kinds of activities do they do outside of work?"

If they saw that the diaspora created a civil association or community centre or religious institution, they rushed to control its agenda and seized whatever money it raised by infiltrating the group. If they failed to do that, they would systematically try to intimidate the leading members of the organization.

One of their first victims was the Eritrean Canadian Community Centre of Metropolitan Toronto (ECCC). It was founded in 1983 by the early arrivers and served the community as a centre of encouragement, guidance, and unity, along with the crucial services it provided to newcomers. It tried to steer clear of politics. Because of its charitable status, it was eligible for federal, provincial, and municipal funds.

The Eritrean consulate office in Toronto wanted to control the centre. It mobilized the PFDJ members and made several attempts to crack down on it. After the regime's undercover agents failed to control the ECCC in 2000, they tried to destroy it by labelling it a hub of opposition. Most elected board members of the ECCC who refused to collaborate with the Eritrean consulate office were subjected to character assassination and isolation.

Once the undercover agents realized they still wouldn't succeed, they founded the Eritrean Canadian Association of Ontario (ECAO) with the help of their supporters. Ever since, the consulate office has used the ECAO to organize events, rent public venues, and recruit individuals for the PFDJ to serve as infiltrators. The consulate office invariably takes advantage of refugees, who often arrive alone with their families waiting back home. It's not unusual for refugees to be forced to donate money to causes they don't believe in, or have 2 percent of their income taken for the development of their home country. If they refuse to collaborate, the regime intimidates them by sending one of its gang members.

Many Eritrean Canadians lived under constant fear of the regime they left behind. Their Achilles' heel was their loved ones back home. That's why most of them didn't want to report the extortion they experienced to law enforcement agents: They were simply too worried about the danger it would inflict on their families. So, the Eritrean consulate office governed the Eritrean Canadians by violating every Canadian law, knowing no one would dare to oppose them. And the refugees who came to find a safe haven found themselves still living under the long arm of the regime that they had fled from. The Eritrean dictator used transnational institutions to enable its supporters and terrorize its opposition.

The sum of such challenges has exacerbated the settlement struggle of Eritrean Canadians for decades. There are about thirty thousand Eritreans living in Canada, most of them in Ontario. While the ECAO was an unacknowledged centre of the Eritrean government supporters, the ECCC was safe — it was only there that many newcomers would get actual settlement services like help with searching for an apartment or a job.

* * *

The first day I visited the ECCC, I met newcomers who had come through the U.S.A. to settle in Canada. One of them was Tesfit, whom I knew from the University of Asmara. It was always refreshing to meet someone I had something in common with. He had travelled through Mexico and the U.S.A. to reach Canada with his girlfriend, Dehab. Like most refugee claimants, his situation was precarious. The three of us — Tesfit, Dehab, and I — took a subway from Pape station, in the eastern end of the city, to downtown Toronto. Unlike in the morning crush, riding a subway around noon was fun. We easily found seats together and chatted and laughed, reminding ourselves how lucky we were to escape the grip of the Eritrean regime. We were loud — and that reminded me of my first experience in the subway.

It was around 8:30 a.m. at Dufferin subway station. Hundreds of people were waiting on both sides of the track when the train arrived. I boarded with everyone else, rubbing shoulders with the commuters. There were no seats left, I had to stand with many others holding the upper bar. Everybody was quiet. The train moved to the next station, then to the next station heading east. I hardly ever heard anyone engage in conversation. Why is no one talking? Compared to the commute I used to sometimes have in a bus in Eritrea, which sounded like a bar, this was basically like a funeral. During the commutes in Eritrea, people would laugh, argue, and engage in casual conversations. You could even strike up a conversation with anyone standing beside you, about anything under the planet. For my first two or three rides in Canada I just assumed it was not allowed or socially awkward to chat in a train until I consulted an employee of the Toronto Transit Commission (TTC).

"That's a good joke, brother," he laughed. "It's a free country. No one would force you not to talk here."

I therefore didn't get worried when I realized we were chatting quite loudly.

Getting off at Dundas Square, we toured along Yonge Street, through the big mall called the Eaton Centre, Queen Street, and King Street. After a one-hour fun walk, we had lunch at one of the fanciest restaurants we could find on King. We guessed it would be expensive, but we went in for the sake of a new experience. It was around two, and most seats were occupied. The receptionist led us to a table and went back to the door. We made ourselves comfortable in the chairs and kept chatting until the waiter would come to take our order. The waiter seemed fully occupied serving one table after the other and didn't seem to notice us. After waiting for about four minutes with menus in our hands, I clapped my hands to finally get his attention. Everyone in the restaurant suddenly turned their head to stare at me in shock. It took me a moment to realize that, and I looked around. I noticed we were the only Black customers. *Is that the reason they are staring at us?* I thought.

"Why are they staring at us?" Tesfit asked.

"I don't know."

Tesfit ignored the situation and quickly got back to the topic we were discussing. I saw the server coming toward our table with a broad smile.

"Good afternoon, sorry for the wait. What can I get you?" he asked politely, and then left quickly to get us the drinks we ordered. A look into the menu had revealed that the beers and meals weren't as expensive as we thought they would be. The server came back with three Corona beers and placed them on the table.

"Thank you, sir," I said. "How long would it take to prepare a meal?"

"Just a few minutes. By the way, where are you from?" he asked.

"Eritrea. It is a small country in northeast Africa."

"Ah, I see, you are new?"

"Yes, we are."

He quickly glanced at the other tables.

"You know, clapping your hand to call a waiter might be okay in Eritrea, but here it is considered rude. I recommend you don't do it," he said politely.

"I am sorry, I didn't —"

He cut me off. "I know, you didn't mean it. I am a Torontonian. I understand — I'm just recommending you not do it again when you go to any other restaurant." He was calm and seemed very sincere in his effort to accustom us to Canadian culture. He was not offended at all.

"Wow, I feel stupid now," I said. "Thank you very much for letting me know. So how do you call the waiter here if he looks in the other direction?"

"You just raise your hand. It is our job to pay attention to every table," he said with a smile as he left.

I would definitely have repeated that mistake again and again if it were not for that server. I admired how he had handled my unintentional rudeness, how he tried to understand me rather than getting offended by my behaviour. Clapping your hand or snapping your fingers to get the attention of a waiter was very common in Eritrea. No one would consider that rude, but in Canada, things were obviously different.

With the help of an ECCC employee, after searching for almost fifteen days I found a two-bedroom apartment in the neighbourhood of Bloor and Parliament that I intended to share with another newcomer Eritrean.

Then I focused on finding a job.

That was a hassle. I applied to jobs that I found in newspapers' classified ads. I visited employment agencies, which usually had something to offer, usually jobs that were physically demanding and paid very little. I had to accept such jobs, any jobs, to pay my rent. I worked as a cashier, a cleaner, a security guard, you name it. Sometimes, I did two or three odd jobs a day to survive. By the time I came home, I would have no energy left to think about how I could get myself out of the dilemma I was in: these jobs would get me nowhere. The minute I hit the pillow, I was gone. I would sleep like a dead person until my alarm went off the next day. Day by day, I would go through the same cycle.

Nevertheless, I never stopped looking for a better job.

One day I went for a job interview at ADT, a company that provides electronic security services to individuals and businesses. There were five people standing outside the building, and I stretched my hand to greet them before asking them if they were here for the interview like me. They hid their hands as if they were trying to protect themselves from something. I didn't get why, and I was really confused. I left the premises without doing the interview.

Puzzled by the weird experience, I asked some Eritreans. They told me Canadians shake hands only if they know you. I hadn't come across that in Regina. I used to shake hands with anyone. I wished social norms were written down, so that you could look them up like traffic rules — red for things you should never do;

yellow for things you should handle with caution to avoid embarrassment; and green for anything else. With something like this in hand, I could apply those invisible rules properly, offending no one.

It was mind-bogglingly difficult to know how I could carry myself or interact. My confidence eroded bit by bit like the bank of a river. I used to joke and strike conversations with strangers, but since I came to Canada, I sensed a loss of my personality and confidence. The sound judgment I had about so many things dissipated. I became reserved and cautious. I didn't think my childhood friends would recognize the new me.

To be in exile is a dramatic, life-altering experience. It often forces you to carry two personalities. Bridging the gap between these two identities, between the two cultures, is a perpetual struggle, and tough to handle. Particularly if you were a journalist or writer in your home country, you feel the pain of a professional crisis. That's what I felt when I thought about the audience I had back home, and the language I had mastered. All of that had no value in my new home. I didn't want to lose my identity as a journalist, but I didn't know how to get it back while I shuffled from one odd job to the other.

What gave me a break was the Hellman-Hammett grant I was awarded by Human Rights Watch in July 2003. That grant came just when I badly needed it. How thoughtful of Lillian Hellman, the American playwright, and novelist Dashiell Hammett to donate their money to Human Rights Watch in order to help writers in financial need, in recognition of all the recipients who suffered simply because they had expressed their views. I imagine thousands of writers and journalists have benefitted from the Hellman-Hammett grant since its inception in 1989. Without a doubt, I believe they all felt the same as I felt. I couldn't stop expressing my gratitude to Hellman and Hammett whenever I hit the bank to withdraw from the five thousand dollar grant deposited in my account. They gave me time to breathe, to explore the city, time to regularly visit the offices of Canadian Journalists for Free Expression (CJFE) and of PEN Canada, which advocates for writers. I was able to connect with other exiled journalists like me.

I remember the first time I visited the CJFE office. I met Julie Payne, a program manager and an engine of the journalists in exile group, a compassionate woman who was passionate to help exiled journalists with whatever she could. Her warm welcome and undivided attention to what I had to share and what I had to say encouraged me to express my challenges with no reservation. She told me about the activities of CJFE, what it could do and what it couldn't do, about the journalists in the exile group and how often they met and the importance of being part of that. She was quite straightforward and didn't try to act as if all one's problems would be solved overnight.

"What I badly need is time to think about what to study," I said. "That's really difficult to do if I have to work long hours in a precarious job. And I don't want to enrol in any program that I might not enjoy or use to get a job afterwards." Julie thought for a moment, then grabbed a piece of paper and scribbled the name and phone number of Anna Luengo.

"Try to speak with Anna," she said, handing me the paper. "She is an administrator of Massey College. She might be able to help." She added that the Donner/CJFE Journalist-at-Risk Fellowship was administered by Massey College, but was granted only to journalists who live outside of Canada. According to this information I would be out of luck for that one, so I could have shut that door for good. But I didn't.

In Eritrea, we have a proverb that says, "Put your hand in the sea; either you will catch a fish or wash your hand." I always took that to heart and never hesitated to follow a lead when I got one, even if I was told my chances were bleak. I remember the one-hour trip I made north of Steeles Avenue to apply for a warehouse job despite their having told me they closed the hiring process. When I showed up at their door, they gave me the job. I hoped it would work that way again.

Immediately, I called Anna from a public phone and she gave me an appointment to meet her on August 28, 2003, at 9 a.m. I was delighted. To get to the appointment, I had to ditch my warehouse work. I could always find jobs like that, but not meetings like this. I didn't care that much when my warehouse boss told me that I would be fired if I didn't show up to work.

I arrived at Massey College a half-hour before my appointment. It is an interdisciplinary graduate residential college at the University of Toronto, which opened in 1963 near busy Bloor Street on the university's downtown campus. The architecture is elegant: it is a modernist building by Ron Thom, with vertical slots on the brick that look Gothic. On the top of the entrance gate, there is a logo of the college carved in limestone. I entered the gate and approached the man who seemed to be in charge of security. I told him the reason for my visit and he confirmed it with Anna, then guided me toward her office, past the fountain in a grassy quadrangle — very refreshing to look at. He pushed open a huge wooden door to enter a corridor, and we walked a bit.

The minute I saw Anna, I could feel her big heart, the compassion she has for people in need. I felt an ease. She welcomed me warmly and led me into her office, which had an artistic window and high ceiling.

"Thank you for taking the time to see me," I said, sitting on the chair. I knew she had another meeting to attend at nine thirty, as she had told me that when we booked the appointment, so I started telling her my story without further delay. I told her how the boat of my life was sinking. How the transition had shaken my confidence that I could overcome my challenges by myself. How I worried about my family, who were being refused an exit visa and still lived in Asmara under the scrutiny of the Eritrean regime.

She listened attentively and compassionately, taking notes of what I had to say, and I felt relieved of my burden, even though I got an answer I didn't want to hear. She told me that the Journalist-at-Risk Fellowship was awarded only to journalists living in exile outside of Canada who were suffering sectarian or ideological violence and intolerance from their own government. Since I was already in Canada, I wasn't eligible. Moreover, that year's grant had already been awarded, to an Iraqi journalist who lived in Tunisia.

"I am sorry," she said earnestly, as if it were her fault. But I had known that my chances were bleak. I thanked her for her time and advice, left my contact information with her, and exited the building.

The funny thing was, though, I felt good for having expanded my network, for trying and knocking on doors I hadn't knocked on before. I could sense I was heading in the right direction if I kept pursuing the advice I was getting. I briefed Julie on how my meeting with Anna went, and went back to chasing down another precarious job.

Weeks passed with no good news. I called my wife and asked her if she had any good stuff to share. She had landed an appointment to get an exit visa if she showed up with a supporting letter from her boss, the minister of education, but that hadn't worked out.

"The minister refused to give me either a release or support letter," she said. "I will try him again."

"That's okay, Mielat, don't worry and don't waste your time. They will not give it to you. As long as I am on their blacklist, it will not happen. We have to find another way. I will mail you the details. Okay, let me chat with my kids now before my calling card is finished," I said, preparing myself to change the tone of my voice.

"Hello, sweetie!"

"Hello, Baba," Frieta said, cheerfully. "How is your study going on?" My kids didn't know the truth about why I left the country. My wife told them that I went to Canada to study. So, my daughter's questions always started like that, and she kept reporting how much she got in the tests or classwork for her various subjects.

"W ... o ... w! I am so proud of you, sweetie!" I said, enthusiastically. "So, are you going to be the number one in your class?"

"Not only in my class, in all grade five classes," she said, confidently. For her, nothing seemed impossible — because she had been number one in grade four, she believed she would succeed again if only she applied the same principles. I liked her confidence and determination. Hearing her articulating her plans and what she was doing to achieve her goals inspired me.

"I don't doubt that, sweetie. I am proud of you, and I love you. Let me please speak with Mussie now."

My son, Mussie, was only four years old, and he liked to sing for me whatever new song he had learned in kindergarten. Listening to how he pronounced the lyrics of the song was always fun, sometimes he added his own words when he forgot the official lyrics, just singing on without interruption. He always made me laugh, even after the call was over.

"Sing *Ertra*, *Ertra*, Mussie!" my wife said. "He learned the Eritrean anthem and he will sing it for you," she added, while encouraging him to start. Mussie began immediately.

"ኤርትራ ኤርትራ፡ (*Ertra, Ertra*, Eritrea, Eritrea)

"ስልጣነ ከነልብሳ ግርማ፡ (*Siltane kenelbisa girma*, We shall honour her with progress),

"ሕድሪ'ለና ክሻ ክንስልማ፡፡ (*Hidri alena kisha kinsilema*, It is our legacy to decorate her with a sack)."

I couldn't stop laughing. The word *kisha* (a sack), doesn't appear in the original lyrics, but he inserted it when he couldn't remember the right word — *gimja* (a crown). However, his word described exactly what the government had been doing for years. Instead of rebuilding the country's economy, empowering its people, earning the country's pride, the president had been doing the opposite — as if his regime had promised itself to shame its people by, instead of crowning itself, dressing in a sack.

"Good job, Mussie!" I said. As I spoke with him, I heard in the background Frieta telling him to ask me if I would come to his birthday party. He did. I felt my heart sinking. I didn't know how to answer that, except by providing a vague answer like a politician would — until he got challenged by a tough journalist, of course.

"I will send you whatever toy you want. Let your mom know. I love you! Let me speak with your mom now, please." Before he passed the phone to his mom, Frieta seized the phone and cornered me with a direct question.

"Baba, so are you going to come?" she paused and waited for me to answer.

I couldn't deceive her, I had to tell the partial truth, painfully.

"I wish, sweetie. But I have exams, and if I don't stay here to study, I will not get the prize like you did. I know you want me to get that prize, right?"

"Yes!"

"I know you do. I love you, sweetie! Now, do me a favour. Make your brother, Evan, laugh, I would like to hear him gurgling."

Chatting with my wife and kids was always the highlight of my week. It refreshed me and reminded me I had a reason to live, a mission to accomplish. On that day, though, after I hung up the phone, I felt down. Anger and sadness overwhelmed me, as I would miss a birthday again because of things I didn't have control of. I missed my wife, my children, my old life. Living in a foreign country alone, working precarious jobs, and not knowing how to overcome my challenges consumed me. I was not in the mood to chat with my roommate or hang out with friends, I just parked myself in my room at three in the afternoon, lying on my bed, staring at the ceiling. My phone rang twice, I let the machine pick it up and listened to Tesfit's message.

"Where are you, buddy? It is three thirty now. You've stood us up for almost an hour, now we are heading to the Rendezvous Restaurant. Please join us there. Bye."

That was unlike me. Missing appointments without notice, even for a social gathering like that, was not part of my DNA, but I did it. I didn't feel guilty for not showing up or for not expressing my regrets. Just like another pillow, I remained in my bed the entire afternoon, the evening, and into the night. It depressed me. My dream was shrinking, my vision was blurring, and my energy hit rock bottom. For two days I didn't leave my room except to use the washroom. I don't know how long it would have lasted if it were not for the call I received on October 2, 2003. I used to leave my answering machine on to pick up any calls I might receive, though I never bothered to call back. But for some reason, the call I received on October 2, at 8:30 a.m., I answered.

"Hello," I said. My voice seemed to come from underwater.

"Good morning, Aaron, it's me, Anna Luengo," she said. She had a very distinctive accent and the timbre of her voice could inspire you to listen to it like music forever. Like a child hearing his mother's voice after hours of separation, I jumped from my bed and sat on my pillow.

"Good morning, Anna."

"Are you awake?" she asked.

"Yes, I am," I said, adjusting myself on the pillow.

"I want to make sure you are awake, because this will sound like a dream," she said.

I laughed and assured her I was, and she broke the glorious news for me instantly: the Iraqi journalist who had been granted the fellowship could not get a visa to come to Canada, so he wouldn't be enrolling at the college. Since the college had already received the CJFE/Donner Foundation grant money, she wanted me to take his place. She said that the committee had awarded it to me.

It really did sound like a dream. A sweet dream that I didn't want to wake up from.

I would be eligible to enrol in any graduate or undergraduate course at the University of Toronto and could use all their facilities for a full academic year. They would pay me a stipend every month; the college would provide accommodation and meals; and the college would cover my travel expenses for three organized trips, local or international.

I literally floated in my imagination, sitting on my bed, thinking how this would change my life, as the news settled into every cell of my body. Before the words came out of my mouth to express my gratitude, tears were rolling down my face. Tears of happiness and relief. The boat of my life had been on the verge of sinking, but had I found an anchor.

Ever since leaving Regina, I had felt insecure. I even questioned the decisions I had made — abandoning the government assistance, moving to a bigger city, and leaving behind the wonderful friendships I cultivated with Chris Mansbridge, Million, and many others. That had left a vacuum in my life when I arrived in Toronto. I felt the insecurity instantly because I had no one that I could trust and turn to for help in navigating the system. However, now, when I realized how hard Anna and Julie Payne had worked to make this happen, and how happy they were for me, I didn't look for other assurance about my safety net. Knowing I had people who actually, really cared for me and that I could trust while I explored this new pattern of life was a blessing. They became like family.

Anna sent her son Alex, a joyful and muscular youth, to help me move from my apartment to Massey College. She invited me occasionally to her house and introduced me to her husband, Tony, her older son, Steve, and her brother with his wife. Since then they have all treated me like family and Anna has treated me like a son.

At Massey, Anna's compassion and energy were contagious. She greeted people warmly, exchanged meaningful conversation when she ran into anyone in the hallway or lounge. She didn't say "good morning" or "how are you doing" for the sake of it, she actually wanted to know how we were doing, and how we were adjusting, and that went not only for journalism fellows but also for the junior and senior fellows of the college. It was not without reason the fellows flocked to her like bees to a flower if she showed up in the lounge. There was always laughter when she was around. The care she showed to anyone that she met was obvious, and was a practical embodiment of the norms of the college. She was indeed the pillar and the face of the college. I always saw her as a symbol of the outstanding personality of Massey College that every one of us should embody. I saw that reflected in my colleagues.

My cohort of journalism fellows — Sandra Martin, a senior arts writer for the *Globe and Mail*; Teddy Katz, a senior national news reporter for CBC Radio; Margo Harper, an assignment editor at CTV news; Philip Preville, a freelance journalist; and Rozima Ali, a Malaysian journalist — became my good friends. They invited me to their houses during Christmas and special holidays. They were there to comfort and support me. My confidence, which had been eroding like soil on the bank of a rushing river just weeks before, now rested like cement on a rock. Massey College became my backbone.

Massey College changed everything for me, by being an actual source of friendship and knowledge. The journalism fellows were there to answer my questions about the Canadian media and its challenges. Since they were outstanding journalists in their mid-career, they had so much to offer. Especially for me. It was like a window to the Canadian media. I dreamt one day to be part of it.

As journalism fellows, we met regularly in informal seminars to discuss current issues with senior politicians and a wide variety of other professionals. Using such occasions I discussed the Eritrea-Ethiopia conflict with former minister of foreign affairs of Canada Lloyd Norman Axworthy when he was United Nations special envoy for Eritrea and Ethiopia. I also met with Bill Graham, who was the current minister of foreign affairs, to discuss the issue of my wife and children. By then, my family's case was in limbo because the Eritrean government was still refusing to give my wife an exit visa. As a result, the visa Canada issued to my wife had expired in her hand. I wrote Minister Graham in detail about what had gone wrong and how difficult it would be to try it again, and I asked that her file be left open, as things were beyond the control of my wife. He promised to discuss my family's case and get back to me, and he did.

Every interaction I had at Massey College with senior or junior members gave me hope and confidence. When John Fraser, the master of Massey College, introduced me to the Massey community and mentioned how the college would help to reunite me with my family, I felt the comfort instantly. He showed me his readiness to help with whatever he could, whenever the issue arose. "It takes a village to raise a kid," as they say. I was groomed by many, particularly in academic circles. I took courses from people like Abe Rotstein and Ursula Franklin in political science and eonomics, and came to an understanding of how the political, social, and economic system of Canada works.

* * *

The fellowship ended in April 2004, but John Fraser allowed me to stay in my accommodations until August, which gave me more leverage to execute my special project — starting a community newspaper. The Eritrean community needed one.

One of the first problems I had observed in the Eritrean Canadian community was a lack of unity. There were die-hard supporters of the Eritrean government despite their limited knowledge of what was going on back there, and there were others who opposed. As a result, there were two community centres and two churches. Instead of working together to overcome whatever challenges they faced in their new home as a community, they were divided because of their political views. They didn't have a platform to communicate with one another and resolve their misunderstandings in a civilized way. It was not difficult to identify who had instigated the division and was crippling the unity of the community, and creating every obstacle to cohesion. It was the Eritrean consulate.

The only way to bring everyone together and show who was behind their problem was by increasing awareness in the community. To make that happen, I launched my newspaper in September 2004 under the name *Meftih*, which means "key." I wanted *Meftih* to be the solution to many problems the Eritrean community faced in Canada, to serve as a key to open doors of opportunity and to increase awareness of how the Eritrean regime was playing a dangerous game to prolong its power. My strategy was simple — to bring everyone onto the same page so they could see what was at stake in their lives and the lives of their children, they had to know who was behind their problems.

Starting the paper didn't require a huge investment, apart from buying a laptop and some design software. I didn't rent an office; I used Starbucks. Therefore, the $2,500 that I earmarked for printing expenses was enough to get me off the ground.

I started this monthly community newspaper in Toronto in 2004, distributing copies to Eritrean stores, restaurants, and community centres. Immediately, both the paper and the car I drove became targets of vandals. The copies of *Meftih* were dumped in the garbage after I distributed them, at several locations. This happened several times during the first year of publication, no doubt by instigation of the Eritrean consulate. But the store owners were reluctant to tell me who was doing it, for fear of the regime and its undercover agents.

I knew I had to do something about this. One day I found three volunteers who wanted to help. I placed them in three different restaurants near Danforth and Greenwood, and Ossington and Bloor. They identified two taxi drivers who took the bundles of *Meftih* newspapers right after they were dropped, for two consecutive months. I confronted the drivers singly, and let them know that I knew what they were doing. They denied it, but never did it again.

I remember vividly the interaction I had with one of them. One of my volunteers had enticed him to come to the Coffee Time near Bloor and Ossington to meet someone. It was a set-up: that someone was me.

"Good afternoon, Zenebe," I said, standing beside him. He jumped and moved his chair away from me. I sat beside him. He didn't say a word but stared at me as if expecting a punch to land on his face. He was sweating.

"Why did you dump my newspaper — *Meftih*?" I could see him swallowing hard.

"I didn't dump your newspaper," he said with a trembling voice.

"Why are you sweating, then?"

"I didn't dump your newspaper."

"Look, Zenebe, I have all the evidence, even your picture. So, I can forgive you for that, but if I catch you doing that stupid work again, I will sue you. This is not Eritrea, this is a country of law.

You don't want to ènd up in jail for this." I stood up and left without waiting to hear his response.

The Eritrean consulate, through their undercover agents, ordered most Eritrean Canadian businesses not to carry *Meftih* in their stores and forbade them to advertise in the paper. Since many of the business owners feared for the safety of family members still living in Eritrea, they complied. They didn't feel free enough or secure enough to reject demands from the Eritrean consulate in Toronto. As a result, some shopkeepers and restaurateurs refused to accommodate *Meftih* in their premises and didn't want to promote their business via *Meftih* even though they had already paid for six months' worth of advertising in advance.

However, there were some brave business owners who did refuse undercover agents' orders. They were fed up with the regime intimidating Eritreans wherever they lived.

"Are you sure you want to do this?" I asked John, an owner of Fiyori restaurant, when he told me he would stand with *Meftih*.

"Yes! I am fed up with their tactics," John said. "This is the only community newspaper we have here, and they wanted to crush it. I won't allow it."

"Thank you, John, for standing for *Meftih*, but aren't you afraid they will campaign against your business, too?"

"I am done with fear now," John said. "Sure, they will do that. They will even label me as a traitor like they labelled you, but I don't care, I will get other customers. What upsets me is their reasoning. When I told them *Meftih* is community oriented and not political, they told me that Aaron constantly criticizes the Eritrean government in articles he writes for other websites. They sound really stupid."

"Can you tell me who visited you, please?" I was keeping a list of names of people who were doing the consulate's dirty work. John didn't want to give me that information.

241

"Look, that is unnecessary," John said. "Please don't ask me. Some of them are friends and some of them are my relatives. What's important is you know they would like to shut your business and destroy you. They are afraid that gradually you will come after them. It doesn't matter for me, I support your mission."

Finally, the collaboration of the community's members played a huge role in the success of *Meftih*. Its circulation grew from three thousand to eight thousand copies. Its enlightening message reached community members both directly and indirectly. *Meftih* even won Best Editorial and Visual Presentation from the National Ethnic Press and Media Council of Canada (NEPMCC), in 2006 and again in 2009, an honour bestowed on me by then Canadian prime minister, Stephen Harper, in 2009.

I repeatedly criticized the Eritrean government's representative in Canada for manipulating the community festival to carry out the regime's political agenda and to raise funds for it.

My coverage of the annual Eritrean festival touched a nerve at the consulate. The festival organizing committee and the consulate were flip sides of the same coin. They operated from the same office in the consulate, suite 309 at 120 Carlton Street. In the October 2006 issue of *Meftih*, I criticized the overall preparation of the Eritrean festival in Toronto, which was usually held in August. Every year, the festival was organized as an Eritrean community event, but the community was barely involved in organizing or setting the festival's agenda. The lack of transparency and the manipulation of the community were the highlight of my coverage. I articulated that the festival was organized by a few individuals who were hand-picked by the Eritrean consulate. I pointed out how the organizers ignored the community's social issues, and focused instead on drumming up money or propagandizing for the Eritrean government. In response to my piece, I received several well orchestrated and intimidating calls from numbers I didn't recognize:

"… we will bury you with your paper"; "… you will pay the price of your actions"; "… we know where you live," etc. Though I didn't want to show it, it did disturb me. I informed the police and presented a list of possible callers since I didn't have concrete proof of identies. The police advised me to return with more evidence.

When the 2007 annual Eritrean festival approached, the chair of the festival organizers, who was also the chair of the Toronto branch of the ruling party (PFDJ), Temesgen Haileab, sent me a letter via email on July 19, 2007. In his letter, he told me not to attend "any venue of the forthcoming Toronto Eritrean Community Festival 2007," adding that it was because I "caused altercations" among the festival participants. It was a complete fabrication, conceived by the Eritrean consulate office to scare me. For the sake of formality I replied to Temesgen right away, though I knew who was behind that letter. I wrote that the allegations stated in the letter were false. I told him clearly that I refused to be intimidated by his letter, and I assured him I would attend the festival as it was a community festival and would be held in a public venue.

Just a few days later, on July 23, I found that, while I was eating lunch with friends in one of the Eritrean restaurants on Bloor near Ossington, the rear tire of my car had been slashed with a knife. From the look of the damage, I guessed the vandals used a butcher knife. I was mad, because there was no way I could catch the vandals, though I knew who or what was behind it. It was an additional message to intimidate me, another warning not to attend the upcoming festival. I would have to take more precautions and conceive different tactics.

I shared the letter I had received from the chair of the festival organizing committee with the executive director of PEN Canada, Isobel Harry; the program manager of the Canadian Journalists for Free Expression (CJFE), Julie Payne; and the Toronto Police Service 14th Division.

Since CJFE and PEN were well informed about the type of government Eritrea had and its animosity toward freedom of the press, they took the matter seriously and reacted quickly. Julie immediately emailed the chair of the festival organizing committee, asking that he renounce his letter. She stressed that freedom of the press is protected in Canada. Isobel also sent a letter via courier to the organizing committee (at the same address as the Eritrean consulate), asking them to permit my participation, but the office refused to accept the letter. PEN Canada sent the same letter again by another courier: again the consulate refused to accept it, saying the chairperson had resigned from his post. Isobel thought this was a ridiculous excuse and expressed her vehement opposition. Her letter stated, "PEN Canada believes that freedom of expression and freedom of the press to observe, record and comment on public events are cornerstones of the free and democratic society that Canada is. An event in a public park is, by its very nature, a public event and that means it must be open to the media to attend and cover it. Any attempt to prevent or restrict media coverage to only selected journalists or news organizations is wrong and should be resisted by everyone who believes in democracy."

The consulate had expected to silence my voice, but the attempt had backfired. It attracted more attention than they wanted. Emboldened by knowing that I had unreserved support from CJFE and PEN Canada, I did attend the festival, in Earlscourt Park near St. Clair and Caledonia, on August 4, 2007. Two friends agreed to watch my back by recording my movements in the Park. There were hundreds of people at the festival, roaming around the bazaar and the tents raising funds in the name of "martyrs' children," and watching the amateur soccer game on the field.

Once I started taking pictures and interviewing people about the event, Temesgen, the chairman whom the organizing committee claimed had resigned from his post, came up to one of my interviewees.

"Why did you speak to him?" Temesgen yelled at the man.

"I didn't say anything bad," the man said in a shaking voice. "I just, I just said it is a good festival." I couldn't believe what I was seeing. Temesgen had four men with him. It was obviously intended as message for the rest of the people not to answer my questions. Then Temesgen and his thugs turned around and asked me to leave.

"We told you not to come. Why are you here? You have to leave right now," Temesgen barked.

I laughed at him and kept taking pictures.

"I said you have to leave now!"

"I am not leaving. You don't have authority to dictate anyone. Remember, this is not Eritrea," I said, looking at him and his men, who restrained him from fighting me.

"This park is Eritrea," he said. "We follow Eritrean rules in this park. We can do whatever we want to do here." The more he barked the sorrier I felt for him. He genuinely believed what he was saying. He lived in Canada, a democratic society, but didn't believe the Eritrean people deserved democracy, freedom of speech, or justice.

The regime always used naive people like him. Most of the undercover agents, like Temesgen, were nationalists. But they had fled to exile while many youths of their age were joining the Eritrean movement to liberate their country from Ethiopia. Now, they were trying to redeem themselves by becoming more Catholic than the priest.

"You have to leave, or I am going to crush you here," he said while trying to get free of the guys holding him back.

"Well, be my guest," I said calmly, moving toward the soccer field to take more pictures.

"You will be dragged out by police, if you choose that," one of the thugs said. I nodded my head and went to the field. Over six hundred people were in the park. Some of them sat under the trees drinking traditional coffee, others were running about with their children, and some were tuned into the game.

An hour later, two Toronto police officers showed up and approached me while I stood beside the soccer field. The attention of the people switched toward us. The PFDJ festival organizing committee had told the police a fabricated story. After we shook hands, they asked me why I was there, despite having been advised by the organizers not to show up.

"They don't have a right to prevent me from attending this festival," I said, abruptly. I explained my role as a journalist, the intention of the festival and how it was manipulated, and how I had criticized the activities of the Eritrean regime and how they dictate to people who live in Canada.

"They said that you created an altercation last year, and for the safety of everyone, it is better if you leave now," the tall officer said.

"They are lying, officer," I said. "The reason they want me to leave is that I criticized the organizers last year for using this festival to raise funds for the dictatorial regime in Eritrea. They are afraid I will do it again."

"I heard that," he said, tersely. "You are repeating yourself. Can you go now?"

I paused and looked at his eyes for a few long seconds without saying a word. The officers had apparently come with a definite purpose and would take no notice of whatever I said. They just kept asking me again and again to leave the park. What they didn't understand was that they were being manipulated by the organizers of the festival.

"Did you have any evidence that I fought with anyone physically last year?"

"Can you go now?" he asked me, ignoring my question.

"I don't think you understand me, officer. They don't have a right to kick anyone out of here, let alone a journalist."

"Sir, they have a permit. Yes, they do have a right to do that. We don't want to have to do this by force," he said. "It is better if you leave voluntarily."

I looked around. Hundreds of people were observing us, wanting to see how the scene would play out. If the members of the community saw me kicked out, they would assume the organizers, working for the Eritrean consulate, had substantial support from the police, and they would be afraid to say no to the organizers about anything. However, if they saw that the organizers could not kick me out even with the help of the police, they would know they could trust the police. To show that the organizers didn't have the power to dictate to anyone in a country run by rule of law, I was ready to hold my ground and argue to the best of my abilities.

"With due respect officers, they don't have that right. Neither do you."

"Excuse me?"

"Before I came here, I showed a letter to your supervisor, and after he learned everything it said, he told me that I have full right to attend any public event. What I don't understand is why you are here. Did someone call you? Have you read the permit?" I paused and looked at both of them. They didn't say a word. "This is a public park, and any event held in the park is open for anyone. That's what the permit said. So, I know my rights and you can't force me to leave this place. Before you try to do anything, please ask your supervisor about public festivals in a public park. Then you may understand what I am saying."

He stared at me for a few seconds and nodded.

"Give us a moment," the tall officer said, stepping away with his partner. I observed them from a distance. They spoke for a few seconds and the tall officer pulled his cellphone out of his pocket and placed a call. He might have been on the phone for ten minutes, but for me it felt like ten hours. Finally, he hung up, spoke with his partner, and approached me to tell me that it was okay to stay. Warning me to watch my back, they left.

It was a victory for me and for anyone who opposed the Eritrean consulate's illegal activities, but a defeat for the so-called organizers.

However, even after the festival, the vandalism didn't stop. After I criticized the Eritrean government "for converting the country into a vast prison camp" on my blog, they smashed the windows of my car.

I remember every incident of that morning — January 3, 2008. It was about minus twenty Celsius, with a wind. I had to go to Oakville that day, so I woke up at six thirty, ate breakfast, and by seven was headed to the parking lot to get my car. Before I saw it, I heard, "What the crap?" It was my neighbour, a chatty Ukrainian. "What happened to your car?" he asked.

"What the heck," I said, opening my mouth in surprise.

"Who did this?" he asked. "I bet it could be your ex. This is not an accident. My ex-wife broke my guitar to make me mad. Don't do anything stupid, learn from me." He tried to tell me his story, but I didn't have time for that.

I went back inside, typed up a detailed complaint, went straight to the police station and informed them what happened, and who could be behind such activities, and how the Eritrean consulate operates. To my disappointment, the officer who stood there to hear my complaint didn't seem to care about learning the background of the story.

"Do you know who did it?" the officer asked in a robotic tone.

"No, but I know who could be behind this."

"Do you have any proof or evidence?"

"Not yet, but I would appreciate it if you can do an investigation on how the Eritrean consulate operate its business here; how they spy, how they intimidate Eritrean Canadians by violating Canadian law," I said. I handed him the detailed complaint I had written.

He glanced at the three pages of stapled paper and put it beside him as he answered a call. I stood there to see him reading and prepared myself to answer whatever questions he would have.

"Okay, you can go now. We will look into it," he said.

I never heard back from him and I didn't follow up. It would be useless to go after those vandals; others would replace them.

To simplify the way refugees or newcomers report their concerns or file their complaints, it would have been useful to have a specific unit or at least contact persons in the law enforcement agencies that could understand the complexities of the issues. Unfortunately, there were none. The law enforcement agents may take adequate training to serve Canadian society. However, as the demography of the country transforms along with the crimes, they may have some catching up to do. They have to understand the perpetrators have come to Canada as diplomats to harass and exploit the victims who have fled from them.

Together with an activist group called the Hidmona Eritrean Human Rights Group, I prepared a petition and lobbied the Canadian government to take action against the Eritrean consulate office in Canada, which was soliciting a 2 percent income tax from Eritreans in Canada, including from people who lived on social welfare, and a three hundred to five hundred dollar forced donation for "national defence." This clearly undermined Canadian sovereignty.

I met with former minister of justice and attorney general of Canada Irwin Cotler to discuss both my colleagues who were in jail and the illegal activities of the Eritrean consulate office. I delivered my testimony in the House of Commons Committee on Human Rights on how the Eritrean consulate office was extorting Eritrean Canadians. We organized demonstrations and reached out to our members of parliament.

What helped us most, though, was the relentless efforts of David Matas, an international human rights lawyer, and the major Canadian media. We had particularly eloquent coverage by Stewart Bell in the *National Post*. He framed the issue elegantly so that the people and the politicians could grasp what was happening under their noses. Then the CBC, the *Toronto Star* and the rest of the mainstream media echoed how the regime was still abusing Eritrean refugees who had come to Canada for safety.

Finally, Canada expelled consul Semere Ghebremariam O. Micael from Toronto in May 2013. It was the highlight of the year, encouraging us to do more and to advocate against the crimes being committed by the Eritrean regime inside the country and abroad.

* * *

While frequenting the offices of PEN Canada and the CJFE, I met writers in exile who had experienced imprisonment, intimidation, and torture. Like me, the uprooting from their home countries had jeopardized their careers as writers and shaken their confidence as newcomers. Hearing similar stories from my fellow writers in exile, from Iran, Afghanistan, Pakistan, Ethiopia, Bosnia, Mexico, and Egypt, comforted me. Whatever uncertainty I felt about going back to my former career, they also felt. We all knew how lucky we were for finding a safe country to live, but we wanted more help to settle properly and find a way to get our careers back. Luckily, PEN Canada and the CJFE realized that welcoming persecuted writers was only a first step.

PEN Canada, under the leadership of Isobel Harry and Haroon Siddiqui, found several placements for writers in exile in academic institutions — George Brown College, Acadia University, York University, Laurentian University, the University of Calgary, and many others. There were teaching or writing residencies, creative writing seminars, screenwriting workshops, student bursaries, and scholarships. I was one beneficiary of such accommodations: I was granted a PEN Lecturer-in-Residence position at George Brown College. It was another turning point of my life. George Brown College valued my contribution and gave credit to the suffering I had gone through because of my professional work, and they gave me a platform to share that with the college students.

One day I spoke to about seventy students on how the security agents made the life of journalists miserable: how they confiscated my laptop and searched my office and my home. The students asked questions: "What did you write?" "How did you escape?" "Why did you criticize the government if you knew it could risk your life?" I exceeded my time limit. After I finished my speech and dismissed the students, two nineteen-year-old students approached the podium.

"That was great, sir," a thin boy said, putting his hand on the podium. "Thank you for telling us about your country. But I have one question, if you don't mind?" He looked at his friend, who stood just beside him for encouragement.

"Sure, please ask anything you want," I said with a broad smile.

"You said that the security agents confiscated your laptop, so are you saying you have computers in Africa?" he asked gently.

I didn't show my surprise. I asked him what he knew about African countries.

"Not much," he said. "I just assume it's still a jungle. Have you seen the movie *The Gods Must Be Crazy*? It's a good movie, but the people live in the forest. I know that was just a movie, but that's the perception I have."

That boy gave me a good topic for future lectures. I started to pay special attention whenever conversation arose about Africa. Many Canadians think of the continent as if it were one country, with one people, language, and culture. *The Gods Must Be Crazy* was a 1980 comedy about Bushmen tribes in Southern Africa. It was widely criticized for racist portrayals. When these young people talked about African dance, they spoke only about the Maasai or the Bushmen. They presented the Maasai and the Bushmen as poster children of Africa, despite the fact that the Maasai are 0.001 percent of Africa's population. So I took it as my duty to tackle the stereotypes of African countries whenever I got a chance to talk to students.

THE INVISIBLE ENEMY

BY FREWEINI (FRIETA) BERHANE

THAT WAS THE LAST CHAPTER MY FATHER WROTE. HE WAS INTENDING TO add a conclusion about how he finally got his family to join him in Canada. I will have to write that conclusion.

When my father left Eritrea, I was just eight and a half years old, my brother, Mussie, was four, and my little brother Evan was only six months. Our father's sudden disappearance from our lives didn't make sense to me. I interrogated my mother daily about his whereabouts. My mother would say he was coming back soon.

Days turned into weeks and weeks turned into months, and still there was no sign of my father coming back. I remember feeling a huge void in my heart and unexplainable anger, which was hard to process with my eight-year-old mind. But I never stopped asking about my father. I can't imagine how difficult it must have been for my mother to not be able to tell me the truth. Even if she had, I doubt I would have been able to understand or comprehend the situation we were in.

Eventually, she told me that he had gone to North America to complete his studies. Although that helped me stop asking repetitive questions, it did not console me. I missed him so much and I just wanted our life to be back the way it was.

I remember hearing his voice for the first time on the phone when he made it safely to Canada. I didn't know what to say. I was overwhelmed by my emotions. Since the calling card allowed him to talk for only a few minutes, he asked me to pass the phone to my mother.

I was so excited to share the good news with my friends.

"Hi guys, my dad is living in Canada now," I said in a high voice, hopping like a bunny.

One of the kids asked, "Where is Canada?"

"Umm, it is in uhhhh ... it's somewhere very far."

"How far?"

I felt a little apprehensive and overwhelmed by their questions. I didn't know anything about Canada, in fact that was the first time I had heard of the country. Our awareness of the West pertained only to the United States, based on the media that we were exposed to.

* * *

From the moment my father arrived in Canada in 2002, he never stopped trying to get us out of Eritrea safely and to reunite our family. Due to the high profile of his case, the government of Canada began to process our application with urgency.

Little did my brothers and I know we were trying to leave our childhood home, our friends and family. I still assumed my father was in Canada to complete his studies. I was under the impression that he would be back shortly and our lives would be back to normal.

At this point, my little brother Evan was growing up with no memory of my father. He never got to celebrate his first birthday with Mom and Dad the way Mussie and I had. He learned how to ride a bike without Dad. So many first milestones were missed.

Even for my brother Mussie, the few memories he had of him were beginning to fade. Mussie used to enjoy going on car rides with Dad so much that after my father left he gave my mother a very hard time. He would refuse to go on a bus, and if he did, he would get upset if the bus driver made a stop to pick up or drop off passengers. My mom also had to transfer him to a new school. The old school had been farther away, and my dad had been the one who used to drop him off and pick him up. Mussie did not like the new school. He misbehaved and got in trouble a lot.

I can't even begin to imagine the stress my mother was under. As if raising three kids without their father was not taxing enough, the government of Eritrea was constantly sending authorities to spy on her and question her about the whereabouts of my father. Like my father, she remained the same loving, caring, and compassionate parent she had always been.

Despite all the strain, the unity and closeness of our entire family made things much easier. My grandmother on my father's side is a spiritual, devoted, and kindhearted woman who taught us to find a blessing in any tough situation. Everyone in the family stepped up to fill the absence of my father.

In 2003, the government of Canada provided us a visa. My parents were exhilarated. But because they didn't want to get our hopes up, especially mine, they did not tell us about the news.

One Sunday morning, my dad called as usual.

"Hello, sweetie," he greeted me with his deep, calm, and comforting voice.

"Hi, Baba, *kemey aleka*?" (how are you?) I said, enthusiastically.

"I am good, and how are you?"

"I am good," and before he could ask another question I asked, "Ummm listen, Baba, when are you coming back?"

After a long pause he responded, "Well, you know I have not completed my studies yet."

"When are you going to finish then?"

"Very soon," he said, which was his usual response. He could sense that I was not satisfied with that answer. "What if you all could come to me instead?"

"To Canada?"

"That's right, sweetie."

I was thrilled. I found myself lost in thoughts about what life would be like in Canada.

Unfortunately, it didn't go as planned. The Eritrean government refused to give us an exit visa. Eventually, our Canadian visa expired.

Things were getting worse in Eritrea. The socio-political instability increased at an astonishing rate and wiped out any economic developments or advancements Eritrea had made. Many citizens were deprived of fundamental human rights and freedom. National service was extended indefinitely, and imprisonment of innocent citizens increased at an alarming rate. Thousands of individuals had been forced to migrate under unsafe conditions.

Under these circumstances, our chances of leaving Eritrea were becoming slim. The only option left was to leave illegally, but my mother did not want to take the risk with three kids. There was a shoot-to-kill order in place near the border.

In addition, I was approaching the end of grade 11. This could be an exciting moment for some people, who live in another part of the world, as it could mark the completion of the first senior year in high school. However, in Eritrea it is a nightmare. The government forces secondary school students to complete their final school year in the Sawa military camp where they are also required to undergo mandatory military training. Thousands of students later end up being conscripted into indefinite government service.

* * *

One Saturday evening, my father and I arranged an online Yahoo chat session. I usually went to the internet café with my cousin or friends, but that evening I decided to go by myself. The connection was slow and required great patience.

After exchanging greeting messages and updates, I felt compelled to discuss a serious matter with him. A matter that I would not feel safe discussing over the phone as the government usually tapped the phones of highly wanted individuals.

As I grew up and the years went by, I had learned the truth about my father's situation and the reason for his disappearance. My mother now kept me well informed and had taught me to be cautious of my surroundings, particularly in matters relating to his situation.

Before the connection went down and my time ran out at the internet café, I typed to my dad that I wanted to talk to him about something.

"Sure, what is it?" Dad wrote.

"My grade 11 is almost done, and I will be heading to Sawa for grade 12. And you know how that is."

"Yes, sweetie, I know."

Although I could not see his reaction in person or hear his voice, I could sense the dread he felt in his heart. Wanting to ease his distress, I typed back, "It is not that bad, Dad. I am mentally prepared for it and I can handle it." I was aware that I would be making getting out of the country more difficult, considering my age, so I suggested he get everybody else out. At this point, it would be hard for me to get a permit to travel within the country, let alone leave the country, so I wrote, "I will join you after I come back from Sawa."

My father was not willing to accept that. He instantly refused to let me go down that path. He knew better. The only option we had left was to cross the border illegally, just as he had done. My mother was terrified by the idea, but staying in Eritrea would be worse, so finally she agreed to it.

Shortly after, my dad started arranging our escape plan. He found smugglers who could help us flee the country as safely as possible. We could not share or discuss this matter with anyone. However, crossing the border wasn't the biggest problem. The smugglers were due to meet us in Teseney, a small town near the border. Travelling there requires a valid government permit for anyone older than fourteen. I was sixteen. My mother already had a valid permit, but I didn't.

"So what do we do now, Mom?" I asked.

"Bring your student ID. As long as you are travelling with your mom and siblings, I believe it should be fine," she said, with some uncertainty.

"I don't think that is a good idea. I will be putting you all at risk and might jeopardize the whole escape plan. I think I should stay and only the three of you should go," I said.

My mom could not bear the idea of leaving me behind. "We have been separated for far too long from your father and we are not going to let that happen with you too. Either we all go together or we stay," she said firmly.

"I don't want to be left behind either but it will be risky."

Before I could say more she stopped me and calmly said, "It will be fine, we will be fine, we will make it miraculously. And we will reunite with your father." It was inspiring to see her courage. It lifted my spirit.

* * *

On May 1, 2009, we said goodbye to our sweet home and began our journey. But that wasn't the most difficult thing. Far more difficult was being unable to say goodbye to my grandmother, aunties, and cousins, as we did not want to put them at risk. We knew that the authorities would come after them regardless, but we also knew it would be better if they didn't know anything about our journey.

To avoid being seen, we left our house in the middle of the night to board the first morning bus to Teseney. My mom told my younger brothers we were going to Teseney to attend a family function. They did not ask too many questions; they were just thrilled to have a getaway weekend. I, on the other hand, was very anxious and was trembling with fear. My heart was racing like I had just run a marathon, my palms were sweating, and I could feel my legs shaking. And I could tell my mom was swamped by the responsibility of crossing a border with her three kids, knowing how dangerous it could be.

I remember her being unable to sleep for weeks as we were arranging the escape plan. Every time I woke up in the night to have a sip of water or to go to the bathroom, the lamp on her nightstand was on. Just weeks before we began our journey, horrifying news circulated about a mother who died crossing the border with her three kids. I am sure my mother was disturbed by that and thought that maybe this was a sign that we shouldn't attempt to flee. But not doing anything was also a risk. We didn't know what would happen next under the corrupt and unstable regime.

We arrived at the bus station around 4 a.m. There were numerous buses lined up and countless people getting ready to board. I did not expect to see that many people, at all. "Where could all these people possibly be going?" I asked my mother. I am not sure whether she didn't hear me or she was too deep in her thoughts, but she didn't reply. I wasn't really expecting an answer anyway. I just thought it might help distract us.

Soon after, the bus driver's assistant began checking tickets and boarding people. As I handed him my ticket I asked, "How long is the journey?"

Snatching the ticket from my hand and not making eye contact, he said, "We will get there at two o'clock. Now hurry, get on the bus, and don't waste my time."

I got on the bus behind my mom and brothers. Most of the front seats were taken, which was fine with us — we did not want to sit close to the front. We found seats at the very back. My father and the smuggler had prepared us well for the journey. So as not to attract attention to ourselves, we had been instructed how to dress and to interact with others in certain ways. We were informed about the multiple checkpoints that we would have to cross. Since I didn't have a valid government document to travel to Teseney, my mother and I were nervous at every checkpoint. Luckily, at the first few checkpoints the guards didn't even bother to come to the back of the bus. That was a big relief. I prayed to God that the rest would go as smoothly. However, to avoid any suspicion I rested my head on Mussie's and Mom's lap and pretended to be asleep. After travelling for a few hours, the driver stopped at a small city called Barentu to take a break. All the passengers were asked to get off the bus to get fresh air and stretch their legs, and come back after half an hour.

We were very hungry so we went to a local restaurant and ordered lunch. My mom and I were happy that we had made it halfway without any problem. We didn't know if security had been relaxed or if we had just got lucky. We ate our food quickly and headed to our bus worrying that it might leave us. We sat in the same arrangement as before and

I rested my head on Mom's lap and pretended to be asleep again. The guy sitting next to my mom started a conversation with her.

He asked, "So are those all your kids?"

"Yes, they are."

"That's nice. So what is your reason for travelling to Teseney?"

I didn't like the guy asking so many questions. For all we knew he could be a spy. And I could tell my mom felt a little apprehensive and her tone changed. She was being very cautious with her words.

"My sister lives in Teseney and she just had a baby. We are going to her baptism."

Since that was our cover story, we had prepared it well. We had brought a baby girl's outfit that my mother pulled out and showed to him.

Suddenly, the bus came to a full stop. "It's another checkpoint," my mother whispered in my ear. Two guards entered the bus and started asking individuals, especially young adults, to show an ID. My heart started racing and my legs were shaking.

I could hear the deep voice of one of the guards. His voice seemed authoritative and intimidating. As he continued to walk toward the back of the bus, I could feel the adrenalin rush in my body. My heart was pounding, my body was covered with sweat, and I started to hyperventilate.

He looked around and gazed toward us.

"Who is that sleeping on your lap?" he asked my mother.

"She is my daughter. She can't handle motion sickness and is resting."

"Can I see your ID?"

My mother handed him her ID.

He looked at it attentively and gave it back to her. "Have a great day," he said, and just walked away.

I couldn't believe it was over. My whole body felt numb and I could barely move my legs. I was amazed how well my mother had handled that situation without being intimidated or showing any fear. Fortunately, we did not encounter any trouble at the remaining checkpoints and made it safely to Teseney after roughly eight hours.

We checked into a hotel until it was time to meet the smuggler. Later, in the evening, he came to the hotel and gave us specific directions on where to meet him still later that night. Upon arriving at the meet-up location, we met the other individuals who would be crossing with us. Once the smuggler showed up with his friend, they took us to a small hut where we were going to spend the night. We were originally supposed to leave for Sudan that same night but because the smugglers changed the plan, we ended up staying at the hut for five days. It was uncomfortable, to say the least. There were fifteen people in total staying in the hut. There was no fan or air conditioning and not enough food to go around. The smugglers had seized our phones and prohibited us from making any outside communication. My father didn't know whether we had been caught or escaped, or even if we were still alive.

On day six, the smugglers told us that we would be leaving that night. We were exhilarated to hear the news.

"The driver is not meeting us here," said one of the smugglers. "We will have to walk for a bit to meet him somewhere else." My mother and the other ladies exclaimed their disapproval. "That was not the plan," my mother said. But the smugglers were unmoved. "It's either this, or you go back," they said.

Most of us had no choice: we did as they said. "Now get some rest and we will wake you up in about two hours, then we begin our journey." With that they left us alone.

My brothers and the other kids fell asleep but the rest of us couldn't. Before we knew it, the smugglers came back and told us to get ready. We packed whatever we had left and started following them. It was pitch dark as we walked through the quiet streets. We could hear the loud sound of crickets and other creatures in the woods. The bright stars lit our path. We walked for about two hours before getting put in the back of a white pickup truck that drove off at 170 or 180 kilometres an hour. I was afraid one of us would fall off and be left stranded in the desert. Luckily we all arrived safely in Kassala, Sudan.

Upon arriving in Kassala, we were able to call my dad for the first time since we left Asmara. He was excited to hear our voices. He had not heard from us for almost a week. This is also when my brothers learned we were heading to Canada. Though excited, they were confused.

"This is where Dad lives?" Evan asked, looking at the desert around us. "This is what Canada looks like?"

We spent several weeks in Kassala organizing our papers before travelling to Khartoum, the capital city of Sudan. In Khartoum, my father had some friends who helped us get settled in and showed us around the city. They were also kind enough to assist us with the completion of our applications and visa processes. Because the earlier visa had already expired, we had to restart the whole process. Luckily, this time things worked in our favour and about a year later we left for Canada.

May 5, 2010, was the day we arrived in Canada. I got to see my father with my own two eyes in the flesh after nearly nine years of separation. That was one of the happiest moments of my life. It took some time getting used to, this new reality of mine. I used to pinch myself to see if it was real and not one of my crazy dreams.

Evan was starstruck the day he met him. It was his first time seeing his father in person. He ran to my mother and whispered in her ear, "Is this really Baba? This is the one I talk to on the phone?"

"Yes, dear, that is him. That is your dad."

Evan was still skeptical. "Can you ask him to call you and I can speak to him on the phone?"

My mother, baffled, asked why he didn't just go up to him.

"I want to make sure the deep cool voice really is his."

Laughing hysterically, she shared what he said with the rest of us. My uncle, Amanuel, who had come along with my father, passed his phone to Evan. My brother enthusiastically grabbed the phone from my uncle's hand and asked Dad to call him. My dad dialed my uncle's number. As soon as it rang, Evan picked it up and said "Hello," and my dad responded, "Hello Evan, how are you?" After hearing the voice he was craving, Evan started hopping like a bunny and saying "It really is you ... it really is you!" That was a beautiful moment.

After our arrival we spent a lot of time together to make up for lost time. He showed us the many wonderful things Toronto had to offer and, since he was well established, he made it easy for us to settle in and navigate the city.

I soon learned about the life my dad created for himself here. I was extremely proud and humbled by his accomplishments. He became my inspiration and role model.

One thing I noticed the most about him was that he was always doing something. He kept himself busy, exploiting opportunities. But despite the busy schedule he had, he always made time for us. He enjoyed spending quality time with his family. He especially enjoyed it when my mother performed the traditional coffee ceremony.

The coffee is made from scratch. First it begins by roasting the beans and perfuming the room with the rich smell. Then the beans are ground into a fine powder and brewed in a clay coffee pot called a *jebena*. The coffee is served in small cups throughout the three stages of the ceremony: *Awol*, *Kali'aytea*, and *Bereka*. As the coffee is brewed at each stage, the cup served at the *Awol*

264

stage is the strongest (similar to espresso) and the cup served at the *Bereka* stage is the weakest. The whole ceremony lasts for two to three hours. It's a beautiful tradition, whose main purpose is simply bonding and celebrating. It also presented me with the perfect opportunity to ask my dad so many unanswered questions I'd had growing up.

* * *

One Sunday afternoon we all sat together to enjoy the coffee ceremony as usual. I asked my dad to tell me about his escape journey from Eritrea in detail. I was eager to learn what exactly had happened to the people who had helped him escape. He stopped sipping his coffee and put it on the table, then began to tell me the story.

When the guards started shooting at my dad, Gebray, and Samson at the border, the three of them were separated and went their own ways. It wasn't until my dad arrived in Canada that he learned exactly what had happened to them. Samson, the smuggler, was able to escape from the guards and returned to Asmara without getting caught. Petros was confident that my dad and Gebray would cross the border successfully. As it was quite late, he decided to spend the night in Girmayka and head to Asmara in the morning.

However, things didn't go as planned. Gebray was captured. The guards interrogated him and found out the identities of everyone involved. The authorities arrested Petros immediately, before he got the chance to return to Asmara, and impounded the vehicle they had driven to Girmayka. During their search of the car, they found out that Petros wasn't the owner. The vehicle belonged to a person named Thomas. The authorities arrested him in Asmara, but Thomas had no idea why. The authorities told him they had

THE BURDEN OF EXILE

seized his vehicle close to the border. He was utterly confused. He had never heard of Petros and had no idea why he had been driving the vehicle that had been rented to someone else — my uncle Amanuel, dad's younger brother. Amanuel was also arrested in Asmara and brought to the Adarset prison, where the others were detained. He took full responsibility and testified that Thomas had had no hand in my dad's escape. Thomas was released after roughly three months.

Samson's luck didn't last for long. He was arrested in Asmara after a couple of weeks and joined the others in Adarset. Amanuel, Petros, Gebray, and Samson were kept separate from the other prisoners and received harsh treatment. They were handcuffed day and night, except during mealtimes and bathroom breaks. They were kept in dark cells, unable to glance at any sunshine for months at a time. They were not allowed visitors, and their family members worried they would not make it out alive.

Eventually, Amanuel, Petros, and Gebray were transferred to a different prison, called Track B. Petros was released after ten months, and Gebray after eleven months. Amanuel spent nearly two and half years in prison. Samson was sent to a special prison intended for smugglers and was detained for nearly four years.

Although my father was forever grateful, he always carried the guilt for what Amanuel, Petros, and Samson had gone through. They paid the price for his escape. But one thing he knew for sure was that if the authorities had arrested him, he would have never made it out alive. All of his colleagues and friends who were arrested in 2002 are either still in prison or died in prison.

Petros and Amanuel left Eritrea after a few years. Amanuel joined my father in Canada in 2008. Petros made it safely to Sweden and now lives there with his family. Gebray had a few unsuccessful attempts at escape but eventually made it out safely and now lives somewhere secure. Samson still resides in Asmara.

* * *

As we all settled in and adjusted to life in Canada, we got busy and did not get to spend as much time together as we did at first. Every time my mother made traditional coffee, however, it brought us together and allowed us to engage in deep and meaningful conversation. Before we knew it, on May 5, 2020, we were celebrating ten years of our family reunited in Canada, and we were all looking forward to celebrating many more years.

The Renaissance scientist Paracelsus once said, "Time is a brisk wind, for each hour it brings something new ... but who can understand and measure its sharp breath, its mystery, and its design?" And just like that, our life took an unexpected turn in 2021.

We all got sick with Covid-19. My mom got severely ill, but my dad's symptoms were relatively mild at the beginning. He cared for and nurtured my mother with love and compassion, as always. At the same time, I was also sick. He would call and check up on me multiple times a day. The fact that I was also carrying my second child worried him immensely.

While he was too busy caring for and worrying about us, the virus was slowly killing him inside. But he remained strong and calm, showing no weakness until he physically couldn't hide it anymore. He was then admitted to the hospital. Due to the restrictions, no one was allowed to go with him. It was unbearable to not be by his side during the time he needed us the most. I would call the hospital staff thousands of times to get updates on his condition. One moment I would be informed he was doing fine, and soon after it would be something else. The unpredictability and uncertainty of the virus made me agitated and frustrated. Unfortunately, as days passed, his condition deteriorated.

His lungs were severely damaged and he was struggling to breathe. The doctors had to put him into a medically induced coma and perform various procedures. On top of that the critical-care command centre, which was managing the transfer of ICU patients between hospitals, decided that the ICU in the Toronto hospital he was in was overwhelmed, and ordered my father transferred to a hospital in Kitchener. We felt completely and utterly helpless. There was nothing we could do to fight the decision.

A few days later, I got a call from the doctor who was looking after my father. He informed me that they had performed another major invasive procedure, which had the potential to bring a better outcome. He also told me that two family members at a time could come and see him. I was thrilled to hear the news.

I went to see him right away. It was a long drive, taking me an hour and half. I worked hard to prepare myself and stay strong. But you can never be prepared for such things. As soon as I stepped foot into the ICU room and saw his body lying on the hospital bed hooked onto multiple tubes, I felt numb and I burst into tears. I was in denial. I refused to believe that the person lying on the bed was my beloved, caring, and courageous father. He seemed unrecognizable and helpless. I desperately wanted to see his beautiful smile. I wanted to hear his deep and comforting voice. I wanted to feel his tight hugs. But all I could hear was the beeping noise the machine was making.

The doctor then walked in, interrupting my deep thoughts. He informed me that things were looking better and that I should remain hopeful. As difficult and painful as the situation was, I decided to pull myself together and stay strong for the sake of my father and my unborn child. As I was leaving the hospital I gave my dad a kiss on the forehead and whispered in his ear, "I love you, Baba, and I can't wait for you to come home."

I called my mom on my way home and briefly updated her about his status without sharing the details. I didn't want to worry her too much as she was still recovering herself. I felt a little relief when I got home that day, and hoped to hear more good news.

Later that night, around nine, I got a call from the hospital. As soon as I saw it was the hospital calling, my heart started racing and I was scared to answer the phone. I couldn't help but wonder whether I was going to hear good news or bad news. So I picked up the phone and answered hesitantly. A voice said, "Hi, I am the on-call doctor who is looking after your father today ... and I have some updates for you."

Overwhelmed with mixed emotions, I asked, "Is my father okay? How is he doing?"

After a long pause, he told me that they had conducted a neurological exam and found my father to be unresponsive. He also told me that a CT scan had revealed an intracranial hemorrhage.

I froze. What the doctor had told me did not make sense at all. I was puzzled and couldn't process the information. How fast things were fluctuating was beyond what I could handle. After gathering all my strength and trying to comprehend the information I said, "I thought ... I thought the other doctor said he was doing fine earlier this morning. He didn't mention anything about brain damage. How could this happen so suddenly?"

The doctor seemed to be himself stunned by the situation. He said, "The severity and complicated course of the virus is quite unpredictable and since there is limited data about the nature of it, it is hard to know for sure what went wrong." He went on to tell me that there was little hope for my father's survival. He advised me to visit him as soon as we could.

After hanging up the phone, I cried until I got a headache. I didn't know how to tell my mother and my brothers. But I had to share the devastating news, while trying to convince them to remain hopeful and pray for a miracle. I couldn't sleep that night. It was a long night and a painful one.

The next day, early morning at six thirty, my phone rang and I jumped out of bed and quickly answered it. It was a nurse from the hospital. The nurse didn't have any good news to share. She had called to tell me that my father was getting worse by the minute, and they could arrange a visit if our family wanted to see him. I got dressed quickly and got ready as my husband prepared breakfast for our little boy. Our place was filled with silence. And my baby girl was kicking hard in my tummy. Maybe she was trying to comfort and distract me. As my little boy was getting ready to eat his breakfast, he suddenly came up to me and kissed my tummy saying, "Hi, baby sister." For a moment I was filled with joy by the sweet gesture. Then I swiftly returned to the sad reality.

I called my family and asked them to get ready so we could go see my father. As I was putting on my shoes and about to leave home, I got another call from the hospital. It was my dad's doctor.

"Hi, Freweini," he said, hesitantly.

"Hi, Doctor," I replied eagerly, hoping to hear some good news.

"I am so very sorry, we did everything we could, but Aaron didn't make it. I am so sorry again."

I was in complete disbelief and couldn't possibly begin to imagine life without my dad.

My father was the most courageous, brave, insightful, caring, kind, resilient, and charismatic person I have known. He encountered many obstacles in his life and overcame them. No matter what he was going through, he always maintained that beautiful smile on his face.

In our tradition, when someone dies, family members and friends get together for weeks to grieve together while comforting each other. We were unable to do that, because of the pandemic and its restrictions. Things seemed to just get worse, and accepting the unfortunate reality became almost too bitter to swallow. However, in the midst of everything, we discovered the wide circle of friends and admirers my father had. They organized a beautiful virtual memorial service that celebrated his life and streamed it live for thousands of people. They spoke about his advocacy, generosity, bravery, accomplishments, and dedication to be a voice for the voiceless. My heart was filled with pride to see how they honoured him. They gave us hope and strength through a difficult time, for which we are truly grateful.

* * *

In collaboration with PEN Canada and George Brown College, where my father was once a writer-in-residence and later on a professor teaching a journalism course, a group of friends worked tirelessly and launched both a scholarship and an ESL program in my father's name at George Brown, dedicated to refugee writers. These initiatives provided us great comfort and pride. My father's legacy will live forever.

ABOUT THE AUTHOR

 Aaron Berhane (1969–2021) was an Eritrean Canadian journalist. Co-founder and former editor-in-chief of Eritrea's now banned largest independent newspaper, *Setit*, he escaped arrest in 2001 by fleeing to Sudan, then Kenya, and subsequently settled in Canada.